P9-DNY-784

With complete nutritional information!

The Super Big Book of EASY, DELICIOUS, & HEALTHY Recipes the *Whole* Family Will Love!

Adams Media
New York London Toronto Sydney New Delhi

Aadamsmedia

Adams Media
An Imprint of Simon & Schuster, Inc.
57 Littlefield Street
Avon, Massachusetts 02322

First Adams Media trade paperback edition January 2019

ADAMS MEDIA and colophon are trademarks of Simon & Schuster.

For information about special discounts for bulk purchases, please contact Simon & Schuster Special Sales at 1-866-506-1949 or business@simonandschuster.com.

The Simon & Schuster Speakers Bureau can bring authors to your live event. For more information or to book an event contact the Simon & Schuster Speakers Bureau at 1-866-248-3049 or visit our website at www.simonspeakers.com.

Interior design by Colleen Cunningham
Interior photographs © Stockfood; Getty Images; Simon & Schuster, Inc.

Manufactured in the United States of America

10 9 8 7 6 5 4 3 2 1

Library of Congress Cataloging-in-Publication Data
Title: The super big book of easy, delicious, and healthy recipes the whole family will love!
Description: Avon, Massachusetts: Adams Media, 2019.
Includes index.
Identifiers: LCCN 2018038264 (print) | LCCN 2018038668 (ebook) | ISBN 9781721400157 (pb) | ISBN 9781721400164 (ebook)
Subjects: LCSH: Quick and easy cooking. | Natural foods. | LCGFT: Cookbooks.
Classification: LCC TX833.5 (ebook) | LCC TX833.5 .S866 2019 (print) | DDC 641.5/12--dc23
LC record available at https://lccn.loc.gov/2018038264

ISBN 978-1-72140-015-7
ISBN 978-1-72140-016-4 (ebook)

Contains material adapted from the following titles published by Adams Media, an Imprint of Simon & Schuster, Inc.: *The Everything® Busy Moms' Cookbook* by Susan Whetzel, copyright © 2013, ISBN 978-1-4405-5925-9; *The Everything® Healthy Cooking for Parties Book* by Linda Larsen, copyright © 2008, ISBN 978-1-5986-9925-8; *The Everything® Gluten-Free Breakfast and Brunch Cookbook* by Jo-Lynne Shane, copyright © 2014, ISBN 978-1-4405-8008-6; *The Everything® Cast-Iron Cookbook* by Cinnamon Cooper, copyright © 2010, ISBN 978-1-4405-0225-5; *The Everything® Calorie Counting Cookbook* by Paula Conway, copyright © 2008, ISBN 978-1-5986-9416-1; *The Everything® Guide to the Blood Sugar Diet* by Emily Barr, copyright © 2016, ISBN 978-1-4405-9255-3; *The Everything® Healthy College Cookbook* by Nicole Cormier, copyright © 2010, ISBN 978-1-4405-0411-2; *The Everything® College Cookbook* by Rhonda Lauret Parkinson, copyright © 2005, ISBN 978-1-59337-303-0; *The Everything® DASH Diet Cookbook* by Christy Ellingsworth and Murdoc Khaleghi, copyright © 2012, ISBN 978-1-4405-4353-1; *The Everything® Wheat-Free Diet Cookbook* by Lauren Kelly, copyright © 2013, ISBN 978-1-4405-5680-7; *The Everything® Southern Cookbook* by Diana Rattray, copyright © 2015, ISBN 978-1-4405-8536-4; *The Everything® Guide to the MIND Diet* by Christy Ellingsworth and Murdoc Khaleghi, copyright © 2016, ISBN 978-1-4405-9799-2; *The Everything® Low-FODMAP Diet Cookbook* by Colleen Francioli, copyright © 2016, ISBN 978-1-4405-9529-5; *The Everything® Guide to the Autoimmune Diet* by Jeffrey McCombs, copyright © 2015, ISBN 978-1-4405-8732-0; *The Everything® Thyroid Diet Book* by Clara Schneider, copyright © 2011, ISBN 978-1-4405-1097-7; *The Everything® Lactose-Free Cookbook* by Jan McCracken, copyright © 2008, ISBN 978-1-5986-9509-0; *The Everything® Quick Meals Cookbook, 2nd Edition* by Rhonda Lauret Parkinson, copyright © 2008, ISBN 978-1-59869-605-9; *The Everything® Cake Mix Cookbook* by Sarah K. Sawyer, copyright © 2009, ISBN 978-1-60550-657-9;; *The Everything® Cooking for Two Cookbook* by David Poran, copyright © 2005, ISBN 978-1-59337-370-2; *The Everything® Gluten-Free College Cookbook* by Carrie S. Forbes, copyright © 2013, ISBN 978-1-4405-6568-7; *The Everything® Easy French Cookbook* by Cecile Delarue, copyright © 2015, ISBN 978-1-4405-8396-4; *The Everything® Eating Clean Cookbook* by Britt Brandon, copyright © 2012, ISBN 978-1-4405-2999-3; *The Everything® Eating Clean Cookbook for Vegetarians* by Britt Brandon, copyright © 2013, ISBN 978-1-4405-5140-6; *The Everything® Flat Belly Cookbook* by Fitz Koehler and Mabelissa Acevedo, copyright © 2009, ISBN 978-1-60550-676-0; *The Everything® Classic Recipes Book* by Lynette Rohrer Shirk, copyright © 2006, ISBN 978-1-59337-690-1; *The Everything® Guide to the Ketogenic Diet* by Lindsay Boyers, copyright © 2015, ISBN 978-1-4405-8691-0; *The Everything® Meals on a Budget Cookbook* by Linda Larsen, copyright © 2008, ISBN 978-1-59869-508-3; *The Everything® Glycemic Index Cookbook, 2nd Edition* by LeeAnn Weintraub Smith, copyright © 2010, ISBN 978-1-4405-0584-3; *The Everything® Freezer Meals Cookbook* by Candace Anderson and Nicole Cormier, copyright © 2010, ISBN 978-1-4405-0612-3; *The Everything® Meals for a Month Cookbook* by Linda Larsen, copyright © 2005, ISBN 978-1-59337-323-8; *The*

Contents

Introduction

Today's families are busy. And after shuffling between school, practices and rehearsals, play dates and group activities, the thought of cooking any meal—let alone one that is nutritionally complete and actually tastes good—can feel overwhelming. Fortunately, *The Super Big Book of Easy, Delicious, & Healthy Recipes the* Whole *Family Will Love!* is here to make mealtime easier. Throughout this book you'll find more than 500 kid- (and parent-) pleasing recipes that are full of flavor and nutrients with no extra additives or empty calories. With recipes ranging from Confetti Scrambled Eggs for breakfast to Chili Mac and Cheese for dinner to Chocolate Cupcakes for dessert, you'll find recipes that taste good and are good for you. Even choosy eaters will love eating their vegetables when they try Baked Zucchini Stacks, Crispy Corn Fritters, and Healthy "Creamed" Spinach. Super snack recipes for Animal Crackers, Baked Potato Chips, English Muffin Pizza Snacks, and Raw Applesauce make it easy to keep hungry, growing kids satisfied between meals.

And, in addition to being delicious and healthy, these recipes are also easy and take less than 30 minutes—including prep time and cook time—to make. Even classic dinnertime favorites like Skillet Chicken Parmesan, Speedy Pork Meatloaf, and Easiest-Ever Vegetarian Lasagna take way less time to make than you'd think. With *The Super Big Book of Easy, Delicious, & Healthy Recipes the* Whole *Family Will Love!*, you'll have a tasty, nutritious meal on the table in no time. Enjoy!

Chapter 1

Simple Ways to Make Healthy Meals Fast

When it comes to being a parent, one of today's biggest challenges is finding time. Time for the children's homework, baths, sports, school, and, of course, eating. So often our meals become a matter of convenience versus nutrition, and on stressful nights, a trip to the drive-through wins out over a home-cooked meal. However, this doesn't have to be the case! The meals in this book can all be prepared in about the same amount of time as it takes to put on your shoes, head out to the car, and make a trip to a restaurant. If you start using some of the strategies found throughout this chapter, meals can be a breeze. Thirty minutes is all it takes from start to finish!

Time-Savers

Sometimes just deciding what to make for your family can derail your meal plan. With multiple family members, all with different taste preferences, how will you ever settle on a dish everyone will enjoy? By being prepared! Doing small things like making a shopping list or planning the week's menu are quick tricks you can use to not only tackle indecision but also cut down on the amount of time it takes to get a nutritious meal on the table.

Shop for the Week

Planning out a week's worth of menus in advance is a helpful tool for creating extra time. Knowing what to expect each day takes away the indecision you may face on a nightly basis when the kids are hungry and you are at a loss for what to prepare.

A weekly menu plan also allows you to shop, list in hand, so that you are prepared for each meal. There is nothing worse than setting out to make a dish only to find you are missing one essential ingredient. Be prepared; it saves time!

Take Advantage of Your Grocer

Many supermarkets today are increasing the amount of convenience foods they offer. Rotisserie chicken, salad bars, prepared vegetables, and desserts can make your life much easier and sometimes more affordable. Deli chicken is often less expensive than buying an uncooked chicken and preparing it yourself. Take advantage! You should also spend more time in the freezer section of the market; frozen vegetables are already cleaned and are preserved at their most nutritious. If chopping and dicing is the last thing you want to do, look no farther than the freezer aisle! Prepared puff pastry and pie crusts found in the freezer section are also wonderful time-savers and rival homemade quality in many cases.

Save Time with Advanced Prep

Upon your return home from the grocery store with the week's menu items, you can save time by preparing many of the items as you put them away. Fresh vegetables can be cleaned and chopped immediately based on the amounts needed for the recipes you plan to prepare; simply clean, chop, and then store the proper amounts in plastic bags for a quick grab when needed.

Make Use of Leftovers

Leftovers are a true luxury and should be viewed as such. It is just as easy to prepare double quantities of many items, such as rice or pasta, for use in a meal later in the week. Simply prepare the night's meal, putting half of the doubled recipe aside and then refrigerating or freezing it until needed. Meats can be prepared in the same fashion. It takes just as much time to prepare eight chicken breasts or hamburgers as it does four, and having the leftovers ready to go later in the week is wonderful when you aren't in the mood to cook.

It is very important to label and store each item appropriately. Many foods can easily be stored in the freezer for later use, but a proper label is critical. Write the contents on each container and the date it was prepared.

Plastic freezer bags are a wonderful convenience, and many have a blank label that you can fill in. Be sure to properly store all items and follow basic hygiene rules for storing and reheating these foods.

A Well-Stocked Kitchen

Being prepared is half the battle when it comes to saving time and energy in the kitchen. Just a few staples will keep you organized and ready to go on those evenings when cooking is the last thing you want to do.

Quality Cookware

A set of stainless steel pots and pans makes meal preparation a breeze. Heavier-bottomed versions are more expensive but allow for more even cooking and easier cleanup than their cheaper counterparts. If your set does not include a wok, consider buying one for stir-frying a variety of dishes.

Heatproof Utensils

A spatula, large spoon, and whisk made out of heat-resistant silicone are a blessing in the kitchen. The soft bottoms do no damage to cookware, there is minimal sticking, and the cleanup is quick and easy.

Bakeware

Invest in at least two good cookie sheets with rimmed edges. While certainly great for cookies, the rimmed edges are also useful for containing juices should you opt to cook meats on them. For larger cuts of meat and roasts, a roasting pan is essential. Buy one with a removable rack for easy cleanup and better roasting results.

Plastic Wrap, Plastic Bags, and Sealable Containers

Plastic bags are the most convenient way to store leftovers or prepared chopped vegetables and fruits for later use. However, for reusable storage, plastic containers with tight-fitting lids are a necessity for large amounts of leftovers. Plastic wrap is also a helpful tool for covering dishes when a lid goes missing, or for keeping splatters from escaping as you microwave food.

Knives

A set of sharp knives stored in a knife block makes for quick and easy food preparation because you always know where the knives are located. It is also safer than keeping loose knives in drawers, where little hands can unknowingly grasp them when you aren't looking.

Mixing Bowls

A set of different-sized mixing bowls, especially a nesting set, is a functional and time-saving kitchen necessity.

Measuring Cups and Spoons

Every recipe benefits from a standard set of measuring cups and spoons. Many take up little drawer space and remain attached, making them easy to find on busy evenings.

Food Processor and Blender

A blender is a wonderful appliance to have in a busy kitchen. Puréeing fruits and vegetables for baby food, smoothies, ice cream toppings, and mixed drinks is substantially easier with the blender. The same is true for the food processor, though this machine can do so much more, depending on the model. Food processors are a true time-saver for chopping vegetables and nuts, putting together piecrusts, and even making cookie dough. Some of the larger, more expensive models will even julienne and evenly slice vegetables for quick dinner preparation.

Mandoline Slicer

Quality truly makes a difference when it comes to mandoline slicers. The plastic versions featured on many infomercials may work fine for small jobs, but a higher-quality metal version will last longer and produce much better results, especially for larger meals. Variable blades and thicknesses will allow for many different uses, from thinly sliced potatoes for potato chips to thicker cuts of vegetables for salads and stews.

Quick and Easy Recipes

The time-saving techniques in this chapter will set you up for success, and the quick and easy recipes in the following pages will help you stay the course and meet your goals of serving your family healthy meals made at home. Flip through these pages to select the recipes you want to prepare this week. Then use the ingredients lists to create your grocery list for the week so you have everything you need on hand. This prep work will make it even easier to get dinner on the table each night. Let's get started.

Chapter 2

Breakfast

Not-Your-Average Scrambled Eggs

Hands-On Time: 15 minutes
Total Time: 15 minutes
Yield: Serves 6

¾ cup chopped mushrooms
1 (3-ounce) package nonfat cream cheese, softened
⅓ cup 1% milk
2 large eggs
2 cups liquid egg substitute
4 large egg whites
¼ teaspoon ground white pepper
2 tablespoons grated Romano cheese

1. Spray a large nonstick saucepan with nonstick cooking spray. Add mushrooms; cook and stir until tender, about 6 minutes.

2. Meanwhile, in food processor or blender combine cream cheese, milk, and eggs; blend until smooth. Add liquid egg substitute, egg whites, pepper, and cheese; process or blend until smooth.

3. Pour egg mixture into saucepan and reduce heat to low. Cook, stirring frequently, until eggs are just set but still moist. Serve immediately.

Per Serving: Calories: 103 | Fat: 2 g | Saturated fat: 1 g | Cholesterol: 6 mg | Sodium: 354 mg | Total carbohydrates: 4 g | Dietary fiber: 0 g | Sugars: 3 g | Protein: 16 g

Fried Potato Pancakes

Hands-On Time: 20 minutes
Total Time: 20 minutes
Yield: Serves 12

6 large Idaho potatoes, peeled and coarsely grated
1 large onion, peeled and grated
2 large eggs, beaten
½ cup potato flour
1 teaspoon salt
¼ teaspoon ground black pepper
½ cup sour cream
½ cup applesauce

1. In a large bowl, mix together the grated potatoes, onions, eggs, potato flour, salt, and pepper.

2. Heat ½″ olive oil in a large skillet over medium heat and spoon in the potato mixture, pressing down to make patties.

3. Fry until golden brown, about 5 minutes per side. Drain, keep warm, and serve with sour cream and applesauce.

Per Serving: Calories: 120 | Fat: 3 g | Saturated fat: 2 g | Cholesterol: 35 mg | Sodium: 210 mg | Total carbohydrates: 21 g | Dietary fiber: 2 g | Sugars: 2 g | Protein: 3 g

Simple Pancakes

Hands-On Time: 10 minutes
Total Time: 10 minutes
Yield: Serves 8

1½ cups flour
2 tablespoons sugar
2 teaspoons baking powder
½ teaspoon salt
1 large egg, beaten
1 cup whole milk
2 tablespoons vegetable oil, divided

1. Stir together the flour, sugar, baking powder, and salt in a large bowl. Whisk together the egg, milk, and 1 tablespoon of oil in a small bowl.

2. Pour the liquid mixture into the dry ingredients. Stir together until all the flour is incorporated but the mixture is still lumpy.

3. Place a griddle over medium heat. Once it's heated through drizzle 1 teaspoon of oil over the pan and swirl to coat. Pour ¼ cup of batter for each pancake.

4. Cook until the bottom of pancake is golden brown and bubbles appear on the top surface. Flip and cook until the other side is golden. Place on a plate and keep warm.

Per Serving: Calories: 156 | Fat: 5 g | Saturated fat: 1 g | Cholesterol: 26 mg | Sodium: 290 mg | Total carbohydrates: 23 g | Dietary fiber: 1 g | Sugars: 5 g | Protein: 4 g

Apple Cinnamon Muffins

Hands-On Time: 10 minutes
Total Time: 30 minutes
Yield: Serves 6

1 teaspoon cinnamon
2 tablespoons granulated sugar
2 cups oat bran
¼ cup brown sugar
1 tablespoon baking powder
2 large egg whites
1 cup buttermilk
½ cup molasses
½ cup unsweetened applesauce
1 cup chopped apple

1. Preheat oven to 450°F. Spray a 6-cup muffin tin with nonstick cooking spray.

2. In a small bowl, combine cinnamon and granulated sugar and set aside.

3. Mix the oat bran, brown sugar, and baking powder in a large bowl. Beat egg whites in a small bowl until foamy. Stir in buttermilk and molasses.

4. Add the buttermilk mixture to the oat bran mixture, then fold in the applesauce and chopped apple.

5. Pour an equal amount of batter into each cup of the prepared muffin tin and sprinkle with cinnamon and sugar. Bake until tops are golden, about 20 minutes.

Per Serving: Calories: 250 | Fat: 3 g | Saturated fat: 1 g | Cholesterol: 5 mg | Sodium: 320 mg | Total carbohydrates: 60 g | Dietary fiber: 6 g | Sugars: 38 g | Protein: 8 g

Whole-Grain Pancakes

Hands-On Time: 25 minutes
Total Time: 25 minutes
Yield: Serves 2

1 cup whole-wheat flour
½ cup buckwheat flour
1½ teaspoons baking powder
2 large egg whites
¼ cup apple juice concentrate
1¼–1½ cups skim milk or milk substitute

1. Sift flours and baking powder together in a medium bowl. In another medium bowl, combine egg whites, apple juice concentrate, and 1¼ cups milk. Add milk mixture to dry ingredients; mix well, but do not overmix. Add remaining milk if necessary to reach desired consistency.

2. Treat a griddle pan with nonstick spray or use a large nonstick skillet. Heat over medium heat. Ladle the batter onto the hot pan with a ¼-cup measuring scoop and cook for 2–3 minutes. When bubbles appear on the surface of the pancake, flip and cook for 2 minutes or until browned. Repeat until all pancake batter is used.

Per Serving: Calories: 490 | Fat: 3 g | Saturated fat: 0 g | Cholesterol: 5 mg | Sodium: 500 mg | Total carbohydrates: 102 g | Dietary fiber: 11 g | Sugars: 34 g | Protein: 22 g

Cinnamon Sugar Doughnuts (pictured)

Hands-On Time: 15 minutes
Total Time: 25 minutes
Yield: Serves 12

2 cups white whole-wheat flour
⅔ cup sugar
1 tablespoon sodium-free baking powder
1 teaspoon ground cinnamon
1 cup low-fat milk
1 teaspoon pure vanilla extract
2 large egg whites
2 tablespoons sugar
¾ teaspoon ground cinnamon
2 tablespoons unsalted butter, melted

1. Preheat oven to 425°F. Lightly spray a doughnut pan with oil and set aside.

2. Measure the flour, sugar, baking powder, and cinnamon into a medium mixing bowl and whisk to combine. Add the milk, vanilla, and egg whites and beat well.

3. Spoon batter into doughnut pan, filling about ⅔ full. Place pan on middle rack in oven and bake for 10 minutes. Remove pan from oven and let rest 5 minutes before gently removing doughnuts from pan.

4. Measure the sugar and cinnamon into a small bowl and mix to combine. Dip doughnuts quickly in melted butter and sprinkle with cinnamon and sugar mixture.

5. Serve immediately or place on wire rack to cool.

Per Serving: Calories: 150 | Fat: 2 g | Saturated fat: 1.5 g | Cholesterol: 5 mg | Sodium: 20 mg | Total carbohydrates: 27 g | Dietary fiber: 2 g | Sugars: 15 g | Protein: 4 g

Quinoa Berry Breakfast

Hands-On Time: 25 minutes
Total Time: 25 minutes
Yield: Serves 4

1 cup quinoa
2 cups water
¼ cup chopped walnuts
1 teaspoon ground cinnamon
1 cup raspberries
1 cup blueberries
¼ cup plain low-fat Greek yogurt

1. Rinse quinoa in fine-mesh sieve before cooking. Place quinoa, water, walnuts, and cinnamon in a 1½-quart saucepan; bring to a boil. Reduce heat to low; cover and cook 15 minutes or until all water has been absorbed.

2. Top each serving with ¼ cup of each of the berries and 1 tablespoon yogurt.

Per Serving: Calories: 250 | Fat: 8 g | Saturated fat: 1 g | Cholesterol: 0 mg | Sodium: 20 mg | Total carbohydrates: 38 g | Dietary fiber: 7 g | Sugars: 7 g | Protein: 9 g

Good-for-You Blueberry French Toast

Hands-On Time: 10 minutes
Total Time: 30 minutes
Yield: Serves 6

12 slices whole-wheat bread
2 cups skim milk
1½ cups fat-free Egg Beaters
1 teaspoon ground cinnamon
2 teaspoons vanilla extract
¾ cup blueberries
½ cup maple syrup

1. Preheat oven to 400°F. Arrange 6 slices of bread in the bottom of a baking dish.

2. Whisk the milk, Egg Beaters, ground cinnamon, and vanilla in a medium bowl. Pour half of the milk mixture over the bread, then top with the remaining bread slices and pour leftover milk mixture atop this.

3. Cover the dish with aluminum foil and bake for 20 minutes. Uncover the dish and bake 5 minutes until the top is golden brown.

4. Serve French toast with blueberries and maple syrup.

Per Serving: Calories: 320 | Fat: 2 g | Saturated fat: 0 g | Cholesterol: 0 mg | Sodium: 430 mg | Total carbohydrates: 62 g | Dietary fiber: 4 g | Sugars: 29 g | Protein: 17 g

Basic Soft-Boiled Eggs

Hands-On Time: 5 minutes
Total Time: 13 minutes
Yield: Serves 2

2 pasteurized eggs, any size

1. Place eggs in medium pot and fill with cold water at least ½″ above the eggs. Bring the water to a rolling boil. Place the eggs in the pot and cook for 3–5 minutes (depending on your own preference for soft-boiled eggs).

2. Remove the eggs from the pot and place in cold water until cool enough to handle. Peel off the shells. These will keep in the refrigerator for up to 1 week.

Per Serving: Calories: 70 | Fat: 5 g | Saturated fat: 1.5 g | Cholesterol: 185 mg | Sodium: 70 mg | Total carbohydrates: 0 g | Dietary fiber: 0 g | Sugars: 0 g | Protein: 6 g

Parmesan Sausage Rolls

Hands-On Time: 20 minutes
Total Time: 40 minutes
Yield: Serves 24

24 pork sausage links
1 (17-ounce) package frozen puff pastry, thawed
1 cup grated Parmesan cheese
1 teaspoon dried thyme
1 large egg, beaten
¼ teaspoon salt
2 teaspoons fennel seeds

1. Preheat oven to 400°F. Line cookie sheets with parchment paper and set aside.

2. In a medium-sized heavy skillet, cook pork sausage links over medium heat until golden brown and cooked through, about 5–7 minutes. Remove and place on paper towels to drain.

3. Unfold puff pastry sheet and place on a lightly floured surface. In a small bowl, combine cheese and thyme and toss to combine. Sprinkle this mixture over the puff pastry, gently pressing it into pastry; roll to a 12″ x 18″ rectangle. Cut into three 12″ x 6″ rectangles, and then cut each rectangle in half to make 6 squares. Cut each square into four 3″ x 3″ squares.

4. Place a cooked and drained sausage on the edge of each square and roll up to enclose sausage; press pastry to seal.

5. In small bowl, beat egg with salt and brush over sausage rolls. Sprinkle with fennel seeds. Place on prepared cookie sheets and bake for 12–18 minutes until puffed and golden brown. Serve hot.

Per Serving: Calories: 140 | Fat: 10 g | Saturated fat: 4 g | Cholesterol: 20 mg | Sodium: 220 mg | Total carbohydrates: 8 g | Dietary fiber: 1 g | Sugars: 3 g | Protein: 5 g

Blueberry Pancakes (pictured)

Hands-On Time: 5 minutes
Total Time: 10 minutes
Yield: Serves 16

½ pint blueberries
1 teaspoon sugar
1 teaspoon grated orange zest
½ cup whole milk
2 large eggs
1½ tablespoons melted butter
1 tablespoon baking powder
1 large banana, peeled
1 cup rice flour
1½ tablespoons cold butter

1. In a medium bowl, mix the berries, sugar, and orange zest. Set aside.

2. In the bowl of a food processor, process the milk, eggs, and melted butter together. Slowly add the baking powder, banana, and flour and process until smooth.

3. Heat a griddle over medium heat. Add cold butter. Pour a half-cupful of pancake batter on the hot griddle and spoon some berries on top. When bubbles rise to the top of the cakes, flip them over and brown on the other side. Repeat with the remaining batter and berries.

Per Serving: Calories: 80 | Fat: 3 g | Saturated fat: 2 g | Cholesterol: 30 mg | Sodium: 15 mg | Total carbohydrates: 12 g | Dietary fiber: 1 g | Sugars: 3 g | Protein: 2 g

Turkey Breakfast Sausages

Hands-On Time: 5 minutes
Total Time: 30 minutes
Yield: Serves 8

2 pounds ground turkey
1 clove garlic, minced
2 teaspoons kosher salt
2 teaspoons ground cumin
2 teaspoons chili powder
1 teaspoon ground black pepper
½ teaspoon cayenne pepper
2 tablespoons olive oil
1 large egg

1. Preheat the oven to 350°F.

2. In a large bowl, combine all the ingredients and mix well with your hands; you can wear gloves if desired.

3. After all the ingredients are well combined, form into thin 2"-diameter patties.

4. Place the patties in a large baking dish. Bake for 20–25 minutes, until browned.

Per Serving: Calories: 190 | Fat: 12 g | Saturated fat: 3 g | Cholesterol: 25 mg | Sodium: 690 mg | Total carbohydrates: 2 g | Dietary fiber: 0 g | Sugars: 0 g | Protein: 25 g

Confetti Scrambled Eggs

Hands-On Time: 10 minutes
Total Time: 10 minutes
Yield: Serves 4

8 large eggs
¼ cup whole milk
½ teaspoon salt
⅛ teaspoon ground black pepper
2 tablespoons butter
1 large tomato, seeded and diced
¼ cup chopped red bell pepper
½ cup finely chopped ham
**1 tablespoon chopped fresh
   parsley**

1. In a medium bowl, whisk together eggs, milk, salt, and pepper until well blended.

2. Melt butter in a large, heavy skillet over medium-low heat. When butter is sizzling hot, pour in egg mixture.

3. Reduce heat slightly. As egg mixture begins to look set on the bottom and sides of the skillet, fold over toward the center with a spatula. Repeat until eggs are almost set, then fold in tomato, bell pepper, and ham. Sprinkle with parsley to serve.

Per Serving: Calories: 240 | Fat: 17 g | Saturated fat: 8 g | Cholesterol: 400 mg | Sodium: 630 mg | Total carbohydrates: 5 g | Dietary fiber: 1 g | Sugars: 2 g | Protein: 16 g

Oven-Baked Apple Pancake

Hands-On Time: 10 minutes
Total Time: 35 minutes
Yield: Serves 8

1 teaspoon olive oil
**2 cups peeled, cored, and sliced
   apples**
1 tablespoon vanilla extract
1 tablespoon baking powder
**½ cup unbleached all-purpose
   flour**
½ cup white whole-wheat flour
⅓ cup unsweetened applesauce
**⅓ cup plus ¼ cup pure maple
   syrup, divided**
¾ cup almond milk
1 tablespoon sugar
½ teaspoon ground cinnamon

1. Preheat oven to 400°F. Lightly oil a large ovenproof skillet with 1 teaspoon olive oil and set aside.

2. Place apple, vanilla, baking powder, flours, applesauce, ⅓ cup maple syrup, and milk in a medium mixing bowl and whisk well to combine. Pour batter into the prepared pan and smooth top to even.

3. Combine sugar and cinnamon in a small bowl and sprinkle evenly over the batter.

4. Place pan on middle rack in oven and bake 25 minutes until golden brown.

5. Remove skillet from oven. Use a rubber spatula and carefully loosen pancake from pan. Slice like a pizza into 8 pieces, drizzle with remaining maple syrup, and serve immediately.

Per Serving: Calories: 150 | Fat: 1 g | Saturated fat: 0 g | Cholesterol: 0 mg | Sodium: 200 mg | Total carbohydrates: 34 g | Dietary fiber: 2 g | Sugars: 20 g | Protein: 2 g

Bacon and Veggie Egg Muffins

Hands-On Time: 10 minutes
Total Time: 30 minutes
Yield: Serves 12

4 slices bacon, diced

½ medium sweet onion, peeled and diced

½ medium red bell pepper, seeded and diced

3 medium spears asparagus, cut into 1" pieces

6 large eggs, beaten

1 cup whole milk

½ cup shredded Cheddar cheese

½ teaspoon salt

⅛ teaspoon ground black pepper

1 clove garlic, minced

1. Preheat oven to 350°F. Butter a 12-cup muffin tin.

2. In a medium skillet over medium heat, sauté the diced bacon until browned and crisp, about 8 minutes. Remove to a paper towel to drain. Add the diced onion, diced bell pepper, and asparagus to the bacon grease in the pan and sauté until soft and starting to brown, about 5 minutes.

3. Meanwhile, in a large liquid measuring cup, whisk together the eggs, milk, cheese, salt, and pepper.

4. Add the garlic to the peppers and onions and continue to cook for 1 minute. Remove the vegetables from the heat.

5. Spoon the vegetable mixture evenly into the 12 muffin cups. Sprinkle the bacon on top of the vegetables. Then pour the egg mixture evenly into each muffin cup so that each cup is almost full.

6. Bake for about 20 minutes or until set. Remove from the oven and cool. Serve warm or cool completely and refrigerate for later.

Per Serving: Calories: 90 | Fat: 6 g | Saturated fat: 3 g | Cholesterol: 105 mg | Sodium: 230 mg | Total carbohydrates: 3 g | Dietary fiber: 0 g | Sugars: 2 g | Protein: 6 g

Delicioso Breakfast Tacos

Hands-On Time: 20 minutes
Total Time: 20 minutes
Yield: Serves 4

4 large eggs
½ cup egg whites
¼ cup lactose-free milk
¼ teaspoon salt
½ teaspoon ground black pepper
4 strips bacon
4 crisp corn taco shells
½ cup shredded light Cheddar cheese
¼ cup diced green bell pepper
½ cup chopped tomatoes

1. In a medium bowl combine eggs, egg whites, milk, salt, and pepper. Beat eggs until fluffy.
2. In a 9" skillet over medium-low heat, add bacon strips and once sizzling, turn heat to low. Flip bacon often or until browned. Remove and place between paper towels to soak up excess oil.
3. Pour egg mixture into skillet and gently push, lift, and fold eggs with spatula until set and cooked to desired doneness. Remove from heat and use the edge of your spatula to cut egg mixture into chunks.
4. Divide egg mixture among taco shells, then add cheese, bacon, bell peppers, and tomatoes.

Per Serving: Calories: 240 | Fat: 14 g | Saturated fat: 5 g | Cholesterol: 200 mg | Sodium: 500 mg | Total carbohydrates: 12 g | Dietary fiber: 1 g | Sugars: 1 g | Protein: 17 g

Savory Cheddar Bread Casserole (pictured)

Hands-On Time: 10 minutes
Total Time: 30 minutes
Yield: Serves 8

2 teaspoons olive oil
½ (8-ounce) loaf rustic bread, cut into 1" cubes
5 large eggs
1½ cups heavy cream
1 cup shredded Cheddar cheese
1 small red onion, peeled and diced
½ teaspoon ground black pepper
2 tablespoons chopped flat-leaf parsley

1. Preheat oven to 375°F.
2. Grease a 2-quart baking pan with olive oil. Place the bread cubes in the dish.
3. Whisk the eggs in a large bowl. Add the cream, cheese, onion, and pepper to the bowl. Stir well. Pour the mixture over the bread cubes. Bake for 25 minutes or until eggs are set and bread is browned.
4. Let rest for 5 minutes and garnish with parsley.

Per Serving: Calories: 320 | Fat: 25 g | Saturated fat: 15 g | Cholesterol: 195 mg | Sodium: 310 mg | Total carbohydrates: 15 g | Dietary fiber: 1 g | Sugars: 1 g | Protein: 11 g

Banana Pancakes

Hands-On Time: 5 minutes
Total Time: 10 minutes
Yield: Serves 16

½ cup whole milk
2 large eggs
1½ tablespoons butter, melted
1 tablespoon baking powder
1 medium banana, peeled
1 cup rice flour (or substitute
  corn, chickpea, or tapioca
  flour)
Extra butter for frying pancakes

1. In the bowl of a food processor, process the milk, eggs, and melted butter together. Slowly add the baking powder, banana, and flour and process until smooth.

2. Heat a griddle pan or large frying pan over medium heat. Drop a teaspoon of butter on it, and when the butter sizzles, start pouring on the batter to about 2″ diameter.

3. When bubbles come to the top, turn the pancakes and continue to fry until golden brown. Place on a plate in a warm oven to keep the pancakes warm while you make the others.

Per Serving: Calories: 70 | Fat: 2 g | Saturated fat: 1 g | Cholesterol: 25 mg | Sodium: 10 mg | Total carbohydrates: 10 g | Dietary fiber: 0 g | Sugars: 1 g | Protein: 2 g

SunButter and Jelly Crepes

Hands-On Time: 30 minutes
Total Time: 30 minutes
Yield: Serves 6

1¼ cups buckwheat flour
3 large eggs
¼ cup plus 1 tablespoon safflower
  oil, divided
¾ cup whole milk
1¼ cups water
½ teaspoon ground cinnamon
⅛ teaspoon salt
½ cup SunButter or other
  sunflower seed butter
1 cup strawberry jam
1 tablespoon confectioners' sugar

1. Place flour in a medium bowl. Add eggs, ¼ cup oil, milk, water, cinnamon, and salt. Mix to combine.

2. Use remaining oil, a little bit at a time, to grease a 9″ round nonstick skillet over medium-high heat. Using a ladle or glass measuring cup, slowly pour ¼ cup batter into skillet; swirl around pan.

3. Cook crepe until golden on bottom, 30–45 seconds. Using a wide spatula, turn crepe over; cook 30 more seconds. Keep in mind that crepes can be finicky, so it may take some practice! Transfer to plate. Make more with remaining batter.

4. Spread equal amounts of sunflower seed butter on each crepe and top with jam. Roll up and place on plates. Lightly dust crepes with confectioners' sugar and serve.

Per Serving: Calories: 510 | Fat: 27 g | Saturated fat: 4 g | Cholesterol: 95 mg | Sodium: 170 mg | Total carbohydrates: 60 g | Dietary fiber: 4 g | Sugars: 38 g | Protein: 11 g

Eggs Benedict

Hands-On Time: 10 minutes
Total Time: 20 minutes
Yield: Serves 4

1 ounce evaporated skim milk

½ cup low-fat mayonnaise

2 teaspoons lemon juice

4 medium eggs

4 slices Canadian bacon

2 (100-calorie) English muffins

1. In a small microwaveable bowl, mix the skim milk with the mayonnaise and lemon juice and heat in the microwave on high for about 40 seconds to warm.

2. Crack each egg into individual microwaveable bowls, being careful not to break the yolks. Cover each bowl with plastic wrap and microwave on high until the whites are cooked and yolks firm, about 2 minutes.

3. In a skillet, cook the bacon. Toast the muffins in the toaster. Place the bacon on two English muffin halves.

4. Add the eggs on the bacon and top each egg with 2 tablespoons of mayonnaise mixture.

Per Serving: Calories: 180 | Fat: 6 g | Saturated fat: 2 g | Cholesterol: 180 mg | Sodium: 610 mg | Total carbohydrates: 17 g | Dietary fiber: 1 g | Sugars: 5 g | Protein: 14 g

Sunday Morning Waffles

Hands-On Time: 30 minutes
Total Time: 30 minutes
Yield: Serves 6

1⅔ cups unbleached all-purpose flour

¼ cup sugar

1 tablespoon sodium-free baking powder

2 large egg whites

1½ cups low-fat milk

2 teaspoons pure vanilla extract

2 tablespoons canola oil

1. Place flour, sugar, and baking powder into a medium mixing bowl and whisk well to combine.

2. Place egg whites into a small mixing bowl and beat until they form stiff peaks. Add milk, vanilla, and canola oil to the dry ingredients and mix well. Let rest for 1–2 minutes to thicken, then gently fold whites into the batter.

3. Heat waffle iron. Spray lightly with oil, then ladle batter onto the hot surface, being careful to avoid the edges (batter will spread once appliance is closed). Close waffle iron and bake until golden brown, roughly 4–5 minutes.

4. Remove baked waffles from iron and repeat process with remaining batter. Serve immediately.

Per Serving: Calories: 230 | Fat: 5 g | Saturated fat: 1 g | Cholesterol: 5 mg | Sodium: 50 mg | Total carbohydrates: 37 g | Dietary fiber: 1 g | Sugars: 12 g | Protein: 8 g

Microwave Scrambled Eggs (pictured)

Hands-On Time: 5 minutes
Total Time: 7 minutes
Yield: Serves 2

3 large eggs
3 tablespoons whole milk
¼ teaspoon salt
⅛ teaspoon black pepper
⅛ teaspoon paprika
1 tablespoon butter

1. In a small bowl, lightly beat the eggs with the milk, salt, pepper, and paprika.

2. Place the butter in a microwave-safe bowl. Microwave on high heat for 30 seconds, and then for 5 seconds at a time until the butter melts (total cooking time should be 30–45 seconds).

3. Pour the egg mixture into the bowl, stirring.

4. Microwave the egg on high heat for 45 seconds. Stir to break up the egg a bit, then continue microwaving for 30 seconds, and then for 15 seconds at a time, stirring each time, until the egg is just cooked through. Serve immediately.

Per Serving: Calories: 173 | Fat: 14 g | Saturated fat: 6 g | Cholesterol: 297 mg | Sodium: 408 mg | Total carbohydrates: 2 g | Dietary fiber: 0 g | Sugars: 1 g | Protein: 10 g

The Perfect Breakfast Potatoes

Hands-On Time: 20 minutes
Total Time: 30 minutes
Yield: Serves 4

4 cups water
1½ teaspoons salt, divided
1½ pounds small red potatoes, quartered
3 tablespoons olive oil
1½ tablespoons chopped fresh thyme
½ teaspoon ground black pepper

1. In a large stockpot, bring the water to a boil and add 1 teaspoon salt.

2. Add the potatoes, cover, and cook over medium to low heat for approximately 7 minutes. (You are just trying to precook the potatoes; you don't want them too soft.) Strain the potatoes.

3. In a large skillet over medium heat, heat the oil. Add the potatoes and immediately season with thyme, ½ teaspoon salt, and pepper.

4. Cook the potatoes 10 minutes until lightly browned, stirring every minute or so.

Per Serving: Calories: 210 | Fat: 10 g | Saturated fat: 1 g | Cholesterol: 0 mg | Sodium: 380 mg | Total carbohydrates: 27 g | Dietary fiber: 3 g | Sugars: 2 g | Protein: 3 g

Blueberry Peach Pie Oatmeal Bowl

Hands-On Time: 10 minutes
Total Time: 10 minutes
Yield: Serves 1

½ teaspoon pumpkin pie spice
1 teaspoon vanilla extract
¾ cup hot cooked oatmeal
¼ cup blueberries
½ medium peach, pitted and sliced
1 tablespoon chopped pecans
2 tablespoons pure maple syrup
½ cup almond milk

1. Stir pumpkin pie spice and vanilla into oatmeal. Spoon into a small bowl.

2. Top with blueberries, peaches, and pecans.

3. Drizzle with maple syrup and pour milk around the edges of the bowl.

Per Serving: Calories: 300 | Fat: 8 g | Saturated fat: 1.5 g | Cholesterol: 0 mg | Sodium: 85 mg | Total carbohydrates: 54 g | Dietary fiber: 5 g | Sugars: 35 g | Protein: 5 g

Cinnamon French Toast

Hands-On Time: 5 minutes
Total Time: 15 minutes
Yield: Serves 2

2 large eggs
½ cup skim milk
½ teaspoon ground cinnamon
½ teaspoon vanilla extract
1 tablespoon confectioners' sugar
4 (45-calorie) slices bread
2 tablespoons pancake syrup

1. Preheat oven to 400°F.

2. Beat eggs and skim milk lightly in a medium bowl. Add the cinnamon, vanilla, and sugar. Soak the bread in the egg mixture and place on a nonstick baking sheet.

3. Bake for about 10 minutes or until golden. Serve with pancake syrup.

Per Serving: Calories: 220 | Fat: 6 g | Saturated fat: 2 g | Cholesterol: 185 mg | Sodium: 350 mg | Total carbohydrates: 30 g | Dietary fiber: 5 g | Sugars: 10 g | Protein: 13 g

Cheese Omelet

Hands-On Time: 10 minutes
Total Time: 10 minutes
Yield: Serves 2

1 cup fat-free Egg Beaters
1 tablespoon fat-free milk
1 teaspoon vegetable oil
½ cup shredded low-fat Cheddar cheese
⅛ teaspoon ground black pepper

1. In a small bowl, combine Egg Beaters and milk.

2. Heat oil in a small skillet on low heat, then pour in the Egg Beaters mixture. Lift the edges of the mixture as it cooks to allow uncooked portions to reach the hot pan surface.

3. Sprinkle the cheese evenly over the mixture and fold into thirds. Flip the omelet to cook evenly. Transfer to a plate and sprinkle with pepper.

Per Serving: Calories: 170 | Fat: 8 g | Saturated fat: 3.5 g | Cholesterol: 20 mg | Sodium: 420 mg | Total carbohydrates: 4 g | Dietary fiber: 0 g | Sugars: 3 g | Protein: 20 g

Country Sweet Potato Breakfast Hash (pictured)

Hands-On Time: 30 minutes
Total Time: 30 minutes
Yield: Serves 6

- 2 tablespoons extra-virgin olive oil, divided
- 3 strips of bacon, diced
- 1 shallot, finely chopped
- 1 sprig rosemary, finely chopped (leaves only)
- 1 small green or yellow zucchini, ¼" diced
- 1 pound small red potatoes, ¼" diced
- 2 large sweet potatoes, peeled and ¼" diced
- ¼ teaspoon paprika
- ¼ teaspoon chili powder
- ½ teaspoon garlic powder
- ¼ teaspoon sea salt
- ⅛ teaspoon ground black pepper

1. Heat a large skillet over medium-high heat and add 1 tablespoon oil and the bacon and shallots. Sauté for 2–3 minutes.
2. Add the rosemary leaves and zucchini and cook about 5 more minutes, until the zucchini is soft and cooked through.
3. Transfer the bacon and zucchini mixture to a plate. Add the potatoes and sweet potatoes along with the remaining oil to the pan. Add the spices, salt, and pepper. Reduce heat to medium-low and cook for about 10 minutes, stirring occasionally. If the potatoes are sticking and appear dry, add another tablespoon of oil.
4. Cook the potatoes until they start to brown, then add the bacon and zucchini back to the pan and stir to combine. Serve hot.

Per Serving: Calories: 174 | Fat: 7 g | Saturated fat: 1 g | Cholesterol: 5 mg | Sodium: 180 mg | Total carbohydrates: 24 g | Dietary fiber: 4 g | Sugars: 5 g | Protein: 5 g

Raspberry-Topped Chocolate Waffles

Hands-On Time: 30 minutes
Total Time: 30 minutes
Yield: Serves 24

- 1 (18.25-ounce) box devil's food cake mix, plus ingredients called for on box
- 1 (8-ounce) tub whipped topping, thawed
- 2 cups fresh raspberries

1. Mix cake batter according to instructions on the box. Prepare waffle iron and bake waffles according to manufacturer's instructions.
2. Top warm waffles with whipped topping and raspberries.

Per Serving: Calories: 160 | Fat: 9 g | Saturated fat: 3.5 g | Cholesterol: 30 mg | Sodium: 170 mg | Total carbohydrates: 19 g | Dietary fiber: 1 g | Sugars: 11 g | Protein: 2 g

Caramel Rolls

Hands-On Time: 10 minutes
Total Time: 30 minutes
Yield: Serves 12

¼ cup caramel fudge ice cream topping
2 tablespoons plus ¼ cup brown sugar, divided
2 tablespoons heavy cream
¼ cup butter, softened
½ teaspoon ground cinnamon
1 (8-ounce) can refrigerated crescent roll dough

1. Preheat oven to 375°F. Spray a 9″ round cake pan with nonstick baking spray.
2. In a small bowl combine ice cream topping, 2 tablespoons brown sugar, and heavy cream and mix well. Spread mixture evenly in the prepared cake pan.
3. In another small bowl, combine butter, ¼ cup brown sugar, and cinnamon and mix well.
4. Unroll dough and separate into 4 rectangles. Press seams to seal. Spread butter mixture over rectangles. Roll up dough, starting at the short edge, and pinch edges of dough to seal. Cut each roll into 3 slices and arrange the twelve rolls on the topping in the cake pan.
5. Bake for 15–20 minutes, until dough is deep golden brown. Invert pan onto serving plate and remove pan. If any caramel remains in pan, spread onto rolls. Serve warm.

Per Serving: Calories: 150 | Fat: 6 g | Saturated fat: 3 g | Cholesterol: 15 mg | Sodium: 170 mg | Total carbohydrates: 22 g | Dietary fiber: 1 g | Sugars: 8 g | Protein: 3 g

Cocoa Pancakes

Hands-On Time: 20 minutes
Total Time: 30 minutes
Yield: Serves 6

Fruit Syrup
¼ cup sugar
1 tablespoon plus 1½ teaspoons
    cornstarch, divided
1¼ cups boiling water
1 (16-ounce) package frozen
    unsweetened blueberries,
    thawed and drained
1 tablespoon lemon juice

Pancakes
1½ cups whole-wheat pastry flour
½ cup unsweetened cocoa
    powder
2 tablespoons granulated sugar
1 teaspoon baking powder
½ teaspoon baking soda
½ teaspoon salt
2 cups chocolate soy milk
1 tablespoon vegetable oil
1½ teaspoons vanilla extract
½ cup carob chips

1. For the syrup: combine sugar and cornstarch in a medium saucepan. Stir in boiling water. Cook over medium heat until mixture comes to a full boil, stirring constantly. Reduce heat and simmer for 1 minute, stirring constantly. Remove from heat. Fold in blueberries and lemon juice. Set syrup aside.

2. For the pancakes: sift flour, cocoa, sugar, baking powder, baking soda, and salt into medium mixing bowl. Add chocolate soy milk and oil, whisking until just combined. Stir in vanilla extract. Let batter sit 5 minutes before cooking.

3. Spray a large nonstick skillet with cooking spray. Heat skillet over medium heat. Pour ¼ cup batter on skillet for each pancake. Sprinkle pancakes with carob chips. Cook for 2 minutes, turning when tops begin to bubble and edges begin looking dry. Cook 2 minutes more and remove from skillet, placing on a warm plate. Serve with fruit syrup.

Per Serving: Calories: 310 | Fat: 6 g | Saturated fat: 2 g | Cholesterol: 0 mg | Sodium: 420 mg | Total carbohydrates: 61 g | Dietary fiber: 9 g | Sugars: 27 g | Protein: 7 g

Chocolate Banana Split Oatmeal Bowl (pictured)

Hands-On Time: 10 minutes
Total Time: 10 minutes
Yield: Serves 1

1 teaspoon vanilla extract
¾ cup prepared oatmeal
1 medium banana, peeled and
    sliced
1 tablespoon sliced almonds
2 tablespoons chopped pecans
2 tablespoons mini chocolate
    chips
1 teaspoon rainbow sprinkles
2 tablespoons pure maple syrup
½ cup almond milk
2 maraschino cherries

1. Stir vanilla into oatmeal, spoon into a small bowl.
2. Top with banana, almonds, pecans, chocolate chips, and sprinkles. Drizzle with maple syrup.
3. Pour milk around the edges of the bowl and top with cherries.

Per Serving: Calories: 570 | Fat: 23 g | Saturated fat: 6 g | Cholesterol: 0 mg | Sodium: 90 mg | Total carbohydrates: 91 g | Dietary fiber: 9 g | Sugars: 58 g | Protein: 8 g

Cranberry Almond Granola

Hands-On Time: 10 minutes
Total Time: 25 minutes
Yield: Serves 6

1 tablespoon whole walnuts
1 tablespoon flaxseeds
3 tablespoons canola oil
3 tablespoons maple syrup
¼ teaspoon vanilla extract
¼ teaspoon almond extract
1 cup gluten-free rolled oats
1 tablespoon sliced almonds
½ teaspoon ground cinnamon
2 tablespoons no-sugar-added
    dried cranberries

1. Preheat oven to 350°F.
2. Using a food processor or blender, add in walnuts and pulse until ground. Add to a large bowl. Next add flaxseed and pulse until finely ground. Add to same large bowl.
3. In a medium bowl, stir together oil, maple syrup, and vanilla and almond extracts.
4. Add oats, almonds, and cinnamon to bowl with walnuts and flaxseed. Pour oil mixture over oats and stir well to combine.
5. Spread granola on a rimmed baking sheet and bake 15 minutes. Stir occasionally to ensure granola turns a light brown color.
6. After removing from oven, add cranberries and stir to combine. Store in an airtight container up to 3 weeks.

Per Serving: Calories: 185 | Fat: 10 g | Saturated fat: 1 g | Cholesterol: 0 mg | Sodium: 0 mg | Total carbohydrates: 21 g | Dietary fiber: 2 g | Sugars: 9 g | Protein: 3 g

Peanut Butter Berry Oatmeal Bowl

Hands-On Time: 10 minutes
Total Time: 10 minutes
Yield: Serves 1

¾ cup prepared oatmeal, heated
2 tablespoons peanut butter
¼ cup raspberries
½ medium banana, peeled and
    sliced
2 tablespoons granola
2 tablespoons pure maple syrup
    or honey
½ cup almond milk

1. Spoon oatmeal into a small bowl. Top with peanut butter, raspberries, banana, and granola.

2. Drizzle with maple syrup and pour almond milk around the edges of the bowl.

Per Serving: Calories: 580 | Fat: 22 g | Saturated fat: 4.5 g | Cholesterol: 0 mg | Sodium: 240 mg | Total carbohydrates: 82 g | Dietary fiber: 10 g | Sugars: 37 g | Protein: 14 g

Raisin Muffins

Hands-On Time: 10 minutes
Total Time: 30 minutes
Yield: Serves 6

2 cups oat bran
¼ cup brown sugar
1 tablespoon baking powder
2 large egg whites
1 cup low-fat buttermilk
½ cup molasses
½ cup unsweetened applesauce
¾ cup raisins

1. Preheat oven to 450°F. Spray a 6-cup muffin tin with nonstick cooking spray.

2. Mix the oat bran, brown sugar, and baking powder in a large bowl. In a small bowl, beat egg whites until foamy; stir in buttermilk and molasses. Add the buttermilk mixture to the oat bran mixture, then fold in the applesauce and raisins.

3. Pour an equal amount of batter into each cup of the prepared muffin tin. Bake until tops are golden, about 20 minutes. Allow to cool slightly before serving.

Per Serving: Calories: 270 | Fat: 2.5 g | Saturated fat: 0.5 g | Cholesterol: 0 mg | Sodium: 350 mg | Total carbohydrates: 67 g | Dietary fiber: 6 g | Sugars: 42 g | Protein: 9 g

Peanut Butter Pancakes

Hands-On Time: 10 minutes
Total Time: 20 minutes
Yield: Serves 2

½ cup sifted all-purpose flour
1 teaspoon baking powder
Pinch of salt
1 large egg
½ cup whole milk
1 tablespoon creamy peanut
    butter
4 teaspoons butter, divided

1. In a medium bowl, mix together the flour, baking powder, and salt. In a small bowl beat the egg and add the milk. Add egg and milk to the flour mixture. In a small bowl, mix the peanut butter with 1 teaspoon melted butter and mix well. Add to the batter.

2. Melt the remaining 3 teaspoons of butter in a nonstick pan or griddle. Pour ¼ cup of the batter into the pan. Heat until small bubbles form on the surface of the pancake. Then flip the pancake. Repeat with the remaining batter. No syrup is necessary for these treats.

Per Serving: Calories: 300 | Fat: 17 g | Saturated fat: 8 g | Cholesterol: 120 mg | Sodium: 490 mg | Total carbohydrates: 30 g | Dietary fiber: 1 g | Sugars: 4 g | Protein: 10 g

Fruity Brunch Pizza

Hands-On Time: 20 minutes
Total Time: 30 minutes
Yield: Serves 4

1 (13.8-ounce) can refrigerated
    pizza crust
2 tablespoons butter, melted
½ cup yellow cake mix
2 tablespoons sugar
½ cup vanilla low-fat yogurt
½ cup sliced strawberries
¼ cup blueberries
½ cup halved red grapes
½ cup blackberries
¼ cup raspberries

1. Preheat oven to temperature specified in pizza crust instructions.

2. Roll out pizza dough on a work surface and cut out 4 equally sized discs or squares. Place on a large ungreased baking sheet.

3. Baste dough with butter and sprinkle with cake mix and sugar. Bake according to pizza crust package instructions.

4. Top with a thin layer of yogurt. Arrange fruit over the yogurt.

Per Serving: Calories: 440 | Fat: 10 g | Saturated fat: 5 g | Cholesterol: 15 mg | Sodium: 890 mg | Total carbohydrates: 83 g | Dietary fiber: 4 g | Sugars: 31 g | Protein: 10 g

Very Veggie Chopped Vegetable Omelet

Hands-On Time: 10 minutes
Total Time: 10 minutes
Yield: Serves 2

4 large egg whites
1 large egg
¼ teaspoon salt
½ cup chopped red bell pepper
½ cup chopped green bell pepper
½ cup chopped eggplant
1 tablespoon olive oil

1. Beat the egg whites and egg in a small bowl. Mix in the salt. Mix the vegetables together in a small bowl.

2. Heat the olive oil in a small skillet on low heat. Pour the egg mixture in to coat the surface. Cook until edges show firmness.

3. Add the vegetable mixture so that it covers the entire egg mixture evenly. Fold one side over the other. Flip the half-moon omelet so both sides are evenly cooked.

Per Serving: Calories: 160 | Fat: 10 g | Saturated fat: 2 g | Cholesterol: 95 mg | Sodium: 440 mg | Total carbohydrates: 6 g | Dietary fiber: 2 g | Sugars: 4 g | Protein: 11 g

Maple Cakes

Hands-On Time: 25 minutes
Total Time: 25 minutes
Yield: Serves 4

2 cups all-purpose flour
5 teaspoons baking powder
1 teaspoon salt
4 tablespoons pure maple syrup, divided
2 cups whole milk
2 large eggs
1 tablespoon butter, melted
1½ cups corn kernels
1 tablespoon vegetable oil

1. In a large bowl, combine the flour, baking powder, and salt. Mix well.

2. Slowly add 2 tablespoons maple syrup, milk, eggs, and butter, whisking to keep it light. Fold in the corn.

3. Heat oil in a large skillet or griddle over medium heat. Drop the batter on the griddle using a ladle. Fry until little bubbles form on the tops of the cakes. Turn and fry on the reverse side until golden brown (about 2–4 minutes per side). Serve with remaining maple syrup.

Per Serving: Calories: 490 | Fat: 13 g | Saturated fat: 6 g | Cholesterol: 115 mg | Sodium: 670 mg | Total carbohydrates: 80 g | Dietary fiber: 3 g | Sugars: 19 g | Protein: 15 g

Chouquettes (Pastry Puffs)

Hands-On Time: 15 minutes
Total Time: 30 minutes
Yield: Serves 40

1 cup water
7 tablespoons butter, diced
¼ teaspoon salt
1 tablespoon sugar
1 cup all-purpose flour
4 large eggs
1 cup pearl sugar

1. First, make the *pâte à choux*, a classic pastry dough. Pour the water into a medium saucepan and bring to a boil over medium heat. Add the butter, salt, and sugar. As soon as the mixture comes back to a boil, remove the pan from the heat.

2. Pour in the flour and stir continuously with a wooden spoon. When the mixture is smooth, put the saucepan back on the stove over low heat and stir until the dough no longer sticks to the spoon and the bottom of the saucepan.

3. Remove from the heat. Break the eggs in the saucepan, one by one, and stir well. The dough must be smooth, but not liquid.

4. Preheat the oven to 350°F.

5. Take 1 tablespoon of dough and make a small ball, then place it on a baking sheet lined with parchment paper. Repeat. Make sure there's plenty of space between each ball, at least 1½″ apart. Sprinkle 1 teaspoon of pearl sugar on each bun. Bake for 15 minutes.

6. Let cool before serving.

Per Serving: Calories: 58 | Fat: 2 g | Saturated fat: 1.5 g | Cholesterol: 25 mg | Sodium: 20 mg | Total carbohydrates: 8 g | Dietary fiber: 0 g | Sugars: 6 g | Protein: 1 g

Chapter 3

Sandwiches and Salads

The Perfect CLT Sandwiches

Hands-On Time: 10 minutes
Total Time: 25 minutes
Yield: Serves 2

1 teaspoon garlic powder

⅛ teaspoon ground black pepper

1 teaspoon Italian seasoning

2 (6-ounce) boneless, skinless
    chicken breasts

1 teaspoon balsamic vinegar

2 100 percent whole-wheat
    hamburger buns

1 cup shredded romaine hearts

2 slices medium beefsteak tomato

1. Prepare a grill with olive oil spray over medium heat.

2. Sprinkle garlic powder, black pepper, and Italian season-ing on the chicken breasts and place on the grill. Cook the chicken for 7–8 minutes, turn, and continue cooking for another 7 minutes or until juices run clear.

3. While the chicken finishes cooking, sprinkle with the balsamic vinegar.

4. Remove the chicken from the grill and place on buns. Top chicken with tomato slices, shredded lettuce, and bun top.

Per Serving: Calories: 330 | Fat: 5 g | Saturated fat: 1.5 g | Cholesterol: 120 mg | Sodium: 270 mg | Total carbohydrates: 22 g | Dietary fiber: 3 g | Sugars: 4 g | Protein: 43 g

Easy Chicken Pita with Cucumber Yogurt

Hands-On Time: 10 minutes
Total Time: 10 minutes
Yield: Serves 2

½ medium cucumber, peeled,
    seeded, and chopped

½ cup plain low-fat Greek yogurt

1 teaspoon chopped fresh dill

2 (10") large pita breads

½ cup shredded lettuce

1½ cups shredded cooked chicken
    breast

¼ cup chopped red onion

1. In a small bowl, combine cucumber, yogurt, and dill and mix well.

2. To assemble, spread the cucumber yogurt on the pita bread. Add lettuce and chicken and garnish with red on-ion. Serve immediately or wrap in wax paper and refrig-erate for up to 4 hours.

Per Serving: Calories: 425 | Fat: 5 g | Saturated fat: 2 g | Cholesterol: 84 mg | Sodium: 478 mg | Total carbohydrates: 48 g | Dietary fiber: 3 g | Sugars: 5 g | Protein: 42 g

Chicken Wrap

Hands-On Time: 10 minutes
Total Time: 10 minutes
Yield: Serves 1

1 (6") small flour tortilla
½ (6-ounce) grilled chicken breast
1 teaspoon minced white onion
2 teaspoons salsa
1 tablespoon shredded fat-free
    Cheddar cheese
¼ cup shredded romaine lettuce

Place tortilla flat on a plate. Slice chicken breast. Pile remaining ingredients in the center of the tortilla. Roll tortilla up burrito-style.

Per Serving: Calories: 250 | Fat: 6 g | Saturated fat: 2 g | Cholesterol: 75 mg | Sodium: 430 mg | Total carbohydrates: 17 g | Dietary fiber: 2 g | Sugars: 2 g | Protein: 32 g

Egg Salad Wraps

Hands-On Time: 10 minutes
Total Time: 25 minutes
Yield: Serves 12

4 large eggs
1 (12-ounce) package firm tofu,
    drained
⅓ cup chopped green onions
4 medium stalks celery, chopped
½ cup low-fat yogurt
½ cup light whipped salad
    dressing
¼ cup Dijon mustard
⅓ cup skim milk
½ teaspoon salt
⅛ teaspoon cayenne pepper
2 cups chopped grape tomatoes
12 (10") whole-wheat tortillas

1. Place eggs in a medium saucepan and cover with cold water. Bring to a boil over high heat. When water boils furiously, remove from heat, cover pan, and let stand for 15 minutes. Drain eggs and run cold water into the pan until the eggs are cold. Crack eggs under water, then peel gently. Chop hard-boiled eggs.

2. Drain the tofu by pressing between paper towels; crumble into large bowl. Add eggs, green onions, and celery and toss gently.

3. In small bowl combine yogurt, salad dressing, mustard, milk, salt, and cayenne pepper and mix well. Add to egg mixture and stir gently to coat. At this point mixture can be refrigerated for up to 24 hours. When ready to eat, fold in grape tomatoes, then make wrap sandwiches with the tortillas.

Per Serving: Calories: 200 | Fat: 8 g | Saturated fat: 3 g | Cholesterol: 60 mg | Sodium: 490 mg | Total carbohydrates: 24 g | Dietary fiber: 5 g | Sugars: 4 g | Protein: 10 g

Apple Banana Sandwich with Peanut Butter (pictured)

Hands-On Time: 10 minutes
Total Time: 10 minutes
Yield: Serves 1

2 slices whole-wheat bread

2 teaspoons peanut butter

1 small apple, cored and thinly sliced

½ medium banana, peeled and sliced

1 teaspoon brown sugar

½ teaspoon ground cinnamon

1. Lightly toast both slices of bread. Spread peanut butter on one slice. Cover with apple and banana. Sprinkle with brown sugar and cinnamon.

2. Place in toaster oven. Broil for 1 minute. Bread should be fairly soft. Remove from toaster oven. Cover with the other piece of toast and slice diagonally.

Per Serving: Calories: 350 | Fat: 8 g | Saturated fat: 1.5 g | Cholesterol: 0 mg | Sodium: 320 mg | Total carbohydrates: 65 g | Dietary fiber: 10 g | Sugars: 31 g | Protein: 11 g

California Bagel

Hands-On Time: 10 minutes
Total Time: 10 minutes
Yield: Serves 2

1 large plain bagel

2 tablespoons fat-free cream cheese

2 thick slices medium tomato

2 slices medium red onion

¼ cup sprouts

½ teaspoon salt

¼ teaspoon ground black pepper

Split and toast bagel. Spread 1 tablespoon cream cheese on each cut half. Top each half with 1 slice of tomato, sliced red onion, and sprouts. Sprinkle with salt and pepper.

Per Serving: Calories: 170 | Fat: 1 g | Saturated fat: 0 g | Cholesterol: 0 mg | Sodium: 670 mg | Total carbohydrates: 33 g | Dietary fiber: 1 g | Sugars: 3 g | Protein: 2 g

Healthier Bacon, Lettuce, and Tomato Sandwich

Hands-On Time: 10 minutes
Total Time: 10 minutes
Yield: Serves 4

6 slices extra-lean bacon

4 tablespoons fat-free Miracle Whip salad dressing

8 slices whole-wheat bread, toasted

1 large tomato, thinly sliced

8 lettuce leaves

Broil the bacon. Spread a thin layer of Miracle Whip on pieces of toasted bread. Arrange bacon and tomato slices on toast with lettuce.

Per Serving: Calories: 320 | Fat: 9 g | Saturated fat: 2.5 g | Cholesterol: 15 mg | Sodium: 630 mg | Total carbohydrates: 46 g | Dietary fiber: 10 g | Sugars: 10 g | Protein: 5 g

Tomato, Mozzarella, and Basil Wraps

Hands-On Time: 10 minutes
Total Time: 10 minutes
Yield: Serves 2

4 medium beefsteak tomato slices

2 (¼") slices fresh mozzarella cheese

2 (8") 100 percent whole-wheat tortillas

2 tablespoons balsamic vinegar

1 teaspoon ground black pepper

4 tablespoons chopped fresh basil leaves

1. Cut tomato slices and cheese slices into thin strips.

2. Lay tortillas flat and layer half of the mozzarella strips down the center of each tortilla, followed by the tomato slices on top. Drizzle the balsamic vinegar and ground black pepper over the mozzarella and tomato, and cover with the chopped basil.

3. Wrap the tortilla tightly and enjoy!

Per Serving: Calories: 240 | Fat: 10 g | Saturated fat: 6 g | Cholesterol: 20 mg | Sodium: 390 mg | Total carbohydrates: 25 g | Dietary fiber: 5 g | Sugars: 5 g | Protein: 11 g

Peanut Butter and Homemade Jam Sandwich

Hands-On Time: 10 minutes
Total Time: 30 minutes
Yield: Serves 1

½ cup hulled strawberries, quartered

1 teaspoon sugar

1 tablespoon natural peanut butter

2 slices bread

1. In a small saucepan over medium heat, combine strawberries and sugar and simmer for 5 minutes or until soft and syrupy. Let cool.

2. Spread peanut butter and cooled strawberry jam over 1 slice of bread, then top with second slice.

Per Serving: Calories: 297 | Fat: 10 g | Saturated fat: 2 g | Cholesterol: 0 mg | Sodium: 298 mg | Total carbohydrates: 44 g | Dietary fiber: 5 g | Sugars: 13 g | Protein: 10 g

Roast Beef Lettuce Wraps

Hands-On Time: 10 minutes
Total Time: 10 minutes
Yield: Serves 4

½ cup mayonnaise

¼ cup chopped chives

8 large green leaf lettuce leaves

8 (8-ounce) thin slices rare roast beef

1. Add mayonnaise and chives to a blender and blend until smooth. Set aside. Wash lettuce leaves and pat them dry, being careful not to rip them. Place 1 slice of roast beef in each lettuce wrap.

2. Spread ½ tablespoon of chive mayonnaise on each piece of roast beef. Roll lettuce up around toppings. Serve immediately with remaining chive mayo for dipping.

Per Serving: Calories: 180 | Fat: 11 g | Saturated fat: 2.5 g | Cholesterol: 50 mg | Sodium: 250 mg | Total carbohydrates: 6 g | Dietary fiber: 1 g | Sugars: 3 g | Protein: 16 g

Tuna Melt English Muffins (pictured)

Hands-On Time: 5 minutes
Total Time: 10 minutes
Yield: Serves 6

¼ teaspoon garlic powder

1 tablespoon lemon juice

½ teaspoon minced fresh thyme

1 large celery stalk, diced

2 tablespoons mayonnaise

½ cup canned tuna, drained

½ cup shredded Cheddar or
 Monterey jack cheese

2 tablespoons Worcestershire
 sauce

6 English muffins, split and
 toasted

1. Stir the garlic powder, lemon juice, thyme, celery, and mayonnaise into the tuna in a small bowl. Stir in the shredded cheese and the Worcestershire sauce.

2. Spoon a heaping tablespoon of the mixture onto each toasted muffin half. Broil briefly in the oven until the cheese is melted and the tuna is heated through. Store the unused portion of the tuna mixture in a sealed container in the refrigerator for 2 days.

Per Serving: Calories: 240 | Fat: 9 g | Saturated fat: 3 g | Cholesterol: 20 mg | Sodium: 470 mg | Total carbohydrates: 29 g | Dietary fiber: 5 g | Sugars: 6 g | Protein: 13 g

Grilled Chicken Patties

Hands-On Time: 15 minutes
Total Time: 15 minutes
Yield: Serves 4

1 pound ground chicken

1 teaspoon ground sweet paprika

½ teaspoon ground black pepper

½ teaspoon ground cumin

½ teaspoon salt-free chili
 seasoning

¼ teaspoon dried red pepper
 flakes

1. Preheat grill.

2. Place ground chicken into a medium mixing bowl. Add the seasonings and mix thoroughly using your hands. Divide mixture into 4 equal portions. Roll each portion into a ball, then flatten to form patties.

3. Once grill is ready, place patties on surface. Grill for 5–6 minutes on the first side, then gently flip patties and grill for another 5–6 minutes on the second side.

4. Remove from grill and serve immediately.

Per Serving: Calories: 170 | Fat: 9 g | Saturated fat: 2.5 g | Cholesterol: 100 mg | Sodium: 70 mg | Total carbohydrates: 1 g | Dietary fiber: 0 g | Sugars: 0 g | Protein: 20 g

Hummus, Carrot, and Parsley Wrap Sandwiches

Hands-On Time: 10 minutes
Total Time: 10 minutes
Yield: Serves 4

1 (9-ounce) package rectangular
    lavash wraps
1 cup hummus
2 medium carrots, shredded
½ cup chopped red cabbage
½ cup chopped fresh parsley

1. Spread the lavash on a clean surface.

2. Measure ¼ cup hummus onto the center of each wrap and spread evenly. Top with a quarter of the shredded carrot, cabbage, and parsley.

3. Fold the top and bottom of the lavash toward the filling, fold one of the sides over the filling to cover, and then carefully roll to close. Repeat with remaining sandwiches. Serve immediately.

Per Serving: Calories: 300 | Fat: 12 g | Saturated fat: 1 g | Cholesterol: 0 mg | Sodium: 540 mg | Total carbohydrates: 40 g | Dietary fiber: 12 g | Sugars: 2 g | Protein: 21 g

Avocado and Chickpea Smash Sandwiches

Hands-On Time: 10 minutes
Total Time: 10 minutes
Yield: Serves 4

1 medium avocado, peeled and
    pitted
⅓ cup hummus
¼ teaspoon salt
⅛ teaspoon ground white pepper
1 cup canned chickpeas, drained
8 slices whole-wheat bread

1. Place avocado in a medium bowl. Top with hummus, salt, and pepper, and mash, leaving some chunks. Fold chickpeas into avocado mixture.

2. Spread avocado mixture on four slices of bread and top with the remaining slices. Cut sandwiches in half and serve.

Per Serving: Calories: 330 | Fat: 12 g | Saturated fat: 2 g | Cholesterol: 0 mg | Sodium: 570 mg | Total carbohydrates: 44 g | Dietary fiber: 10 g | Sugars: 5 g | Protein: 13 g

Egg-cellent Sandwich

Hands-On Time: 25 minutes
Total Time: 25 minutes
Yield: Serves 1

1 teaspoon olive oil

1 teaspoon minced garlic

¼ cup spinach leaves

1 large poached egg

1 high-fiber English muffin, toasted

2 tablespoons ricotta cheese

2 tomato slices

1. Heat oil in a small skillet over medium-high heat. Add garlic and sauté 30 seconds. Add spinach and cook 1 minute or until wilted. Set aside.

2. Spread ricotta on English muffin half. Top with tomatoes, spinach mixture, and egg. Serve immediately.

Per Serving: Calories: 300 | Fat: 15 g | Saturated fat: 4 g | Cholesterol: 200 mg | Sodium: 320 mg | Total carbohydrates: 29 g | Dietary fiber: 5 g | Sugars: 6 g | Protein: 16 g

Banana Nutter Sandwich

Hands-On Time: 10 minutes
Total Time: 10 minutes
Yield: Serves 6

1 loaf gluten-free bread

½ cup natural peanut butter

3 large bananas, peeled and sliced

1. Slice loaf of bread into 12 slices.

2. Spread peanut butter on 6 slices, then add sliced bananas. Place remaining bread slices on top to make a sandwich.

Per Serving: Calories: 410 | Fat: 15 g | Saturated fat: 1.5 g | Cholesterol: 0 mg | Sodium: 540 mg | Total carbohydrates: 64 g | Dietary fiber: 5 g | Sugars: 16 g | Protein: 7 g

Tuna Salad Sandwich

Hands-On Time: 10 minutes
Total Time: 10 minutes
Yield: Serves 4

- 1 (6-ounce) can tuna packed in water, drained
- ¼ cup diced sweet pickles
- 2 tablespoons mayonnaise
- 1 tablespoon lemon juice
- ¼ teaspoon salt
- 4 green lettuce leaves
- 8 slices toasted whole-wheat bread

Combine tuna, pickles, mayonnaise, lemon juice, and salt in a medium bowl with a rubber spatula. Place 1 lettuce leaf on a slice of bread. Add a scoop of tuna salad and top with another slice of bread. Repeat with remaining lettuce leaves and bread slices.

Per Serving: Calories: 262 | Fat: 8 g | Saturated fat: 1.5 g | Cholesterol: 20 mg | Sodium: 600 mg | Total carbohydrates: 30 g | Dietary fiber: 4 g | Sugars: 7 g | Protein: 17 g

Barbecue Chicken Wrap (pictured)

Hands-On Time: 10 minutes
Total Time: 30 minutes
Yield: Serves 4

- 3 (4-ounce) boneless, skinless chicken breasts
- ¼ cup barbecue sauce
- 4 (6") gluten-free tortillas
- ½ cup shredded Cheddar cheese
- 2 large romaine lettuce leaves, halved

1. Place chicken breasts in a medium pan and cover with water. Place pan over medium heat, bring to a boil, then simmer 10–12 minutes or until chicken meat is cooked through. Allow chicken to cool on a plate and then shred with forks.

2. In a small saucepan over low heat, add barbecue sauce and chicken and stir to combine. Keep warm while you begin making wraps.

3. Warm a small skillet over low heat and add a tortilla. Sprinkle on cheese and wait until cheese is melted. Remove from heat and place wrap on a wide plate or clean work surface.

4. Add ¼ of barbecue chicken and top with lettuce. Place wrap horizontally in front of you, fold bottom and top edges over, rotate wrap, and roll up from bottom. Repeat with remaining tortillas. Place any leftover barbecue chicken in an airtight container.

Per Serving: Calories: 214 | Fat: 9 g | Saturated fat: 3 g | Cholesterol: 30 mg | Sodium: 520 mg | Total carbohydrates: 24 g | Dietary fiber: 5 g | Sugars: 7 g | Protein: 11 g

Meatball Sandwich

Hands-On Time: 10 minutes
Total Time: 20 minutes
Yield: Serves 2

6 (2") cooked meatballs

1 cup marinara sauce

2 (6") sub buns

½ cup shredded mozzarella
   cheese

1. Preheat oven to 350°F.

2. In a medium pan, heat the meatballs in the sauce over medium heat, until sauce starts to bubble, about 5–7 minutes.

3. Open the buns flat and put 3 meatballs with sauce on each half. Sprinkle mozzarella cheese on top of meatballs, then top with other bun half.

4. Heat sandwiches in the oven until cheese melts, about 3–4 minutes.

Per Serving: Calories: 523 | Fat: 15 g | Saturated fat: 7 g | Cholesterol: 60 mg | Sodium: 1,800 mg | Total carbohydrates: 64 g | Dietary fiber: 7 g | Sugars: 10 g | Protein: 33 g

French Toasted–Ham Sandwiches

Hands-On Time: 15 minutes
Total Time: 15 minutes
Yield: Serves 6

3 teaspoons prepared yellow
   mustard

12 slices firm white bread

12 thin slices cooked ham

6 slices Swiss cheese

2 large eggs, lightly beaten

½ cup whole milk

¼ teaspoon salt

⅛ teaspoon ground black pepper

3 tablespoons butter

1. Spread a thin layer of mustard over each slice of bread. On each of 6 slices, place 2 slices of ham and 1 slice of cheese. Top with remaining 6 slices of bread, mustard side down.

2. In a shallow bowl, whisk eggs with milk, salt, and pepper.

3. Melt butter in a large skillet over low heat.

4. Dip sandwiches in egg mixture, turning to coat well. Depending on the size of the skillet, cook 2 or 3 at a time. Place sandwiches in the hot skillet and brown well on each side.

Per Serving: Calories: 390 | Fat: 18 g | Saturated fat: 10 g | Cholesterol: 120 mg | Sodium: 460 mg | Total carbohydrates: 35 g | Dietary fiber: 1 g | Sugars: 2 g | Protein: 20 g

Clubhouse Sandwich

Hands-On Time: 10 minutes
Total Time: 10 minutes
Yield: Serves 4

12 slices whole-wheat bread
3 tablespoons mayonnaise
1 medium head romaine lettuce
4 large tomatoes, thickly sliced
12 slices extra lean bacon, broiled
½ pound thinly sliced smoked turkey
¼ teaspoon salt
⅛ teaspoon ground black pepper
12 toothpicks or cocktail sticks

1. Toast bread. Spread mayonnaise thinly on 4 slices of bread. Cut romaine leaves to fit the bread. Place 2 tomato slices on top of lettuce. Place bacon on top of the tomato. Top with turkey slices, salt, and pepper, and finish with another slice of bread.

2. Repeat for the second layer. Cover with a final bread slice. Cut sandwich into 4 pieces diagonally. Place toothpick or cocktail stick into center of each little sandwich to hold it together.

Per Serving: Calories: 570 | Fat: 18 g | Saturated fat: 4 g | Cholesterol: 35 mg | Sodium: 1,560 mg | Total carbohydrates: 68 g | Dietary fiber: 4 g | Sugars: 12 g | Protein: 18 g

Pressed Ham and Cheese Sandwich

Hands-On Time: 10 minutes
Total Time: 10 minutes
Yield: Serves 1

1 teaspoon butter
2 slices whole-wheat bread
3 ounces prosciutto or deli ham
1 slice Gruyère cheese
1 teaspoon Dijon mustard

1. Melt butter in a large skillet over medium heat.
2. Make sandwich with bread, ham, cheese, and mustard and place into buttered pan. Place a second heavy pan on top of the sandwich.
3. Cook sandwich for 2–3 minutes on each side or until cheese melts and the bread is golden brown.

Per Serving: Calories: 490 | Fat: 23 g | Saturated fat: 11 g | Cholesterol: 120 mg | Sodium: 600 mg | Total carbohydrates: 28 g | Dietary fiber: 4 g | Sugars: 3 g | Protein: 42 g

Mixed-Berry and Greens Salad (pictured)

Hands-On Time: 10 minutes
Total Time: 10 minutes
Yield: Serves 8

4 cups mixed baby lettuces

2 cups baby spinach

¾ cup raspberry vinaigrette dressing

1 cup blueberries

1 cup raspberries

Combine lettuce and spinach in serving bowl. Add vinaigrette and toss to combine. Top with berries and serve immediately.

Per Serving: Calories: 60 | Fat: 2 g | Saturated fat: 0 g | Cholesterol: 0 mg | Sodium: 80 mg | Total carbohydrates: 9 g | Dietary fiber: 2 g | Sugars: 6 g | Protein: 1 g

Tomato Cucumber Basil Salad

Hands-On Time: 15 minutes
Total Time: 15 minutes
Yield: Serves 4

2 medium cucumbers, chopped

4 ripe medium tomatoes, quartered

1 small red onion, thinly sliced

¼ cup chopped fresh basil

3 tablespoons red wine vinegar

1 tablespoon olive oil

1 clove garlic, minced

¼ teaspoon ground black pepper

1. Place cucumbers in a medium bowl. Add the tomatoes, onion, and basil.
2. Place the remaining ingredients into a small bowl and whisk well to combine.
3. Pour the dressing over the salad and toss to coat. Serve immediately or cover and refrigerate until ready to serve.

Per Serving: Calories: 80 | Fat: 3.5 g | Saturated fat: 0 g | Cholesterol: 0 mg | Sodium: 25 mg | Total carbohydrates: 9 g | Dietary fiber: 2 g | Sugars: 5 g | Protein: 2 g

Cottage Cheese and Fruit Salad

Hands-On Time: 10 minutes
Total time: 10 minutes
Yield: Serves 4

2 cups cottage cheese
1 teaspoon ground cinnamon
½ teaspoon ground nutmeg
1 large red apple, cored and thinly sliced
2 tablespoons apple juice
½ teaspoon salt
¼ teaspoon ground black pepper

Combine all ingredients in a medium mixing bowl. Cover bowl with plastic wrap and chill until ready to serve.

Per Serving: Calories: 130 | Fat: 3 g | Saturated fat: 1 g | Cholesterol: 10 mg | Sodium: 670 mg | Total carbohydrates: 13 g | Dietary fiber: 2 g | Sugars: 10 g | Protein: 14 g

Canadian Bacon, Egg, and Cheese Muffin

Hands-On Time: 15 minutes
Total Time: 15 minutes
Yield: Serves 2

2 slices Canadian bacon
1 tablespoon butter
2 large eggs, beaten
2 gluten-free English muffins, split
1 tablespoon mayonnaise
2 slices Cheddar cheese

1. In a small frying pan over medium heat, cook the Canadian bacon until lightly browned on each side, 4–5 minutes. Remove from the pan.

2. Add the butter to the pan and fry the eggs for about 3 minutes per side. If you prefer the eggs scrambled, you can break them up in the pan while they're cooking.

3. Meanwhile, toast the English muffins. Spread the insides with ½ tablespoon mayonnaise each.

4. When the eggs are almost done, flip them and lay a slice of cheese on top of each. Cook for another 30 seconds before removing from the pan.

5. Assemble sandwich by layering the bottom of an English muffin with an egg topped with cheese, a slice of bacon, and finally the top of the English muffin. Repeat with the second sandwich. Serve immediately.

Per Serving: Calories: 462 | Fat: 27 g | Saturated fat: 11 g | Cholesterol: 235 mg | Sodium: 750 mg | Total carbohydrates: 35 g | Dietary fiber: 3 g | Sugars: 3 g | Protein: 18 g

Curried Chicken Salad Wraps

Hands-On Time: 10 minutes
Total Time: 10 minutes
Yield: Serves 4

1½ cups cooked, cubed chicken
   breast
⅓ cup mayonnaise
3 tablespoons mango chutney
1 teaspoon curry powder
¼ cup golden raisins
⅓ cup pine nuts
4 (8") flour tortillas
4 iceberg lettuce leaves

1. In a medium bowl, combine chicken, mayonnaise, chutney, curry powder, raisins, and pine nuts.

2. Place flour tortillas on work surface and top with lettuce leaves. Divide chicken mixture among tortillas. Roll up each tortilla, enclosing filling, then cut in half crosswise.

Per Serving: Calories: 440 | Fat: 26 g | Saturated fat: 4 g | Cholesterol: 50 mg | Sodium: 420 mg | Total carbohydrates: 29 g | Dietary fiber: 3 g | Sugars: 9 g | Protein: 21 g

Gourmet Grilled Cheese Sandwiches

Hands-On Time: 20 minutes
Total Time: 20 minutes
Yield: Serves 8

½ cup ricotta cheese
1 cup shredded sharp white
   Cheddar cheese
1 cup shredded Swiss cheese
1 cup shredded white American
   cheese
1 tablespoon butter
½ teaspoon dried basil leaves
16 slices white sandwich bread
8 tablespoons butter

1. In medium bowl, combine ricotta cheese with Cheddar cheese and mix well. Add Swiss and American cheese, 1 tablespoon butter, and basil leaves and mix until blended.

2. Spread about 3 tablespoons of the mixture between two slices of bread. Butter the outsides of the bread with 1 tablespoon on each slice, then cook in a skillet over medium heat until the bread is toasted and cheese melts.

Per Serving: Calories: 438 | Fat: 30 g | Saturated fat: 17 g | Cholesterol: 83 mg | Sodium: 636 mg | Total carbohydrates: 26 g | Dietary fiber: 5 g | Sugars: 3 g | Protein: 17 g

Macaroni Salad (pictured)

Hands-On Time: 10 minutes
Total Time: 15 minutes
Yield: Serves 4

2 cups elbow macaroni, cooked according to package directions

⅓ **cup diced celery**

⅓ **cup finely chopped red onion**

⅓ **cup Miracle Whip salad dressing**

3 tablespoons fat-free sour cream

1 teaspoon dry mustard

1 teaspoon Splenda

½ **teaspoon salt**

½ **teaspoon ground black pepper**

In a large bowl, mix all ingredients together. Cover, refrigerate until cold, and serve.

Per Serving: Calories: 170 | Fat: 5 g | Saturated fat: 1 g | Cholesterol: 10 mg | Sodium: 220 mg | Total carbohydrates: 27 g | Dietary fiber: 1 g | Sugars: 3 g | Protein: 4 g

Broccoli Ranch Coleslaw

Hands-On Time: 10 minutes
Total Time: 10 minutes
Yield: Serves 4

1 (12-ounce) bag broccoli coleslaw

⅓ **cup diced celery**

¼ **cup sunflower seeds**

½ **cup dried cranberries**

½ **cup ranch salad dressing**

1. Mix the broccoli slaw, celery, sunflower seeds, and cranberries together in a large bowl.

2. Drizzle salad dressing into the bowl and toss to coat. Serve immediately or chill in fridge for up to 12 hours before serving.

Per Serving: Calories: 240 | Fat: 17 g | Saturated fat: 2 g | Cholesterol: 10 mg | Sodium: 330 mg | Total carbohydrates: 20 g | Dietary fiber: 4 g | Sugars: 13 g | Protein: 4 g

Fruit Salad

Hands-On Time: 25 minutes
Total Time: 25 minutes
Yield: Serves 6

½ cup cubed cantaloupe
½ cup cubed honeydew melon
½ cup cubed watermelon
1 kiwi, peeled and cut into sticks
½ cup red grapes
½ cup sliced strawberries
½ cup fresh pineapple chunks
½ cup peeled mango chunks

Toss all the fruits together gently in a large bowl. Chill fruit salad before serving.

Per Serving: Calories: 51 | Fat: 0 g | Saturated fat: 0 g | Cholesterol: 0 mg | Sodium: 5 mg | Total carbohydrates: 12 g | Dietary fiber: 1 g | Sugars: 10 g | Protein: 1 g

Spinach Salad with Warm Bacon Dressing

Hands-On Time: 15 minutes
Total Time: 15 minutes
Yield: Serves 4

1 pound baby spinach, trimmed of coarse stems
6 slices bacon, chopped crosswise into julienne strips
1 clove garlic, peeled and crushed
½ cup red wine vinegar
½ teaspoon salt
¼ teaspoon black pepper
2 tablespoons thinly sliced chives

1. Wash the spinach well in several changes of cold water, dry very well, then bundle in paper towels and refrigerate while preparing dressing.

2. To prepare the dressing, brown the bacon in a large heavy skillet over medium heat for 3–5 minutes until crisp. Remove the bacon with a slotted spoon and set it aside on paper towels to drain.

3. Add the garlic to the bacon drippings in the pan and sauté over low heat for 1 minute, until soft. Mix in the vinegar, salt, and pepper and bring to a boil. Mound the spinach in a large heatproof salad bowl. Pour the mixture over the spinach, sprinkle in the bacon bits and chives, and toss well to mix. Serve immediately.

Per Serving: Calories: 210 | Fat: 17 g | Saturated fat: 6 g | Cholesterol: 30 mg | Sodium: 660 mg | Total carbohydrates: 5 g | Dietary fiber: 3 g | Sugars: 1 g | Protein: 8 g

Quick Potato Salad

Hands-On Time: 10 minutes
Total Time: 30 minutes
Yield: Serves 8

2 pounds Yukon gold potatoes
1 cup plain low-fat yogurt
½ teaspoon celery seed
½ teaspoon dry mustard
½ teaspoon white pepper
⅔ cup thinly sliced yellow onion
2 tablespoons chopped parsley
2 tablespoons chopped scallions

1. In a large pot, boil potatoes. Once they have cooled, peel the skin and cut into chunks.
2. Whisk yogurt, celery seed, mustard, and white pepper together in a large mixing bowl. Add the potatoes and toss them gently to coat. Place the onion slices on top and sprinkle with parsley and scallions. Serve immediately.

Per Serving: Calories: 110 | Fat: 1 g | Saturated fat: 0 g | Cholesterol: 0 mg | Sodium: 30 mg | Total carbohydrates: 23 g | Dietary fiber: 3 g | Sugars: 4 g | Protein: 4 g

Coleslaw

Hands-On Time: 10 minutes
Total Time: 25 minutes
Yield: Serves 8

3 cups shredded cabbage
¼ cup shredded purple cabbage
¼ cup shredded carrot
¼ cup chopped green onion
2 tablespoons chopped parsley
½ cup mayonnaise
1 tablespoon whole milk
1 teaspoon sugar
1 tablespoon cider vinegar
1 teaspoon celery seed
¼ teaspoon salt
⅛ teaspoon ground black pepper

1. Mix all ingredients together in a medium bowl.
2. Refrigerate at least 15 minutes before serving.

Per Serving: Calories: 107 | Fat: 10 g | Saturated fat: 1.5 g | Cholesterol: 5 mg | Sodium: 170 mg | Total carbohydrates: 3 g | Dietary fiber: 2 g | Sugars: 3 g | Protein: 1 g

Dilly Brussels Sprouts Slaw (pictured)

Hands-On Time: 20 minutes
Total Time: 20 minutes
Yield: Serves 4

1 pound Brussels sprouts,
  trimmed

1½ tablespoons extra-virgin olive
  oil

1 tablespoon lemon juice

½ teaspoon kosher salt

½ teaspoon ground black pepper

1 small cucumber, quartered and
  thinly sliced

½ small red onion, peeled and
  diced

1 tablespoon chopped fresh dill

1. Slice Brussels sprouts as thinly as possible using the slicing blade of a food processor or a chef's knife. Place them in a medium bowl.

2. Toss with remaining ingredients and let sit at room temperature 1 hour before serving. This salad can be kept in the refrigerator for up to 3 days.

Per Serving: Calories: 90 | Fat: 5 g | Saturated fat: 1 g | Cholesterol: 0 mg | Sodium: 210 mg | Total carbohydrates: 10 g | Dietary fiber: 4 g | Sugars: 3 g | Protein: 3 g

Bean Salad with Orange Vinaigrette

Hands-On Time: 10 minutes
Total Time: 10 minutes
Yield: Serves 6

1 (15-ounce) can black beans,
  drained and rinsed

1 (15-ounce) can chickpeas,
  drained and rinsed

1 (15-ounce) can cannellini beans,
  drained and rinsed

1 small red onion, peeled and
  sliced

1 medium red bell pepper, seeded
  and diced

3 medium green onions, trimmed
  and sliced

⅓ cup apple cider vinegar

¼ cup pure maple syrup

2 tablespoons orange juice

1 tablespoon olive oil

1 teaspoon grated orange zest

½ teaspoon ground black pepper

1. Place beans in a large mixing bowl. Add onion and bell pepper and stir to combine.

2. Measure remaining ingredients into a small bowl and whisk well to combine. Pour dressing over bean salad and toss to coat.

3. Serve immediately or cover and refrigerate until ready to serve.

Per Serving: Calories: 300 | Fat: 4.5 g | Saturated fat: 0.5 g | Cholesterol: 0 mg | Sodium: 240 mg | Total carbohydrates: 52 g | Dietary fiber: 14 g | Sugars: 13 g | Protein: 14 g

Greek Pasta Salad

Hands-On Time: 30 minutes
Total Time: 30 minutes
Yield: Serves 8

1 clove garlic, peeled
½ teaspoon plus 1 tablespoon salt, divided
¼ cup olive oil
1 tablespoon lemon juice
1 tablespoon white wine vinegar
1 teaspoon chopped fresh oregano
⅛ teaspoon ground black pepper
1 (16-ounce) box orzo
1 small red onion, peeled and finely chopped
1 small red bell pepper, seeded and chopped
1 small green bell pepper, seeded and chopped
1 small yellow bell pepper, seeded and chopped
¼ cup chopped sundried tomatoes
1 cup pitted kalamata olives
1 teaspoon chopped fresh parsley
½ cup crumbled feta cheese

1. In large bowl, combine garlic and ½ teaspoon salt; work together with back of spoon until a paste forms. Gradually whisk in olive oil until smooth. Stir in lemon juice, vinegar, oregano, and black pepper. Set aside.

2. In a large stockpot over high heat, bring 6 quarts of water to a boil. Add 1 tablespoon salt and orzo. Cook, stirring occasionally, for 9 minutes. Drain well and immediately add to bowl with the dressing. Toss well. Add the remaining ingredients and toss well again. Serve warm or chilled.

Per Serving: Calories: 370 | Fat: 16 g | Saturated fat: 2.5 g | Cholesterol: 10 mg | Sodium: 590 mg | Total carbohydrates: 48 g | Dietary fiber: 1 g | Sugars: 4 g | Protein: 10 g

Watermelon Salad with Feta and Mint

Hands-On Time: 10 minutes
Total Time: 10 minutes
Yield: Serves 6

2 tablespoons extra-virgin olive
   oil
3 tablespoons fresh lemon juice
1 teaspoon sea salt
¼ teaspoon ground black pepper
1 teaspoon apple cider vinegar
1 small seedless watermelon,
   chilled, peeled, and cut into 1"
   cubes
¼ cup fresh mint leaves
½ cup crumbled feta cheese

1. In a large bowl, whisk oil, lemon juice, salt, pepper, and vinegar. Add watermelon and mint to the bowl. Toss gently to combine all ingredients. Sprinkle feta over the top.

2. Serve immediately.

Per Serving: Calories: 140 | Fat: 8 g | Saturated fat: 2.5 g | Cholesterol: 10 mg | Sodium: 510 mg | Total carbohydrates: 16 g | Dietary fiber: 1 g | Sugars: 13 g | Protein: 3 g

French-Style Carrot Salad

Hands-On Time: 15 minutes
Total Time: 15 minutes
Yield: Serves 6

2 pounds carrots, peeled and
   grated
1 tablespoon chopped flat-leaf
   parsley
1 tablespoon chopped fresh
   thyme leaves
Zest and juice of 1 lemon
1 teaspoon Dijon mustard
1 large clove garlic, minced
¼ cup extra-virgin olive oil
1 teaspoon salt
½ teaspoon ground black pepper

1. In a large bowl, toss grated carrots with parsley, thyme, and lemon zest.

2. Combine the lemon juice, mustard, garlic, oil, salt, and pepper in a medium-sized glass jar with a tight-fitting lid. Shake well to blend. Pour over salad and toss to coat well.

Per Serving: Calories: 145 | Fat: 9 g | Saturated fat: 1 g | Cholesterol: 0 mg | Sodium: 503 mg | Total carbohydrates: 15 g | Dietary fiber: 4.5 g | Sugars: 7 g | Protein: 2 g

Cobb Salad Bowl

Hands-On Time: 10 minutes
Total Time: 10 minutes
Yield: Serves 2

4 cups chopped romaine lettuce
2 tablespoons olive oil
1 tablespoon apple cider vinegar
2 large hard-boiled eggs, sliced
1 (6-ounce) grilled and shredded chicken breast
1 small avocado, peeled, pitted, and sliced
2 large tomatoes, chopped
1 medium cucumber, peeled and chopped

1. In a large bowl combine romaine lettuce, olive oil, and vinegar and toss to coat.

2. Place even amounts of salad mixture into each of two serving bowls and top each with half the egg slices, chicken, avocado, tomato, and cucumber. Serve cold.

Per Serving: Calories: 540 | Fat: 51 g | Saturated fat: 7 g | Cholesterol: 215 mg | Sodium: 140 mg | Total carbohydrates: 25 g | Dietary fiber: 12 g | Sugars: 12 g | Protein: 31 g

Chapter 4

Soups, Stews, and Chilis

Creamy Mushroom and Rice Soup

Hands-On Time: 10 minutes
Total Time: 20 minutes
Yield: Serves 4

3 cups water, divided
4 cups chopped mushrooms
2 teaspoons minced garlic
2 teaspoons sea salt
3 teaspoons ground black pepper
2 cups cooked brown rice
1 cup low-fat plain Greek yogurt

1. In a large saucepan, heat 4 tablespoons water over medium-high heat. Add mushrooms, garlic, salt, and pepper and cook, stirring, for about 5 minutes or until tender. Add remaining water and bring to a boil. Reduce heat to low and simmer for about 10 minutes.

2. Remove from the heat, add the rice to the pot, and allow to cool slightly. Stir to combine, add the yogurt, and blend well.

Per Serving: Calories: 170 | Fat: 2 g | Saturated fat: 1 g | Cholesterol: 5 mg | Sodium: 970 mg | Total carbohydrates: 29 g | Dietary fiber: 3 g | Sugars: 4 g | Protein: 10 g

Frozen Garden Vegetable Soup

Hands-On Time: 10 minutes
Total Time: 25 minutes
Yield: Serves 4

2 teaspoons olive oil
1 medium onion, peeled and chopped
2 medium stalks celery, chopped
1 teaspoon minced garlic
1 teaspoon dried parsley
1 (16-ounce) package frozen vegetables (carrots, green beans, peas, and corn)
2 cups low-sodium beef broth
1 cup water
½ cup dried ditalini pasta
¼ teaspoon salt
⅛ teaspoon ground black pepper
½ teaspoon Tabasco sauce

1. In a medium saucepan, heat the olive oil over medium-high heat. Add the onion and celery. Sauté for about 4 minutes until softened. Add garlic and parsley and sauté 1 minute more.

2. Add the frozen vegetables. Cook for about 4–5 minutes until they are thawed and heated through, using a rubber spatula to break them up while cooking.

3. Add the beef broth and water. Bring to a boil and add pasta. Stir in the salt, pepper, and Tabasco sauce. Reduce heat to medium and simmer for 8 minutes until pasta is tender. Serve immediately.

Per Serving: Calories: 172 | Fat: 4 g | Saturated fat: 0 g | Cholesterol: 2.5 mg | Sodium: 403 mg | Total carbohydrates: 30 g | Dietary fiber: 5 g | Sugars: 7 g | Protein: 6 g

Fresh Broccoli Cream Soup

Hands-On Time: 15 minutes
Total Time: 30 minutes
Yield: Serves 8

1½ pounds broccoli
2 cups water
1 large stalk celery, peeled and chopped
1 medium onion, peeled and chopped
2 tablespoons butter
2 tablespoons all-purpose flour
2½ cups chicken broth
½ cup whole milk
½ teaspoon salt
½ teaspoon ground black pepper

1. Cut the broccoli into florets. Chop the broccoli stem.
2. In a large saucepan or steamer, boil the water and immediately add the chopped broccoli stem, celery, and onion. Simmer for 10 minutes.
3. Meanwhile, steam the broccoli florets until tender, about 5 minutes, then shock them in ice water. Drain and set aside, covered.
4. In a medium saucepan, melt the butter and whisk in the flour, stirring until it is smooth. Take the saucepan off the heat and allow to cool slightly. Whisk the chicken broth into the flour mixture. Bring to a boil, stirring it for 1 minute.
5. Add all the vegetables except the steamed broccoli to the sauce and bring to a boil. Add the florets, then remove from heat. Stir in the milk, salt, and pepper.

Per Serving: Calories: 80 | Fat: 3 g | Saturated fat: 2 g | Cholesterol: 10 mg | Sodium: 300 mg | Total carbohydrates: 8 g | Dietary fiber: 2 g | Sugars: 2 g | Protein: 2 g

Potato Vegetable Soup

Hands-On Time: 10 minutes
Total Time: 30 minutes
Yield: Serves 6

1 tablespoon olive oil
2 cloves garlic, minced
1 medium onion, peeled and chopped
6 cups fat-free vegetable broth
1 pound small potatoes, peeled and sliced
3 large carrots, peeled and sliced
1 medium zucchini, sliced
1 teaspoon dried dill weed
2 tablespoons fresh parsley
½ teaspoon salt
⅛ teaspoon ground black pepper

1. In a medium sauté pan, heat the olive oil over medium heat. Add the garlic and onion and sauté for 4 minutes or until the onion is soft. Add the broth, potatoes, carrots, zucchini, dill, parsley, salt, and pepper and bring to a boil.
2. Reduce the heat to low and cook, covered, until the potatoes are tender, about 20 minutes.

Per Serving: Calories: 120 | Fat: 3 g | Saturated fat: 0 g | Cholesterol: 0 mg | Sodium: 930 mg | Total carbohydrates: 22 g | Dietary fiber: 3 g | Sugars: 5 g | Protein: 5 g

Classic Chicken Noodle Soup (pictured)

Hands-On Time: 15 minutes
Total Time: 25 minutes
Yield: Serves 4

2 cups cooked, shredded chicken
2 medium carrots, peeled and sliced
1 medium stalk celery, sliced
1 small onion, peeled and diced
3 cloves garlic, minced
4 cups low-sodium chicken broth
1 teaspoon all-purpose salt-free seasoning
½ teaspoon ground sage
¼ teaspoon ground rosemary
¼ teaspoon ground black pepper
1½ cups yolkless egg noodles

1. Combine all the ingredients except noodles in a large stockpot. Bring to a boil over high heat.

2. Once boiling, add the noodles, reduce heat to medium-low, and simmer 10 minutes.

3. Remove from heat. Ladle soup into bowls and serve immediately.

Per Serving: Calories: 130 | Fat: 1 g | Saturated fat: 0 g | Cholesterol: 40 mg | Sodium: 190 mg | Total carbohydrates: 10 g | Dietary fiber: 2 g | Sugars: 3 g | Protein: 18 g

Garden Tomato Soup

Hands-On Time: 20 minutes
Total Time: 30 minutes
Yield: Serves 4

1 tablespoon olive oil
3 cups chopped, peeled, and seeded tomatoes
1 cup chopped onion
1 cup chopped red bell pepper
1 tablespoon minced garlic
4 cups low-sodium vegetable broth
2 tablespoons no-salt-added tomato paste
⅛ teaspoon ground black pepper
1 tablespoon chopped fresh basil
1 teaspoon chopped fresh oregano
½ teaspoon chopped fresh thyme

1. Heat the oil in a large stockpot over medium heat. Add the tomatoes, onion, bell pepper, and garlic and cook, stirring, for 10 minutes.

2. Add broth, tomato paste, and black pepper and stir to combine. Raise heat to high and bring to a boil. Once boiling, reduce heat to low, cover, and simmer for 10 minutes.

3. Remove from heat and purée using a blender or food processor. Serve immediately, garnished with herbs.

Per Serving: Calories: 110 | Fat: 4 g | Saturated fat: 0.5 g | Cholesterol: 0 mg | Sodium: 160 mg | Total carbohydrates: 17 g | Dietary fiber: 4 g | Sugars: 10 g | Protein: 3 g

Chicken Soup with Carrots and Rice

Hands-On Time: 10 minutes
Total Time: 30 minutes
Yield: Serves 6

8 cups chicken broth

1 small onion, peeled and chopped

2 cloves garlic, minced

1 teaspoon dried thyme

4 large carrots, peeled and chopped

2 cups shredded cooked chicken breast

3 cups cooked white rice

1 teaspoon ground black pepper

1. Into a large stockpot over medium-high heat, add broth, onion, garlic, thyme, and carrots. Bring to a boil, reduce heat to low, and simmer for 20 minutes until carrots are tender.

2. Add shredded chicken and rice; simmer for 10 more minutes until chicken and rice are warmed through. Season with pepper.

Per Serving: Calories: 268 | Fat: 3 g | Saturated fat: 1 g | Cholesterol: 46 mg | Sodium: 629 mg | Total carbohydrates: 30 g | Dietary fiber: 3 g | Sugars: 3 g | Protein: 28 g

Fresh Tomato Basil Soup

Hands-On Time: 15 minutes
Total Time: 30 minutes
Yield: Serves 6

1 tablespoon butter

¼ cup chopped onion

4 cups (2 pounds) crushed tomatoes

¼ cup loosely chopped fresh basil leaves

1 cup low-sodium chicken broth

2 ounces reduced-fat cream cheese or Neufchâtel

1. Melt butter in large soup pot. Add onion and sauté until soft. Add crushed tomatoes, basil, and chicken broth.

2. Bring mixture to a boil. Reduce heat; cook for another 15 minutes. Remove from heat; stir in cream cheese until melted.

3. Transfer to food processor or blender; purée until smooth. Depending on size of processor or blender, you may need to purée a portion at a time. Transfer to serving bowls.

Per Serving: Calories: 70 | Fat: 3.5 g | Saturated fat: 2 g | Cholesterol: 10 mg | Sodium: 135 mg | Total carbohydrates: 7 g | Dietary fiber: 2 g | Sugars: 5 g | Protein: 2 g

Manhattan-Style Seafood Stew

Hands-On Time: 15 minutes
Total Time: 30 minutes
Yield: Serves 6

1½ teaspoons olive oil

1 large onion, diced

4 cloves garlic, minced

2 (15-ounce) cans no-salt-added
    diced tomatoes, with juice

2 medium potatoes, diced

2 cups low-sodium chicken or
    vegetable broth

2 medium carrots, sliced

½ pound white-fleshed fish, cut
    into 1" chunks

1 medium jalapeño pepper, seeded
    and minced

1 large bay leaf

¼ pound small frozen, raw shrimp,
    peeled and cleaned

⅓ cup chopped fresh cilantro

½ teaspoon grated orange zest

½ teaspoon ground black pepper

1. Heat the oil in a small stockpot over medium heat. Add the onion and garlic and cook, stirring, for 3 minutes. Add the tomatoes with juice, potatoes, broth, carrots, fish, minced jalapeño pepper, and bay leaf and stir to combine. Cover the pot and cook, stirring occasionally, for 15 minutes.

2. Add the shrimp, cilantro, orange zest, and black pepper and stir well. Simmer until shrimp are pink, 5 minutes or less, then remove from heat.

3. Carefully remove bay leaf and serve immediately.

Per Serving: Calories: 170 | Fat: 3.5 g | Saturated fat: 0.5 g | Cholesterol: 45 mg | Sodium: 190 mg | Total carbohydrates: 20 g | Dietary fiber: 3 g | Sugars: 5 g | Protein: 13 g

Spring Asparagus Soup

Hands-On Time: 20 minutes
Total Time: 30 minutes
Yield: Serves 4

1 tablespoon olive oil

3 medium scallions, chopped

½ cup finely chopped sweet onion

1 clove garlic, minced

2 small potatoes, peeled and chopped

1 pound asparagus

4 cups low-sodium chicken broth

1 tablespoon lemon juice

1 teaspoon grated lemon zest

2 tablespoons minced thyme leaves, divided

⅛ teaspoon ground white pepper

1 cup fat-free half-and-half

¼ cup plain low-fat Greek yogurt

1. In large soup pot, heat olive oil over medium heat. Add scallions, sweet onion, and garlic; cook and stir for 3 minutes. Then add potatoes; cook and stir for 5 minutes longer.

2. Snap the asparagus spears and discard ends. Chop asparagus into 1" pieces and add to pot along with broth. Bring to a boil, reduce heat, cover, and simmer for 10 minutes.

3. Using an immersion blender, purée the soup until smooth. Add lemon juice, lemon zest, 1 tablespoon thyme, pepper, and half-and-half. Heat until steaming. Top soup with Greek yogurt and remaining thyme.

Per Serving: Calories: 90 | Fat: 2 g | Saturated fat: 1 g | Cholesterol: 0 mg | Sodium: 320 mg | Total carbohydrates: 13 g | Dietary fiber: 2 g | Sugars: 4 g | Protein: 5 g

Cream of Cauliflower and Potato Soup (pictured)

Hands-On Time: 10 minutes
Total Time: 25 minutes
Yield: Serves 4

1 large head cauliflower, chopped

1 large potato, peeled and chopped

1 medium carrot, peeled and chopped

2 cloves garlic, minced

1 medium onion, peeled and chopped

2 teaspoons ground cumin

½ teaspoon ground black pepper

1 tablespoon chopped parsley

¼ teaspoon dried dill

1. In a large soup pot or Dutch oven, combine the cauliflower, potato, carrot, garlic, onions, cumin, and pepper.

2. Add enough water to cover the ingredients in the pot. Bring to a boil over high heat.

3. Reduce heat to low. Simmer about 10 minutes or until the vegetables are tender.

4. Stir in the parsley and dill before serving.

Per Serving: Calories: 70 | Fat: 1 g | Saturated fat: 0 g | Cholesterol: 0 mg | Sodium: 40 mg | Total carbohydrates: 16 g | Dietary fiber: 4 g | Sugars: 4 g | Protein: 3 g

Cream of Cauliflower Soup

Hands-On Time: 10 minutes
Total Time: 20 minutes
Yield: Serves 4

1 large head cauliflower, chopped

3 medium stalks celery, chopped

2 cloves garlic, minced

1 medium onion, chopped

2 teaspoons cumin

½ teaspoon ground black pepper

1 tablespoon chopped fresh chives

1 teaspoon chopped fresh dill,
    plus additional for garnish

4 slices bacon, cooked and
    crumbled

1. In a large soup pot or Dutch oven, combine cauliflower, celery, garlic, onion, cumin, and pepper. Add enough water to just cover ingredients in pot. Bring to a boil over high heat.

2. Reduce heat to low. Simmer about 8 minutes or until vegetables are tender.

3. Stir in chives and dill. Garnish with bacon and additional chives before serving.

Per Serving: Calories: 100 | Fat: 3.5 g | Saturated fat: 1.5 g | Cholesterol: 5 mg | Sodium: 240 mg | Total carbohydrates: 15 g | Dietary fiber: 6 g | Sugars: 6 g | Protein: 7 g

Skillet Chili

Hands-On Time: 10 minutes
Total Time: 30 minutes
Yield: Serves 4

1½ pounds stew beef, cubed

1¼ teaspoons salt, divided

½ teaspoon ground black pepper

1 tablespoon chili powder

1 tablespoon cornstarch

3 tablespoons olive oil, divided

1 teaspoon minced ginger

2 tablespoons chopped jalapeño peppers

1 teaspoon minced garlic

1 small onion, peeled and chopped

1 medium red bell pepper, seeded and diced

1 (15-ounce) can red beans,

1 (15-ounce) can diced tomatoes, drained

2 tablespoons chopped chipotle peppers

1 tablespoon of the adobo sauce (from chipotle peppers)

1 teaspoon ground cumin

½ cup chicken stock

1. Place the beef in a large bowl and add 1 teaspoon salt, black pepper, chili powder, and cornstarch. Set aside.

2. Heat a large wok or skillet over medium-high heat and add 2 tablespoons oil. When the oil is hot, add the minced ginger. Stir-fry for 30 seconds or until aromatic.

3. Add the beef. Let sit for 1 minute, then stir-fry for 2–3 minutes or until it is no longer pink and is nearly cooked through. Remove from the pan and drain on a plate lined with paper towels.

4. Heat 1 tablespoon oil. When the oil is hot, add the chopped jalapeño peppers. Stir-fry for 5 seconds, then add the minced garlic. Add the onion and stir-fry for about 2 minutes, until it is softened.

5. Add the diced bell pepper. Stir-fry for 1 minute, adding remaining ¼ teaspoon salt.

6. Stir in the red beans, diced tomatoes, and the chipotle peppers and adobo sauce.

7. Stir in the cumin and chicken stock and bring to a boil.

8. Stir in the beef. Turn down the heat, cover, and simmer for about 10–15 minutes. Serve hot.

Per Serving: Calories: 480 | Fat: 18 g | Saturated fat: 5 g | Cholesterol: 110 mg | Sodium: 790 mg | Total carbohydrates: 31 g | Dietary fiber: 9 g | Sugars: 9 g | Protein: 45 g

Black Bean and Corn Soup (pictured)

Hands-On Time: 5 minutes
Total Time: 30 minutes
Yield: Serves 6

4 cups canned black beans,
1 teaspoon olive oil
1 clove garlic, minced
½ teaspoon all-purpose seasoning
2 cups frozen corn
2 cups diced tomatoes
2 cups crushed tomatoes
1 small red chili pepper, seeded
  and sliced
2 tablespoons chili powder
1 teaspoon ground cumin
1 cup chicken broth
1 cup water

1. Combine all ingredients in a large saucepan over medium heat. Cook for 15 minutes.

2. Reduce heat to low, simmer for another 10 minutes, then serve.

Per Serving: Calories: 250 | Fat: 2 g | Saturated fat: 0 g | Cholesterol: 0 mg | Sodium: 510 mg | Total carbohydrates: 47 g | Dietary fiber: 11 g | Sugars: 10 g | Protein: 13 g

Quick and Easy Miso Soup

Hands-On Time: 5 minutes
Total Time: 15 minutes
Yield: Serves 4

8 cups water
1 teaspoon instant dashi powder
6 ounces or ½ block firm tofu cut
  into ¼" cubes
2 medium green onions, trimmed
  and thinly sliced
½ sheet nori, cut into 16 squares
¼ cup white miso paste

1. Add the water to a large pot and bring to a boil. Reduce heat to medium and add the instant dashi, whisking to dissolve. Add the tofu, half the green onions, and nori and cook for 1 minute.

2. Remove pot from heat. Place the miso paste into a medium bowl and ladle a little of the broth onto the miso. Using chopsticks, gently mix the miso with the hot broth, then pour the miso mixture into the pot. Serve immediately, garnishing each bowl with the remaining green onions.

Per Serving: Calories: 70 | Fat: 2 g | Saturated fat: 0.5 g | Cholesterol: 0 mg | Sodium: 570 mg | Total carbohydrates: 8 g | Dietary fiber: 2 g | Sugars: 2 g | Protein: 6 g

Hearty Beef and Green Bean Stew

Hands-On Time: 10 minutes
Total Time: 25 minutes
Yield: Serves 4

1 tablespoon olive oil
12 ounces beef round, cut into 1"
    cubes
1 cup chopped onion
2 cups (1" pieces) chopped
    potatoes
½ cup (1" pieces) peeled and
    chopped carrots
½ cup (1" pieces) peeled and
    chopped parsnip
1 tablespoon parsley
¼ teaspoon Tabasco sauce
1 cup low-sodium V8 juice
¼ teaspoon salt
1 tablespoon all-purpose flour
¼ cup water
1 cup fresh green beans, trimmed

1. Heat olive oil in pressure cooker and brown meat. Add onions, potatoes, carrots, parsnip, parsley, Tabasco, V8, and salt.

2. Close cover securely; place pressure regulator on vent pipe and cook for 10–12 minutes with pressure regulator rocking slowly (or follow manufacturer instructions for your pressure cooker). Cool down pressure cooker at once (nonelectric pressure cookers). Add green beans and cook uncovered for 5 minutes.

3. Make paste of 1 tablespoon flour and ¼ cup water; stir into stew to thicken. Heat and stir liquid until thickened.

Per Serving: Calories: 270 | Fat: 6 g | Saturated fat: 1.5 g | Cholesterol: 45 mg | Sodium: 240 mg | Total carbohydrates: 26 g | Dietary fiber: 4 g | Sugars: 6 g | Protein: 26 g

Dumplings in Broth

Hands-On Time: 15 minutes
Total Time: 30 minutes
Yield: Serves 8

1 cup all-purpose flour
2 teaspoons baking powder
½ teaspoon kosher salt
1 large egg
⅔ cup whole milk
1 quart simmering chicken broth
2 tablespoons chopped parsley

1. In a large bowl, sift together all-purpose flour, baking powder, and salt. Mix together egg and milk.

2. Make a well in the center of the flour mixture and pour in milk mixture. Blend together just until a dough is formed.

3. Drop dough by heaping spoonfuls (about ¼ cup) into pot with simmering broth. Cover and simmer 10–15 minutes. Sprinkle with parsley and serve immediately.

Per Serving: Calories: 78 | Fat: 1 g | Saturated fat: 1 g | Cholesterol: 25 mg | Sodium: 600 mg | Total carbohydrates: 12 g | Dietary fiber: 0 g | Sugars: 2 g | Protein: 4 g

Cannellini Minestrone

Hands-On Time: 5 minutes
Total Time: 30 minutes
Yield: Serves 6

3 cups canned cannellini beans, drained and rinsed
2 cups diced tomatoes
2 cups water
1 cup frozen spinach
1 cup sliced white mushrooms
½ cup chopped onions
½ cup chopped celery
1 clove garlic, minced
1 teaspoon dried parsley
1 teaspoon dried basil
½ teaspoon all-purpose seasoning
½ teaspoon crushed red pepper

1. Combine all ingredients in a large saucepan. Cook over medium-high heat for 15 minutes.

2. Reduce heat to low and simmer for another 10 minutes, then serve.

Per Serving: Calories: 140 | Fat: 1 g | Saturated fat: 0 g | Cholesterol: 0 mg | Sodium: 430 mg | Total carbohydrates: 26 g | Dietary fiber: 8 g | Sugars: 3 g | Protein: 9 g

Vegetable Chowder

Hands-On Time: 15 minutes
Total Time: 30 minutes
Yield: Serves 8

3 tablespoons butter
1 medium onion, peeled and chopped
1 cup chopped celery
2 cups sliced carrots
1 cup fresh corn kernels
½ cup water
2 cups low-sodium vegetable broth
3 medium potatoes, peeled and diced
2 cups whole milk
¼ cup all-purpose flour

1. Melt butter in a large, deep skillet over medium heat. Add onion, celery, carrots, and corn and sauté until tender, about 10 minutes. Add the water, broth, and potatoes and increase heat to high. Boil for 15 minutes or until potatoes are tender.

2. Reduce heat to medium. Combine milk and flour in a measuring cup and add to soup. Cook and stir 5 minutes until thickened.

Per Serving: Calories: 170 | Fat: 7 g | Saturated fat: 4 g | Cholesterol: 20 mg | Sodium: 140 mg | Total carbohydrates: 23 g | Dietary fiber: 3 g | Sugars: 8 g | Protein: 5 g

Vegetable Bean Soup with Pesto (pictured)

Hands-On Time: 15 minutes
Total Time: 30 minutes
Yield: Serves 6

½ cup chopped onion
½ cup chopped carrots
¼ cup chopped celery
2 tablespoons olive oil
2 cloves garlic, minced
1 cup chopped cabbage
4 cups chicken stock
1 cup chopped, peeled tomatoes
2 cups chopped zucchini
½ cup cooked navy beans
½ cup cooked chickpeas
½ teaspoon salt
¼ teaspoon ground black pepper
¼ cup basil pesto

1. In a large pan, sauté the onions, carrots, and celery in the olive oil over medium-high heat for 15 minutes. Add garlic and cabbage and cook until cabbage is wilted. Add chicken stock, tomatoes, zucchini, navy beans, and chickpeas and bring to a boil. Reduce heat to medium-low and simmer 15 minutes. Season with salt and pepper.

2. Serve hot with pesto.

Per Serving: Calories: 203 | Fat: 10 g | Saturated fat: 1 g | Cholesterol: 3 mg | Sodium: 598 mg | Total carbohydrates: 21 g | Dietary fiber: 6 g | Sugars: 7 g | Protein: 10 g

Roman Egg Drop Soup

Hands-On Time: 15 minutes
Total Time: 15 minutes
Yield: Serves 8

2 quarts (32 ounces) chicken
   stock
½ teaspoon kosher salt, divided
4 large eggs
½ cup grated Parmigiano-
   Reggiano cheese, divided
½ teaspoon ground black pepper
¼ teaspoon ground nutmeg
3 tablespoons chopped fresh dill
2 tablespoons olive oil

1. In a medium pot, bring stock to a simmer with ¼ tea-spoon salt for 4 minutes.

2. Meanwhile, in a medium bowl, whisk together eggs, ¼ cup cheese, remaining ¼ teaspoon salt, and pepper.

3. Add a ⅓ of egg mixture to stock and continuously whisk. Add nutmeg and remaining eggs in 2 more batches and allow soup to return to a boil. If any large clusters of eggs form, whisk until you see more shreds of eggs. Serve soup with remaining cheese and garnish with dill and a drizzle of olive oil.

Per Serving: Calories: 110 | Fat: 8 g | Saturated fat: 2.5 g | Cholesterol: 100 mg | Sodium: 440 mg | Total carbohydrates: 2 g | Dietary fiber: 0 g | Sugars: 1 g | Protein: 8 g

Turkey Chili

Hands-On Time: 20 minutes
Total Time: 20 minutes
Yield: Serves 8

1 medium onion, diced
2 garlic cloves, minced
Nonstick cooking spray
2 pounds lean ground turkey
1 medium jalapeño pepper,
   seeded and minced
1 (1.25-ounce) package chili spice
   mix
2 pounds fresh tomatoes, seeded
   and diced
1 (15-ounce) can kidney beans
1 teaspoon salt

1. In large pan, sauté onions and garlic in cooking spray on low heat until transparent. Add ground turkey, browning until done. Stir continuously.

2. Add jalapeño, chili mix, tomatoes, beans, and salt. Simmer for 10 minutes for the flavors to blend. Serve hot.

Per Serving: Calories: 240 | Fat: 9 g | Saturated fat: 2.5 g | Cholesterol: 75 mg | Sodium: 500 mg | Total carbohydrates: 14 g | Dietary fiber: 4 g | Sugars: 5 g | Protein: 26 g

Kidney Bean and Corn Chili

Hands-On Time: 5 minutes
Total Time: 15 minutes
Yield: Serves 4

2 tablespoons canola oil

1 medium green bell pepper,
    seeded and chopped

1 medium celery stalk, chopped

1 small onion, peeled and
    chopped

1 clove garlic, minced

1 (16-ounce) can diced tomatoes

1 (16-ounce) can cooked kidney
    beans, drained and rinsed

1 cup tomato sauce

¼ cup water

2 teaspoons chili powder

¼ teaspoon hot pepper sauce

1 teaspoon ground basil

1 teaspoon oregano

¾ teaspoon black pepper

1 cup cooked corn kernels

1. In a large saucepan or soup pot, heat the oil over medium heat. Sauté the green pepper, celery, onion, and garlic for 3 minutes.

2. Add the remaining ingredients. Bring to a boil, reduce to a simmer, and cook for 10 more minutes.

Per Serving: Calories: 240 | Fat: 9 g | Saturated fat: 1 g | Cholesterol: 0 mg | Sodium: 230 mg | Total carbohydrates: 35 g | Dietary fiber: 10 g | Sugars: 7 g | Protein: 10 g

Simplified Chicken Stew (pictured)

Hands-On Time: 5 minutes
Total Time: 20 minutes
Yield: Serves 4

1 cup sliced baby carrots

1 medium stalk celery, finely diced

1 large onion, peeled and diced

4 large potatoes, peeled and diced

1 teaspoon Mrs. Dash Garlic & Herb
or Original Seasoning Blend

2 tablespoons extra-virgin olive oil

2 cups chicken broth

4 (4-ounce) boneless, skinless
chicken breasts, chopped

¼ teaspoon salt

⅛ teaspoon ground black pepper

Put all the ingredients in a pressure cooker. Lock the lid and bring to high pressure; maintain pressure for 10 minutes. Remove from heat and quick-release the pressure. Remove the lid, stir.

Per Serving: Calories: 511 | Fat: 10 g | Saturated fat: 2 g | Cholesterol: 61 mg | Sodium: 468 mg | Total carbohydrates: 72 g | Dietary fiber: 9 g | Sugars: 9 g | Protein: 33 g

Potato Asparagus Soup

Hands-On Time: 15 minutes
Total Time: 25 minutes
Yield: Serves 4

1 tablespoon olive oil

3 medium scallions, chopped

½ cup finely chopped sweet onion

1 clove garlic, minced

2 new medium potatoes, peeled
and chopped

1 pound asparagus

4 cups chicken stock

1 tablespoon lemon juice

1 teaspoon lemon zest

1 tablespoon fresh thyme leaves

⅛ teaspoon ground white pepper

1 cup half-and-half

1. In large soup pot, heat olive oil over medium heat. Add scallions, sweet onion, and garlic; cook and stir for 3 minutes. Then add potatoes; cook and stir for 5 minutes longer.

2. Snap the asparagus spears and discard ends. Chop asparagus into 1" pieces and add to pot along with stock. Bring to a boil, reduce heat, cover, and simmer for 10 minutes.

3. Using an immersion blender, purée soup until smooth. If you do not have an immersion blender, purée soup in 4 batches in blender or food processor, then return to pot and continue with recipe.

4. Add lemon juice, lemon zest, thyme, pepper, and half-and-half; heat until steaming and serve. You can also serve this soup chilled.

Per Serving: Calories: 231 | Fat: 11 g | Saturated fat: 4.5 g | Cholesterol: 26 mg | Sodium: 470 mg | Total carbohydrates: 23 g | Dietary fiber: 4 g | Sugars: 5 g | Protein: 13 g

Creamy Zucchini, Cilantro, and Avocado Soup

Hands-On Time: 10 minutes
Total Time: 10 minutes
Yield: Serves 2

½ cup peeled and chopped
  zucchini
1 tablespoon minced jalapeño
  pepper
1 clove garlic, minced
2 tablespoons fresh cilantro
2 tablespoons lime juice
1 cup water
1 cup peeled, pitted, and chopped
  avocado

Place all ingredients except the water and avocado in a blender and blend. Gradually add the water, ¼ cup at a time, until the mixture becomes smooth. Add the avocado last and blend until creamy.

Per Serving: Calories: 130 | Fat: 11 g | Saturated fat: 1.5 g | Cholesterol: 0 mg | Sodium: 15 mg | Total carbohydrates: 9 g | Dietary fiber: 5 g | Sugars: 1 g | Protein: 2 g

Half-Purée of Chickpeas

Hands-On Time: 15 minutes
Total Time: 30 minutes
Yield: Serves 4

2 tablespoons extra-virgin olive oil
1 small white onion, peeled and
  diced
2 cloves garlic, minced
1 medium celery stalk, small-diced
1 small carrot, peeled and diced
2 teaspoons ground coriander
1 (15.5-ounce) can chickpeas and
  liquid
3 cups chicken broth
¼ teaspoon salt
⅛ teaspoon ground black pepper
2 tablespoons chopped fresh
  parsley

1. Heat the olive oil in a medium saucepan over medium-high heat until barely smoking. Add the onion, garlic, celery, carrot, and coriander. Sauté for about 3 minutes, until the vegetables begin to soften.

2. Add the chickpeas with liquid and the broth. Simmer for 15 minutes, uncovered. Season with salt and pepper.

3. Purée half of the soup in a blender and return it to the unpuréed portion in the pot. Divide the soup between 2 warmed bowls and top with the parsley.

Per Serving: Calories: 210 | Fat: 10 g | Saturated fat: 1.5 g | Cholesterol: 0 mg | Sodium: 530 mg | Total carbohydrates: 21 g | Dietary fiber: 6 g | Sugars: 2 g | Protein: 10 g

Quick Creamy Pumpkin Soup

Hands-On Time: 10 minutes
Total Time: 30 minutes
Yield: Serves 4

2 cups puréed pumpkin

4 cups water

1 cup whole milk

1 large onion, peeled and chopped

2 cloves garlic, minced

¼ teaspoon ground nutmeg

1. Combine pumpkin, water, milk, onion, and garlic in a medium stockpot over medium-high heat. Bring to a boil and then reduce heat to medium low. Simmer for 20 minutes. Stir in nutmeg.

2. Blend the soup in batches in a blender or use an immersion blender to process until smooth and creamy.

Per Serving: Calories: 100 | Fat: 3 g | Saturated fat: 1.5 g | Cholesterol: 10 mg | Sodium: 40 mg | Total carbohydrates: 17 g | Dietary fiber: 4 g | Sugars: 6 g | Protein: 4 g

Slow Cooker Bone Broth

Hands-On Time: 10 minutes
Total Time: 24 hours, 10 minutes
Yield: Serves 16

1 large yellow onion, peeled and chopped

3 medium carrots, peeled and chopped

3 medium celery stalks, trimmed and chopped

6 cloves garlic, chopped

4 pounds beef or pork marrow bones

2 tablespoons apple cider vinegar

3 dried bay leaves

15 peppercorns

1. Add vegetables and garlic to the bottom of a 6-quart slow cooker. Place marrow bones on top of the chopped vegetables and pour apple cider vinegar over the bones. Fill slow cooker with just enough water to cover bones.

2. Add bay leaves and peppercorns. Cover slow cooker and set it to low. Let simmer for 24 hours.

3. Strain and discard solids. Cool by submerging the pot in an ice-water bath. Place in freezer-safe containers and store in freezer until ready to use.

Per Serving: Calories: 32 | Fat: 0.4 g | Saturated fat: 0.1 g | Cholesterol: 8 mg | Sodium: 8 mg | Total carbohydrates: 0.3 g | Dietary fiber: 0.1 g | Sugars: 0.1 g | Protein: 6 g

Simple Italian Wedding Soup (pictured)

Hands-On Time: 20 minutes
Total Time: 25 minutes
Yield: Serves 8

1 tablespoon butter

1 medium sweet onion, peeled and diced

2 small carrots, peeled and chopped

1 pound mild or hot Italian sausage

4 cups low-sodium chicken broth

1 cup water

½ teaspoon salt

1 cup orzo or other small pasta

2 ounces grated Parmesan cheese

2 cups finely chopped kale

1. Heat butter in a large pot or Dutch oven over medium heat. Add onions and carrots and sauté until soft, about 5 minutes.

2. Use your fingers to squeeze small (around ½" in diameter) balls of sausage meat from the casings. Add each directly into the pot with the onion mixture. Stir occasionally as you make all the sausage balls. Discard casings. Stir to combine.

3. Add broth and water, cover, and increase heat to high. Bring to a boil and add the salt and pasta. Reduce heat to low and simmer, stirring occasionally, until the pasta is al dente, about 5–6 minutes.

4. Add Parmesan and kale and cook for 1 minute. Serve immediately.

Per Serving: Calories: 280 | Fat: 14 g | Saturated fat: 6 g | Cholesterol: 35 mg | Sodium: 540 mg | Total carbohydrates: 25 g | Dietary fiber: 2 g | Sugars: 4 g | Protein: 12 g

Hearty Salmon, Cheddar, and Corn Chowder

Hands-On Time: 20 minutes
Total Time: 20 minutes
Yield: Serves 8

2 tablespoons butter

½ cup chopped scallions

2 tablespoons all-purpose flour

⅛ teaspoon ground black pepper

3 cups whole milk

2 cups cooked and diced Yukon Gold potatoes

1 cup frozen whole-kernel corn, cooked and drained

1 (14.75-ounce) can salmon, drained and flaked

2 cups shredded Cheddar cheese

1. In a large saucepan over medium-low heat, melt butter. Add scallions and sauté until tender, about 5 minutes. Stir in flour and pepper; continue cooking, stirring constantly, until smooth and bubbly.

2. Gradually stir in milk. Continue to cook, stirring constantly, until bubbly and thickened.

3. Stir in potatoes, corn, and salmon. Heat through. Add cheese, gently stirring just until melted.

Per Serving: Calories: 360 | Fat: 18 g | Saturated fat: 10 g | Cholesterol: 95 mg | Sodium: 420 mg | Total carbohydrates: 24 g | Dietary fiber: 2 g | Sugars: 1 g | Protein: 25 g

Carrot Ginger Soup

Hands-On Time: 15 minutes
Total Time: 40 minutes
Yield: Serves 5

1 cup diced onion
2 cloves garlic, crushed
1 teaspoon olive oil
6 medium carrots, diced
5 cups spring water
1½ teaspoons sweet white miso
¼ teaspoon ginger juice
¼ cup chopped parsley

1. In a large soup pot, sauté onion and garlic in olive oil over medium-high heat until translucent, about 5–7 minutes.

2. Add carrots and water. Bring to boil, reduce heat to medium-low, and simmer, covered, until carrots are soft, about 20 minutes.

3. In a small bowl, purée miso in a little cooking liquid. Add miso purée to soup.

4. Add ginger juice. Simmer 3 more minutes.

5. Purée soup in a food mill or blender. Garnish with parsley.

Per Serving: Calories: 90 | Fat: 1 g | Saturated fat: 0 g | Cholesterol: 0 mg | Sodium: 180 mg | Total carbohydrates: 18 g | Dietary fiber: 5 g | Sugars: 0 g | Protein: 2 g

Cream of Spinach Soup

Hands-On Time: 15 minutes
Total Time: 35 minutes
Yield: Serves 6

2 packages (10 oz.) frozen chopped spinach
1 cup chopped white onion
6 cups chicken stock
¼ teaspoon salt
¼ teaspoon ground black pepper
⅛ teaspoon ground nutmeg
2 cups half-and-half at room temperature

1. Combine the spinach, onions, and stock in a large saucepan over medium-high heat. Bring to a low boil and reduce heat to a simmer. Cook until the spinach is tender, about 10 minutes, stirring occasionally. Remove from heat, add the salt, pepper, and nutmeg, and let cool for 5 minutes.

2. Transfer the spinach mixture to a food processor fitted with a metal blade (or a blender). Process until smooth. Work in batches if necessary.

3. Transfer the spinach mixture back to the saucepan over medium-high heat and slowly add the half-and-half, stirring constantly to combine. Reheat gently until heated throughout, about 6–8 minutes; do not boil. Serve hot.

Per Serving: Calories: 80 | Fat: 2 g | Saturated fat: 0 g | Cholesterol: 0 mg | Sodium: 300 mg | Total carbohydrates: 15 g | Dietary fiber: 4 g | Sugars: 7 g | Protein: 3 g

Quick and Easy Hot and Sour Soup

Hands-On Time: 10 minutes
Total Time: 20 minutes
Yield: Serves 6

1 cup chicken broth

6 cups water

1 teaspoon salt

1 teaspoon sugar

2 tablespoons soy sauce

½ cup canned bamboo shoots

2 medium shiitake mushrooms, sliced

½ cup cooked boneless pork loin, chopped

3 tablespoons rice vinegar

¼ teaspoon ground white pepper

1 tablespoon cornstarch

¼ cup water

1 large egg, lightly beaten

1 medium green onion, trimmed and minced

3–4 drops sesame oil

1. In a large saucepan, bring the chicken broth and water to a boil. Add the salt, sugar, soy sauce, bamboo shoots, mushrooms, and cooked meat.

2. Bring back to a boil and add the rice vinegar and white pepper. Test the broth and adjust the taste if required. Mix the cornstarch and water and slowly pour it into the soup, stirring. When the soup thickens, turn off the heat.

3. Pour in the beaten egg and stir quickly to form thin shreds. Stir in the green onion. Drizzle with the sesame oil. Give a final stir and serve hot.

Per Serving: Calories: 50 | Fat: 2 g | Saturated fat: 0.5 g | Cholesterol: 40 mg | Sodium: 890 mg | Total carbohydrates: 4 g | Dietary fiber: 1 g | Sugars: 1 g | Protein: 6 g

Garlic White Bean and Kale Soup

Hands-On Time: 10 minutes
Total Time: 15 minutes
Yield: Serves 8

1 medium white onion, peeled and
    diced
1½ teaspoons olive oil
4 cloves garlic, minced
4 cups vegetable broth
2 (15-ounce) cans white beans,
    drained and rinsed
3 cups chopped kale
3 tablespoons lemon juice

1. In a large stockpot, sauté onion in olive oil over medium heat until translucent, about 5–7 minutes. Add garlic and sauté another 1–2 minutes until fragrant.

2. Add broth and beans; bring to a boil.

3. Fill pot with kale, cover, and remove from heat. Allow kale to cook down for 5 minutes.

4. Serve with lemon juice squeezed over soup.

Per Serving: Calories: 190 | Fat: 2 g | Saturated fat: 0 g | Cholesterol: 0 mg | Sodium: 700 mg | Total carbohydrates: 32 g | Dietary fiber: 8 g | Sugars: 1 g | Protein: 12 g

Spicy Sweet Potato Soup

Hands-On Time: 10 minutes
Total Time: 30 minutes
Yield: Serves 4

3 cups water
2 medium sweet potatoes
½ teaspoon cayenne pepper
½ teaspoon all-natural sea salt

1. In a medium pot over medium-high heat, add water.

2. Peel sweet potatoes, rinse thoroughly, and cut into ¼" slices.

3. Add sweet potato slices to pot and bring to a boil. Reduce heat to simmer and cook until sweet potatoes are fork tender, about 15–20 minutes. Remove from heat and reserve water from pot in a separate measuring cup.

4. Sprinkle sweet potatoes with ¼ teaspoon of the cayenne and add ¼ cup of removed water back to pot. Using an immersion blender, emulsify potatoes, adding removed water as needed until desired thickness is achieved. While emulsifying, add remaining cayenne and salt.

Per Serving: Calories: 50 | Fat: 0 g | Saturated fat: 0 g | Cholesterol: 0 mg | Sodium: 330 mg | Total carbohydrates: 12 g | Dietary fiber: 2 g | Sugars: 4 g | Protein: 1 g

Greek Chicken Lemon Soup

Hands-On Time: 15 minutes
Total Time: 15 minutes
Yield: Serves 4

4 cups chicken stock
4 large eggs
4 tablespoons fresh lemon juice
Thin slices of whole lemon,
    seeded, for garnish
1 tablespoon olive oil, for serving

1. In a medium-sized saucepan, bring the chicken stock to a boil.

2. In a medium bowl, beat the eggs with a whisk until they are frothy, then add the lemon juice.

3. Slowly ladle 2 cups of the hot chicken stock into the egg mixture, whisking constantly. Pour the egg mixture back into the remaining stock, whisking over low heat until the soup thickens. This will take about 4 minutes. Serve in warm bowls garnished with a slice of lemon and a drizzle of olive oil.

Per Serving: Calories: 190 | Fat: 11 g | Saturated fat: 3 g | Cholesterol: 195 mg | Sodium: 410 mg | Total carbohydrates: 10 g | Dietary fiber: 0 g | Sugars: 4 g | Protein: 12 g

Spicy Turkey Chili with Chocolate

Hands-On Time: 10 minutes
Total Time: 25 minutes
Yield: Serves 6

1 pound lean ground turkey
½ cup diced red bell pepper
½ cup diced onion
1 clove garlic, minced
½ teaspoon all-purpose seasoning
2 tablespoons Splenda brown
    sugar substitute
1 teaspoon crushed red pepper
1 teaspoon ground cumin
3 cups canned kidney beans,
    drained and rinsed
1 cup crushed tomatoes
½ teaspoon ground black pepper
1 cup chicken broth
1 tablespoon cocoa powder
¼ cup chocolate syrup

1. Coat a large saucepan with nonstick spray. On medium-high heat, brown ground turkey with bell peppers, onions, garlic, and all-purpose seasoning for 10 minutes.

2. Add remaining ingredients to saucepan and simmer for 15 minutes.

Per Serving: Calories: 290 | Fat: 8 g | Saturated fat: 2 g | Cholesterol: 60 mg | Sodium: 360 mg | Total carbohydrates: 34 g | Dietary fiber: 7 g | Sugars: 5 g | Protein: 23 g

Chapter 5

Appetizers

Asparagus and Green Bean Fries

Hands-On Time: 30 minutes
Total Time: 30 minutes
Yield: Serves 6

½ cup vegetable oil
1½ cups all-purpose flour
½ teaspoon salt
½ teaspoon ground black pepper
2 tablespoons whole milk
2 large eggs
1 pound asparagus, trimmed
½ pound green beans, trimmed

1. In a large frying pan, heat vegetable oil over medium-high heat.

2. In a shallow dish, whisk together flour, salt, and pepper. In a second shallow dish, whisk together milk and eggs.

3. One at a time, dip the asparagus stalks and green beans into the egg mixture and then into the flour mixture. Repeat until well coated.

4. Place the batter-coated vegetables into the hot oil. Fry until golden brown. Transfer to a paper towel–lined plate to drain before serving.

Per Serving: Calories: 190 | Fat: 5 g | Saturated fat: 1 g | Cholesterol: 60 mg | Sodium: 220 mg | Total carbohydrates: 29 g | Dietary fiber: 3 g | Sugars: 3 g | Protein: 8 g

Sweet Potato Tempura

Hands-On Time: 15 minutes
Total Time: 15 minutes
Yield: Serves 4

¾ cup rice flour
¼ cup tapioca flour
2 tablespoons sugar
½ teaspoon salt
1 cup seltzer water
3 cups vegetable oil
3 large sweet potatoes, peeled and sliced

1. In a medium bowl, mix rice flour, tapioca flour, sugar, and salt. Add water slowly until mixture is thick enough to coat the potatoes, about the consistency of pancake batter.

2. Heat oil in medium frying pan over medium-high heat. Dip sweet potato pieces in the batter and fry in oil that has been heated to 350°F until golden, about 5 minutes. Turn the pieces halfway to evenly brown the sweet potatoes. Drain on paper towels.

Per Serving: Calories: 308 | Fat: 7 g | Saturated fat: 1 g | Cholesterol: 0 mg | Sodium: 344 mg | Total carbohydrates: 58 g | Dietary fiber: 4 g | Sugars: 10 g | Protein: 4 g

Zucchini Roll-Ups

Hands-On Time: 15 minutes
Total Time: 15 minutes
Yield: Serves 4

¾ cup part-skim ricotta cheese
½ teaspoon minced garlic
1 tablespoon grated lemon zest
1½ tablespoons chopped fresh basil
½ teaspoon salt
½ teaspoon ground black pepper
1 medium zucchini
1 tablespoon extra-virgin olive oil
¼ cup large basil leaves

1. In a small bowl, mix cheese, garlic, zest, chopped basil, salt, and pepper.
2. Cut zucchini into thin slices, lengthwise, using a mandoline or sharp knife.
3. Starting from a short side, roll up each zucchini slice into a cup and secure with a toothpick. Fill the center of each roll-up with ricotta mixture using a piping bag or plastic zip-top bag with the corner cut off.
4. Place roll-ups on serving dish, drizzle with olive oil, and garnish with whole basil leaves.

Per Serving: Calories: 103 | Fat: 7 g | Saturated fat: 3 g | Cholesterol: 14 mg | Sodium: 340 mg | Total carbohydrates: 5 g | Dietary fiber: 1 g | Sugars: 1 g | Protein: 6 g

Goat Cheese–Stuffed Mushrooms

Hands-On Time: 10 minutes
Total Time: 30 minutes
Yield: Serves 12

12 large white mushrooms
½ small zucchini, trimmed and minced
½ medium red bell pepper, seeded and minced
1 teaspoon garlic powder
1 tablespoon water
¼ cup crumbled goat cheese

1. Preheat oven to 375°F.
2. Clean the mushrooms with a dry paper towel; remove and reserve stems. Mince the mushroom stems.
3. Prepare a medium skillet with olive oil spray and place it over medium heat. Add the zucchini and red pepper and sauté for about 2–3 minutes. Add mushroom stems and garlic powder and continue to sauté until all vegetables are tender, about 4–5 minutes. Add water to skillet as needed to prevent sticking and promote steaming. Remove sautéed vegetables from heat and stuff mushroom caps full with the mixture.
4. Place stuffed mushrooms on a baking sheet and top with goat cheese. Bake for 20 minutes.

Per Serving: Calories: 20 | Fat: 0.5 g | Saturated fat: 0 g | Cholesterol: 5 mg | Sodium: 15 mg | Total carbohydrates: 1 g | Dietary fiber: 0 g | Sugars: 1 g | Protein: 1 g

Easy Cheese Fries (pictured)

Hands-On Time: 5 minutes
Total Time: 30 minutes
Yield: Serves 4

1 (12-ounce) package frozen steak fries
½ cup fat-free shredded Cheddar cheese
1 teaspoon salt

1. Preheat oven to 450°F.
2. Bake fries on a nonstick baking sheet for 15–20 minutes, flipping fries once. Remove fries from oven and sprinkle with cheese.
3. Bake for 3 more minutes or until cheese has melted. Sprinkle with salt. Serve hot.

Per Serving: Calories: 140 | Fat: 3 g | Saturated fat: 0 g | Cholesterol: 5 mg | Sodium: 980 mg | Total carbohydrates: 22 g | Dietary fiber: 2 g | Sugars: 0 g | Protein: 7 g

Garlic Toasted Triangles

Hands-On Time: 10 minutes
Total Time: 10 minutes
Yield: Serves 12

¾ cup butter, softened
¾ teaspoon garlic powder
⅛ teaspoon salt
⅛ teaspoon ground black pepper
½ teaspoon dried basil leaves
1 teaspoon lemon juice
1 teaspoon balsamic vinegar
12 (1") slices crusty French bread

1. Preheat the broiler on high heat. Spray a broiling rack with nonstick cooking spray.
2. In a small bowl, beat together the softened butter, garlic powder, salt, pepper, basil, lemon juice, and balsamic vinegar.
3. Spread the garlic butter over one side of the bread slices (about 1½ tablespoons per bread slice). Store any leftover garlic butter in a sealed container in the refrigerator.
4. Lay the bread slices on the rack, butter side up. Broil the toast about 1 minute, watching carefully, until the butter has melted and the bread is toasted. Cut each bread slice diagonally into quarters.

Per Serving: Calories: 180 | Fat: 12 g | Saturated fat: 7 g | Cholesterol: 31 mg | Sodium: 197 mg | Total carbohydrates: 15 g | Dietary fiber: 1 g | Sugars: 1 g | Protein: 3 g

Buttermilk Fried Green Tomatoes

Hands-On Time: 30 minutes
Total Time: 30 minutes
Yield: Serves 8

4 large green tomatoes
1 large egg
¼ cup buttermilk
½ cup cornmeal
½ cup all-purpose flour
1 teaspoon baking powder
⅛ teaspoon ground white pepper
¼ cup canola oil

1. Slice tomatoes into ⅓" rounds and pat dry with paper towels. In shallow bowl, combine egg and buttermilk and whisk until blended. On plate, combine cornmeal, flour, baking powder, and pepper and mix well.

2. Heat oil in a heavy skillet over medium heat until temperature reaches 375°F. Dip tomato slices into egg mixture, then into cornmeal mixture. Fry tomatoes in hot oil, four at a time, turning once, until golden brown, about 3–6 minutes per side. Drain on paper towels and serve immediately.

Per Serving: Calories: 100 | Fat: 2 g | Saturated fat: 0 g | Cholesterol: 25 mg | Sodium: 60 mg | Total carbohydrates: 18 g | Dietary fiber: 2 g | Sugars: 4 g | Protein: 4 g

Easy Falafel Patties

Hands-On Time: 15 minutes
Total Time: 30 minutes
Yield: Serves 4

1 (15-ounce) can chickpeas, drained
½ medium onion, peeled and minced
1 tablespoon all-purpose flour
1 teaspoon ground cumin
¾ teaspoon garlic powder
¾ teaspoon salt
Egg substitute for 1 large egg
¼ cup chopped fresh parsley
2 tablespoons chopped fresh cilantro

1. Preheat oven to 375°F.

2. Place chickpeas in a large bowl and mash with a fork until coarsely mashed. Combine chickpeas with onion, flour, cumin, garlic powder, salt, and egg substitute, mashing together to combine. Add parsley and cilantro.

3. Shape mixture into 2" balls or 1"-thick patties and bake in oven for 15 minutes or until crisp.

Per Serving: Calories: 110 | Fat: 2 g | Saturated fat: 0 g | Cholesterol: 0 mg | Sodium: 680 mg | Total carbohydrates: 19 g | Dietary fiber: 4 g | Sugars: 3 g | Protein: 6 g

Potato Skins

Hands-On Time: 10 minutes
Total Time: 30 minutes
Yield: Serves 6

6 medium baking potatoes, washed
½ teaspoon salt
⅛ teaspoon black pepper
½ cup fat-free shredded Cheddar cheese
¼ cup sliced green onions

1. Preheat oven to 475°F.
2. Cut potatoes in half and scoop out 90 percent of the pulp. Coat a large cookie sheet with nonstick spray.
3. Place potato halves on sheet and sprinkle with salt and pepper. Bake potatoes for 10–15 minutes or until crispy.
4. Sprinkle potatoes with cheese and return to oven for 2 minutes. Sprinkle potatoes with onions and serve.

Per Serving: Calories: 40 | Fat: 0 g | Saturated fat: 0 g | Cholesterol: 5 mg | Sodium: 290 mg | Total carbohydrates: 5 g | Dietary fiber: 1 g | Sugars: 1 g | Protein: 4 g

Bacon-Wrapped Jalapeño Poppers

Hands-On Time: 5 minutes
Total Time: 25 minutes
Yield: Serves 4

½ cup cream cheese, softened
½ cup shredded Pepper Jack cheese
8 medium jalapeño peppers, seeded and halved
16 slices bacon

1. Preheat oven to 425°F.
2. Mix cream cheese and Pepper Jack cheese together in a small bowl. Divide filling into 16 equal portions and stuff each pepper half with cheese filling.
3. Wrap each pepper in bacon. Lay flat on a cookie sheet lined with aluminum foil and bake for 15–20 minutes or until bacon is crispy. Serve hot or at room temperature.

Per Serving: Calories: 50 | Fat: 0.5 g | Saturated fat: 0 g | Cholesterol: 0 mg | Sodium: 5 mg | Total carbohydrates: 12 g | Dietary fiber: 5 g | Sugars: 7 g | Protein: 2 g

Corn Dog Muffins (pictured)

Hands-On Time: 15 minutes
Total Time: 30 minutes
Yield: Serves 12

1 cup all-purpose flour
1 cup yellow cornmeal
¼ cup turbinado sugar
2 teaspoons baking powder
½ teaspoon salt
1 cup whole milk or buttermilk
2 large eggs
¼ teaspoon vanilla extract
¼ cup butter, softened
¼ cup unsweetened applesauce
1 (16-ounce) package beef, turkey, chicken, or veggie hot dogs, chopped into ¼" pieces

1. Preheat the oven to 425°F. Spray muffin tins with non-stick cooking spray or line with muffin liners.

2. In a medium-sized bowl, mix together flour, cornmeal, sugar, baking powder, and salt. Stir in milk, eggs, vanilla, butter, and applesauce, and mix until smooth. Add chopped hot dogs to corn bread batter. Stir well. Fill ¾ of each muffin tin with batter.

3. Bake until muffins become light brown and center is thoroughly cooked, about 12–15 minutes. Cool for 5 minutes before serving.

Per Serving: Calories: 270 | Fat: 17 g | Saturated fat: 8 g | Cholesterol: 60 mg | Sodium: 690 mg | Total carbohydrates: 23 g | Dietary fiber: 1 g | Sugars: 6 g | Protein: 8 g

Fried Zucchini Sticks

Hands-On Time: 15 minutes
Total Time: 15 minutes
Yield: Serves 4

¾ cup all-purpose flour
½ teaspoon garlic powder
¾ teaspoon Italian seasoning
¼ teaspoon salt
4 medium zucchini, cut into sticks
2 cups vegetable oil

1. In a large bowl or pan, combine the flour, garlic powder, Italian seasoning, and salt.

2. Lightly toss the zucchini sticks with the flour mixture, coating well.

3. Heat oil in a large skillet or frying pan on medium heat. When oil is hot, gently add zucchini to pan. Fry until lightly golden brown on all sides.

Per Serving: Calories: 230 | Fat: 14 g | Saturated fat: 2 g | Cholesterol: 0 mg | Sodium: 160 mg | Total carbohydrates: 22 g | Dietary fiber: 2 g | Sugars: 5 g | Protein: 5 g

Peppered Parmesan Crisps

Hands-On Time: 5 minutes
Total Time: 10 minutes
Yield: Serves 15

1 cup shredded (not grated) Parmesan cheese
1 teaspoon ground black pepper

1. Preheat oven to 325°F. Line a cookie sheet with parchment paper.

2. Place rounded teaspoons of the shredded cheese on the parchment, equally spaced with about 2–2½" between each mound. Lightly flatten each mound with your fingertips to a circle about 1½" across. Sprinkle with pepper. Bake, checking after 3 minutes, until the cheese just starts to melt and very lightly begins to brown. Remove immediately and transfer the crisps to a rack to cool. Store in airtight containers.

Per Serving: Calories: 30 | Fat: 1.5 g | Saturated fat: 1 g | Cholesterol: 5 mg | Sodium: 90 mg | Total carbohydrates: 0 g | Dietary fiber: 0 g | Sugars: 0 g | Protein: 2 g

Prosciutto-Wrapped Cantaloupe

Hands-On Time: 15 minutes
Total Time: 15 minutes
Yield: Serves 12

1 medium cantaloupe, chilled
2 teaspoons lime juice
12 slices prosciutto
½ cup small mint leaves

1. Cut cantaloupe in half and remove seeds. Using a melon baller, scoop 36 balls and transfer to a medium bowl. Pour lime juice over melon.

2. To assemble, cut prosciutto into strips and wrap around melon balls.

3. Garnish with mint leaves.

Per Serving: Calories: 46 | Fat: 2 g | Saturated fat: 1 g | Cholesterol: 10 mg | Sodium: 270 mg | Total carbohydrates: 4 g | Dietary fiber: 0.4 g | Sugars: 4 g | Protein: 4 g

Asian Sesame Chicken Skewers

Hands-On Time: 10 minutes
Total Time: 25 minutes
Yield: Serves 8

24 (6") wooden skewers
½ cup low-sodium chicken stock
2 tablespoons low-sodium soy sauce
2 tablespoons sesame oil
2 garlic cloves, minced
4 drops hot sauce
1½ pounds boneless, skinless chicken breasts

1. Place the wooden skewers in a tall glass of water to soak for at least 15 minutes while preparing the chicken.

2. Combine the stock, soy sauce, sesame oil, garlic, and hot sauce in a medium-sized bowl; whisk until blended.

3. Rinse the chicken under cold running water and pat dry with paper towels. Cut the chicken into ½"-wide strips the length of the breast. You should have about 18–24 strips. (The strips will vary somewhat in size.) Add the chicken strips to the marinade, cover, and refrigerate for 15 minutes.

4. Just before preparing to serve, lightly oil a broiler rack and position it about 4" from the heat source. Preheat oven broiler to medium.

5. Remove the chicken strips from the marinade and discard the marinade. Thread one strip on a presoaked wooden skewer. Thread the remaining chicken on the remaining skewers. (Threading the strips in the form of an *S* will help them stay on the skewer.)

6. Place the skewers on the broiler rack and broil for about 3 minutes. Turn the skewers over and broil for another 3–4 minutes, until the chicken is no longer pink. Remove from the oven and serve hot.

Per Serving: Calories: 110 | Fat: 3 g | Saturated fat: 1 g | Cholesterol: 60 mg | Sodium: 50 mg | Total carbohydrates: 0 g | Dietary fiber: 0 g | Sugars: 0 g | Protein: 19 g

Delicious Deviled Eggs

Hands-On Time: 20 minutes
Total Time: 20 minutes
Yield: Serves 12

6 large eggs, hard-boiled, cooled,
    and peeled
½ cup low-fat plain yogurt
1 medium stalk celery, minced
1 teaspoon garlic powder
1 teaspoon onion powder
1 teaspoon ground white pepper
½ teaspoon paprika

1. Halve the eggs lengthwise and remove yolks to a medium mixing bowl. Mash the yolks and mix with the yogurt, celery, garlic powder, onion powder, and white pepper.

2. Spoon the mixture into each of the egg white halves. Sprinkle the eggs with paprika, cover, and refrigerate until ready to serve.

Per Serving: Calories: 50 | Fat: 3 g | Saturated fat: 1 g | Cholesterol: 95 mg | Sodium: 40 mg | Total carbohydrates: 2 g | Dietary fiber: 0 g | Sugars: 1 g | Protein: 4 g

Tex-Mex Quesadillas (pictured)

Hands-On Time: 10 minutes
Total Time: 20 minutes
Yield: Serves 4

1 cup cooked black beans
1 cup fresh corn kernels
1 cup chopped tomato
½ cup chopped onion
1 teaspoon cumin
1 teaspoon garlic powder
2 (6") whole-wheat tortillas

1. Preheat the oven to 400°F. Line a baking sheet with foil and spray foil with nonstick cooking spray.

2. In a medium mixing bowl, combine the black beans, corn, tomato, onion, and spices.

3. Lay the tortillas on the baking sheet and spoon the black bean mixture onto ½ of each tortilla, folding the empty half over. Press lightly to close.

4. Bake for 5 minutes, turn, and continue baking for 5 minutes or until golden brown.

Per Serving: Calories: 160 | Fat: 3 g | Saturated fat: 1 g | Cholesterol: 0 mg | Sodium: 470 mg | Total carbohydrates: 27 g | Dietary fiber: 6 g | Sugars: 3 g | Protein: 6 g

Deep-Fried Rice Bombs

Hands-On Time: 15 minutes
Total Time: 30 minutes
Yield: Serves 10

3 cups vegetable oil

4 cups cooked jasmine rice

¼ cup cooked wild rice

2 teaspoons chili garlic sauce

1 tablespoon soy sauce

1 tablespoon sugar

1. Line a large baking sheet with parchment paper. Heat oil in a large, high-sided skillet to 350°F.
2. Combine remaining ingredients in a large bowl and mix well.
3. Form the rice mixture into 1″ balls and place on prepared baking sheet. Fry rice balls in batches until golden, about 2 minutes per batch. Drain on paper towels.

Per Serving: Calories: 120 | Fat: 3 g | Saturated fat: 0.5 g | Cholesterol: 0 mg | Sodium: 120 mg | Total carbohydrates: 21 g | Dietary fiber: 0 g | Sugars: 1 g | Protein: 2 g

Miniature Crab Cakes

Hands-On Time: 20 minutes
Total Time: 30 minutes
Yield: Serves 8

8 ounces canned crabmeat

¼ cup mayonnaise

1½ tablespoons lemon juice

2 teaspoons grated lemon zest

1 large egg

1 tablespoon chili sauce

2 tablespoons minced sweet
    white onion

1 teaspoon dried dill weed

2 teaspoons Dijon-style mustard

½ cup panko bread crumbs

1. Preheat oven to 450°F. Prepare a baking sheet with non-stick spray.
2. Mix crabmeat, mayonnaise, lemon juice, zest, egg, chili sauce, onion, dill, and mustard together in a bowl. Spread the panko crumbs on a piece of waxed paper.
3. Make little burgers using about 1 tablespoon of the crab mixture. Coat with panko. Place on prepared baking sheet.
4. Bake for 5 minutes. Turn and bake for another 5 minutes or until very crisp. Serve hot or at room temperature.

Per Serving: Calories: 80 | Fat: 3.5 g | Saturated fat: 0.5 g | Cholesterol: 55 mg | Sodium: 320 mg | Total carbohydrates: 7 g | Dietary fiber: 0 g | Sugars: 1 g | Protein: 6 g

Bruschetta

Hands-On Time: 15 minutes
Total Time: 15 minutes
Yield: Serves 18

1½ pounds ripe tomatoes

2 tablespoons minced red onion

2 tablespoons chopped fresh basil

2 tablespoons plus ¼ cup extra-virgin olive oil, divided

1 teaspoon balsamic vinegar

½ teaspoon sea salt

¼ teaspoon ground black pepper

3 cloves garlic, peeled and divided

1 loaf Italian bread

1. Chop tomatoes in a ¼" dice and place in a large bowl with red onion, basil, 2 tablespoons olive oil, balsamic vinegar, sea salt, and black pepper. Mince 1 clove garlic and stir into tomato mixture.

2. Slice bread diagonally into 24 pieces, about ½" thick. Grill on each side until browned, about 1 minute per side. Use the remaining 2 cloves garlic to rub directly on one side of the grilled bread and brush with remaining olive oil.

3. To serve, place the tomato mixture in a serving bowl and center on a serving platter. Arrange bread with the garlic and oil side up on the platter around the bowl.

Per Serving: Calories: 80 | Fat: 5 g | Saturated fat: 1 g | Cholesterol: 0 mg | Sodium: 150 mg | Total carbohydrates: 8 g | Dietary fiber: 1 g | Sugars: 1 g | Protein: 2 g

Stuffed Celery

Hands-On Time: 10 minutes
Total Time: 10 minutes
Yield: Serves 12

Wide ends of 6 medium celery stalks, cut in half

5 ounces Brie cheese, softened

2 tablespoons capers

3 tablespoons chopped walnuts, toasted and finely chopped

1. Lay the celery pieces on a cool serving plate. Remove the skin from the Brie and mash with a fork. Mix in the capers.

2. Stuff each piece of celery with the filling and garnish with toasted walnuts.

Per Serving: Calories: 50 | Fat: 4 g | Saturated fat: 2 g | Cholesterol: 10 mg | Sodium: 125 mg | Total carbohydrates: 1 g | Dietary fiber: 0 g | Sugars: 0 g | Protein: 3 g

Crostini with Ricotta, Radishes, and Chives (pictured)

Hands-On Time: 10 minutes
Total Time: 20 minutes
Yield: Serves 10

1 large baguette, cut into ½" slices
1½ cups fresh ricotta
12 medium red radishes, thinly sliced
½ cup chopped chives

1. Preheat oven to 300°F.
2. Place the baguette slices in a single layer on a baking sheet. Bake for 5 minutes or until lightly toasted. Remove from oven and cool.
3. Spread about 1 tablespoon of ricotta over toasted baguette slices. Top with radish slices and a sprinkling of chives.

Per Serving: Calories: 135 | Fat: 5 g | Saturated fat: 3 g | Cholesterol: 19 mg | Sodium: 185 mg | Total carbohydrates: 15 g | Dietary fiber: 1 g | Sugars: 1 g | Protein: 7 g

Pan-Fried Salmon Balls

Hands-On Time: 20 minutes
Total Time: 20 minutes
Yield: Serves 10

2 pounds fresh salmon fillet, skinned and cut into 1" pieces
1 medium yellow onion, peeled and chopped
1 clove garlic
¼ medium bunch fresh cilantro
¼ cup bread crumbs
1 large egg, lightly beaten
¼ teaspoon salt
¼ teaspoon ground black pepper
1 tablespoon olive oil

1. Add salmon, onion, garlic, and cilantro to a food processor. Pulse 3–5 times until mixture is ground and combined.
2. In a large mixing bowl, combine salmon mixture, bread crumbs, egg, salt, and pepper. Form the mixture into 2" balls.
3. Heat the oil in a large skillet over medium heat. Add the salmon balls and fry until golden brown and cooked through.
4. Transfer the balls to paper towels to drain. Serve as desired.

Per Serving: Calories: 150 | Fat: 6 g | Saturated fat: 1 g | Cholesterol: 60 mg | Sodium: 154 mg | Total carbohydrates: 3 g | Dietary fiber: 0.3 g | Sugars: 0.6 g | Protein: 20 g

Pork Egg Rolls

Hands-On Time: 30 minutes
Total Time: 30 minutes
Yield: Serves 25

1 pound lean ground pork
1 tablespoon dark soy sauce
2 tablespoons oyster sauce
1 teaspoon minced garlic
1 teaspoon minced ginger
1 cup matchstick-cut carrots
2 medium scallions, finely
    chopped
1 teaspoon sesame oil
1 teaspoon black pepper
25 (6" x 6") egg roll wrappers
2 large eggs, beaten
2 cups peanut oil

1. In a large bowl, mix together the ground pork, soy sauce, oyster sauce, garlic, ginger, carrots, scallions, sesame oil, and black pepper.

2. One at a time, place an eggroll wrapper on a flat surface with one of the points facing toward you. Spoon about 2 tablespoons of the filling in a line toward the bottom half of the wrapper. Brush the top corner and sides with the beaten egg. Fold in the sides of the wrapper and tightly roll it up until it is closed. Press to seal, set aside, and continue with the remaining ingredients.

3. Heat the oil in a large wok over high heat to 375°F. In batches, fry the egg rolls until golden brown, about 5–6 minutes. Remove the fried egg rolls to plates lined with paper towels to drain. Serve hot.

Per Serving: Calories: 120 | Fat: 4 g | Saturated fat: 1 g | Cholesterol: 30 mg | Sodium: 230 mg | Total carbohydrates: 14 g | Dietary fiber: 0 g | Sugars: 0 g | Protein: 6 g

Baked Stuffed Shrimp

Hands-On Time: 15 minutes
Total Time: 23 minutes
Yield: Serves 4

1 tablespoon unsalted butter
2 cloves garlic, smashed
2 tablespoons grated Parmesan
    cheese
6 tablespoons bread crumbs
1½ tablespoons lemon juice
1 teaspoon dried oregano
½ teaspoon salt
1 teaspoon ground black pepper
16 raw jumbo shrimp, peeled

1. Preheat the oven to 500°F. Melt the butter in a medium saucepan over medium heat. Sauté the garlic for about 4 minutes.

2. Stir in the next 6 ingredients and mix well. Place the shrimp on a baking pan. Mound the stuffing on each shrimp.

3. Bake for about 8 minutes or until the shrimp have turned pink and the stuffing is light brown.

Per Serving: Calories: 130 | Fat: 4.5 g | Saturated fat: 2.5 g | Cholesterol: 105 mg | Sodium: 840 mg | Total carbohydrates: 10 g | Dietary fiber: 1 g | Sugars: 1 g | Protein: 13 g

Garlic Roasted Tomatoes

Hands-On Time: 10 minutes
Total Time: 30 minutes
Yield: Serves 6

4 large ripe tomatoes, thickly
   sliced
6 cloves garlic, sliced
2 tablespoons extra-virgin olive oil
1 teaspoon kosher salt
1 teaspoon ground black pepper

1. Preheat oven to 400°F. Spray a baking sheet with non-stick cooking spray.
2. Place tomatoes on baking sheet.
3. In a small bowl, toss together garlic, olive oil, salt, and pepper. Spread evenly over tomato slices.
4. Bake for 20 minutes or until tomatoes are soft and aromatic. Serve hot.

Per Serving: Calories: 66 | Fat: 5 g | Saturated fat: 1 g | Cholesterol: 0 mg | Sodium: 326 mg | Total carbohydrates: 6 g | Dietary fiber: 2 g | Sugars: 3 g | Protein: 1 g

Cucumber Slices with Smoked Salmon and Dill Cream

Hands-On Time: 20 minutes
Total Time: 20 minutes
Yield: Serves 12

2 medium cucumbers
3 tablespoons chopped fresh dill
8 ounces Neufchâtel cheese at
   room temperature
½ tablespoon lemon juice
½ teaspoon ground black pepper
3 ounces smoked salmon

1. Cut the cumbers into slices about ¼" thick. Place the slices on paper towels to drain while you prepare the dill cream.
2. Combine the dill, Neufchâtel cheese, lemon juice, and pepper in a food processor; blend until smooth.
3. Fit a pastry bag with the tip of your choice and spoon the dill cream into the bag. Pipe 1 teaspoon of the dill cream atop each cucumber slice.
4. Top the cream cheese with the salmon. Serve immediately.

Per Serving: Calories: 66 | Fat: 5 g | Saturated fat: 2.5 g | Cholesterol: 16 mg | Sodium: 208 mg | Total carbohydrates: 3 g | Dietary fiber: 0.4 g | Sugars: 2 g | Protein: 4 g

Fresh Tomato and Basil Bruschetta over Portobellos

Hands-On Time: 15 minutes
Total Time: 23 minutes
Yield: Serves 12

6 medium plum (Roma) tomatoes, seeded and chopped

2 tablespoons extra-virgin olive oil

½ small red onion, peeled and minced

4 cloves garlic, minced

2 tablespoons balsamic vinegar

3 tablespoons torn fresh basil

1 tablespoon grated Parmesan cheese

½ teaspoon salt

½ teaspoon ground black pepper

6 large portobello mushroom caps, wiped clean, stems removed

cooking spray

8 ounces fresh mozzarella, thinly sliced

1. Preheat the oven to 425°F.
2. In a large bowl, combine the tomatoes, olive oil, onion, garlic, vinegar, basil, and Parmesan cheese. Add salt and pepper and mix well.
3. Slice each mushroom cap in half, leaving two half circles, and place on a baking sheet sprayed with gluten-free nonstick cooking spray. Lightly spray each portobello mushroom cap with nonstick cooking spray. Bake for 5 minutes. Remove from oven.
4. Spoon bruschetta mixture on each mushroom half. Top with mozzarella and bake for 2–3 minutes more until cheese is melted. Serve warm.

Per Serving: Calories: 100 | Fat: 6 g | Saturated fat: 3 g | Cholesterol: 10 mg | Sodium: 230 mg | Total carbohydrates: 5 g | Dietary fiber: 1 g | Sugars: 2 g | Protein: 6 g

Grilled Kale (pictured)

Hands-On Time: 10 minutes
Total Time: 10 minutes
Yield: Serves 4

1 large bunch kale, stems removed

2 tablespoons olive oil

¼ teaspoon salt

1. Preheat grill to medium heat.
2. Toss the kale with the olive oil and salt.
3. Arrange the kale in a single layer on the grill. Close the cover and cook for 1–2 minutes. Use tongs to carefully turn the leaves of kale.
4. Close the cover again and cook for another 2 minutes. The kale is done when it is no longer limp and the edges are crisp. Larger pieces may need additional time. Remove from the grill and serve immediately.

Per Serving: Calories: 80 | Fat: 7 g | Saturated fat: 1 g | Cholesterol: 0 mg | Sodium: 161 mg | Total carbohydrates: 4 g | Dietary fiber: 2 g | Sugars: 1 g | Protein: 2 g

Smoked Salmon Hand Rolls

Hands-On Time: 20 minutes
Total Time: 20 minutes
Yield: Serves 6

6 nori sheets, perforated
1½ cups cooked sushi rice, cooled
6 ounces smoked salmon slices
1 medium avocado, peeled,
   pitted, and cut into eighths

1. Tear each nori sheet in half. Moisten your hands and divide rice into 6 portions, forming into balls.

2. Pick up nori sheet and hold shiny side down in the palm of your hand (if you're right-handed, hold nori sheet in left hand and vice versa). Moisten your hand again and place 1 rice ball at a slight angle to far left of sheet; press to a ¼" thickness leaving space between rice and edges of nori sheet; press your index finger into middle to make an indentation the size of your finger.

3. Keep the nori in your hand and add salmon and avocado. Still holding nori in one hand, use your other hand and tightly roll up bottom left-hand corner on a diagonal, over rice and filling. Create a cone by tightly wrapping opposite right-hand edge around. Fold and tuck to create a cone shape. With a moist finger, place a piece or two of rice on the corner to secure inside edge of nori to outside.

Per Serving: Calories: 124 | Fat: 5 g | Saturated fat: 1 g | Cholesterol: 10 mg | Sodium: 210 mg | Total carbohydrates: 12 g | Dietary fiber: 3 g | Sugars: 0 g | Protein: 8 g

Tangy Grilled Scallops with Bacon

Hands-On Time: 20 minutes
Total Time: 20 minutes
Yield: Serves 4

12 large scallops
1½ tablespoons lemon juice
½ teaspoon salt
½ teaspoon ground black pepper
6 slices bacon, cut in half
4 wooden skewers

1. Rinse the scallops in cold water and dry on paper towels. Sprinkle the scallops with lemon juice, salt, and pepper.

2. In a medium skillet over medium-high heat, fry the bacon on one side.

3. Wrap the scallops in bacon with the cooked side in (the raw side will get cooked on the grill). Thread 3 scallops on each skewer. If the bacon is not tightly wrapped, secure it with toothpicks.

4. Set the gas grill to medium or wait until the coals have plenty of ash.

5. Grill until the bacon is crisp, turning once. This should take no more than 3–4 minutes per side.

Per Serving: Calories: 100 | Fat: 5 g | Saturated fat: 1.5 g | Cholesterol: 25 mg | Sodium: 670 mg | Total carbohydrates: 2 g | Dietary fiber: 0 g | Sugars: 0 g | Protein: 10 g

Crab Rangoon with Green Onions

Hands-On Time: 15 minutes
Total Time: 1 hour, 5 minutes
Yield: Serves 24

48 wonton wrappers
1 cup fresh or canned crabmeat
1 cup cream cheese
½ teaspoon Worcestershire sauce
½ teaspoon soy sauce
⅛ teaspoon ground white pepper
2 teaspoons minced onion
1½ medium green onions, thinly sliced
1 large clove garlic, minced
Water for wetting wontons
4 cups oil for deep-frying

1. Cover wonton wrappers with a damp towel to prevent drying. Set aside.

2. If using canned crabmeat, drain thoroughly. Flake crabmeat with a fork into a large bowl. Add cream cheese, then mix in Worcestershire sauce, soy sauce, white pepper, onion, green onion, and garlic.

3. Lay a wrapper in a diamond shape or circle, depending on the shape of wonton wrappers you are using. Add a heaping teaspoon of filling in the middle; spread out evenly but not too near the edges. Spread water along all 4 sides. Fold the bottom over the top to form a triangle (round wrappers will form a half moon). Seal the edges, adding more water if needed. Cover filled wontons with a damp towel to prevent drying.

4. Heat 4 cups oil in a 16" preheated wok to 375°F. Slide in wontons 3 at a time and deep-fry for 2–3 minutes until they turn golden brown. Remove with a slotted spoon and drain on paper towels. Cool and serve.

Per Serving: Calories: 110 | Fat: 7 g | Saturated fat: 2.5 g | Cholesterol: 15 mg | Sodium: 150 mg | Total carbohydrates: 10 g | Dietary fiber: 0 g | Sugars: 0 g | Protein: 3 g

Cheddar Bacon Potato Skins

Hands-On Time: 15 minutes
Total Time: 30 minutes
Yield: Serves 16

16 small potatoes, scrubbed and baked
1 stick salted butter or margarine
½–1 cup shredded Cheddar cheese
½ pound bacon, fried and crumbled

1. Preheat oven to 450°F.

2. Cut the potatoes in half lengthwise. Carve out the inside of each of the potatoes and reserve for another use. In a small saucepan, melt the butter over medium heat. Once melted, brush on the inside and outside of each potato skin.

3. Top each potato skin with desired amount of grated Cheddar cheese and bacon.

4. Place potato skins on a baking sheet and bake for 10–15 minutes or until the edges are brown and the cheese has melted. Serve hot.

Per Serving: Calories: 241 | Fat: 12 g | Saturated fat: 6 g | Cholesterol: 35 mg | Sodium: 350 mg | Total carbohydrates: 26 g | Dietary fiber: 2 g | Sugars: 1 g | Protein: 9 g

Caribbean Meatballs

Hands-On Time: 20 minutes
Total Time: 28 minutes
Yield: Serves 10

1 large egg
½ teaspoon ground ginger
¼ teaspoon ground cloves
¾ teaspoons granulated sugar
½ cup bread crumbs
¼ cup minced green bell pepper
1 pound ground beef
1 tablespoon skim milk
½ cup sweet-and-sour sauce

1. Preheat oven broiler. In a small bowl, beat the egg well and set aside.

2. In a medium bowl, mix the ginger, cloves, and sugar thoroughly with the bread crumbs. In a small bowl, mix the green pepper with the ground beef.

3. Add the beaten egg, the bread crumb mixture, and milk to the ground beef and pepper mixture. Add more milk if the mixture is a bit dry.

4. Roll the mixture into small balls about 1½" in diameter (slightly smaller than a golf ball).

5. Spray a rack with nonstick cooking spray and place the rack in a shallow roasting pan. (A baking sheet won't allow the fat to drain from the meatballs.) Place the meatballs on the rack and broil for 8 minutes, until cooked through. Serve with sweet-and-sour sauce.

Per Serving: Calories: 140 | Fat: 7 g | Saturated fat: 3 g | Cholesterol: 50 mg | Sodium: 100 mg | Total carbohydrates: 7 g | Dietary fiber: 0 g | Sugars: 3 g | Protein: 9 g

Rosemary Parmesan Twists (pictured)

Hands-On Time: 10 minutes
Total Time: 25 minutes
Yield: Serves 16

2 (8-ounce) cans refrigerated crescent roll dough
2 teaspoons extra-virgin olive oil
½ cup shredded Parmesan cheese
1 tablespoon finely chopped fresh rosemary

1. Preheat oven to 375°F and line a baking sheet with parchment paper.

2. On a lightly floured work surface, lay out one of the crescent dough sheets. Brush the top with half the olive oil, then evenly sprinkle the Parmesan cheese and rosemary over the top. Lay out the second dough sheet, brush with the reserved olive oil, and lay oil side down on top of the first sheet.

3. Cut the two sheets in half horizontally, then cut each half into eight strips. Twist each strip, then lay it on the prepared baking sheet.

4. Bake for 13–15 minutes or until the twists are golden brown. Serve warm.

Per Serving: Calories: 130 | Fat: 7 g | Saturated fat: 3 g | Cholesterol: 0 mg | Sodium: 260 mg | Total carbohydrates: 11 g | Dietary fiber: 0 g | Sugars: 2 g | Protein: 3 g

Pigs in a Blanket with Cheese

Hands-On Time: 15 minutes
Total Time: 25 minutes
Yield: Serves 8

2 cups gluten-free pancake and
  baking mix
1 cup boiling water
4 gluten-free hot dogs, cut in half
  crosswise
1 cup shredded Cheddar cheese

1. Preheat oven to 375°F. Line a baking sheet with parchment paper.

2. In a medium bowl, stir pancake and baking mix with boiling water until you have a soft dough. Divide dough into 8 equal pieces. Roll or pat dough out into 4" x 4" squares. Place a hot dog half and a tablespoon of cheese in the middle of each square and roll dough around hot dog. Pinch end of dough to secure. Place wrapped hot dogs on baking sheet.

3. Bake for 10–15 minutes or until golden-brown, the cheese is melted, and the hot dogs are sizzling.

Per Serving: Calories: 208 | Fat: 9 g | Saturated fat: 4 g | Cholesterol: 15 mg | Sodium: 350 mg | Total carbohydrates: 25 g | Dietary fiber: 1 g | Sugars: 3 g | Protein: 7 g

Vegetarian Quinoa Black Bean Cakes

Hands-On Time: 30 minutes
Total Time: 30 minutes
Yield: Serves 8

3 tablespoons grapeseed oil,
  divided
½ cup finely chopped green bell
  pepper
3 cloves garlic, chopped
1 medium onion, peeled and finely
  chopped
½ cup finely chopped plum
  tomatoes
1 (15-ounce) can black beans,
  thoroughly rinsed and drained
2 cups cooked quinoa
1 tablespoon fresh cilantro leaves
½ teaspoon ground cumin
½ teaspoon red pepper flakes
½ teaspoon salt
½ teaspoon ground black pepper
1 large egg white, beaten
1 cup bread crumbs

1. Heat 2 tablespoons oil in a large skillet over medium heat. Add the green pepper and sauté until soft, about 3 minutes.

2. Add the garlic, onion, and tomatoes, and continue to sauté until soft, about 3–4 minutes.

3. Remove from heat, combine with beans, quinoa, cilantro, cumin, red pepper flakes, salt, and black pepper. Allow to cool for 5 minutes. Place in food processor and pulse until chunky but not completely smooth.

4. Add the beaten egg white and mix well. Form into patties and dredge in bread crumbs. Heat remaining oil in a large skillet over medium-high heat. Sauté patties at least 5 minutes on each side.

Per Serving: Calories: 220 | Fat: 7 g | Saturated fat: 0.5 g | Cholesterol: 0 mg | Sodium: 320 mg | Total carbohydrates: 30 g | Dietary fiber: 6 g | Sugars: 3 g | Protein: 8 g

Deep-Fried Mushrooms

Hands-On Time: 35 minutes
Total Time: 35 minutes
Yield: Serves 10

20 medium shiitake mushrooms, stems removed
1 teaspoon baking powder
¾ cup flour
½ teaspoon sugar
¼ teaspoon salt
2 tablespoons vegetable oil
¾ cup water
¼ cup cornstarch
4 cups vegetable oil for deep-frying

1. Wipe mushrooms with a damp cloth.

2. To make the batter: In a medium bowl, sift baking powder into the flour. Add sugar, salt, and vegetable oil, stirring. Add water and stir into a smooth batter. Add a bit more water if the batter is too dry, or more flour if it is too wet. Use a wooden spoon to test the batter—it should drop slowly and coat the back of the spoon.

3. Lightly dust mushrooms with cornstarch and coat with the batter, using your fingers.

4. Add oil to a large preheated wok and heat to 350°F. When oil is ready, add about 5 mushrooms at a time and deep-fry until golden brown, about 3–5 minutes. Drain on paper towels. Cool and serve.

Per Serving: Calories: 150 | Fat: 10 g | Saturated fat: 1 g | Cholesterol: 0 mg | Sodium: 110 mg | Total carbohydrates: 13 g | Dietary fiber: 1 g | Sugars: 1 g | Protein: 2 g

Chapter 6

Pasta Main Dishes

Angry Ziti

Hands-On Time: 15 minutes
Total Time: 25 minutes
Yield: Serves 6

2 tablespoons olive oil

1 medium onion, thinly sliced

¼ teaspoon crushed red pepper flakes

4 cloves garlic, minced

1 cup chopped plum tomatoes

2 (14-ounce) cans crushed tomatoes, undrained

¼ cup white wine

¼ cup tomato paste

¼ teaspoon salt

⅛ teaspoon cayenne pepper

1 (16-ounce) package ziti pasta

¼ cup grated Parmesan cheese

1. Bring a large pot of water to a boil. Meanwhile, in large skillet, heat oil over medium heat. Add onions, red pepper flakes, and garlic and sauté until crisp-tender, about 5 minutes. Add all of the tomatoes, white wine, tomato paste, salt, and cayenne pepper. Sauté until blended, stirring frequently, about 5 minutes.

2. Cook pasta in boiling water until al dente according to package directions; drain the pasta and add to skillet. Cook, stirring and tossing, for 1 minute, then sprinkle with cheese and serve.

Per Serving: Calories: 440 | Fat: 8 g | Saturated fat: 2 g | Cholesterol: 5 mg | Sodium: 320 mg | Total carbohydrates: 75 g | Dietary fiber: 8 g | Sugars: 8 g | Protein: 16 g

Hawaiian Chicken Pasta

Hands-On Time: 15 minutes
Total Time: 20 minutes
Yield: Serves 6

1 (16-ounce) box angel hair pasta

1 tablespoon olive oil

1½ pounds boneless, skinless chicken breasts, cut into bite-sized pieces

1 tablespoon sesame oil

½ tablespoon garlic powder

2 teaspoons ground ginger

½ teaspoon poppy seeds

¼ teaspoon salt

¼ teaspoon ground black pepper

1 medium sweet onion, peeled and diced

1 medium green pepper, seeded and chopped

3 medium carrots, peeled and thinly sliced

1 (20-ounce) can pineapple chunks, drained (reserve the juice)

1½ tablespoons cornstarch

¼ cup soy sauce

1. In a large stockpot, prepare pasta according to package directions.

2. While pasta cooks, in a large wok or skillet, heat olive oil over medium-high heat. Add chicken pieces. Add sesame oil, garlic powder, ginger, poppy seeds, salt, and pepper. Cook for 5 minutes until lightly browned.

3. Add onion, green pepper, carrots, pineapple chunks, and ¼ cup pineapple juice. Stir-fry until vegetables are tender, about 8 minutes.

4. In a small bowl, combine ½ cup pineapple juice, cornstarch, and soy sauce. Whisk until smooth.

5. Add pasta to pan and top with the pineapple/soy sauce. Stir to coat.

Per Serving: Calories: 570 | Fat: 8 g | Saturated fat: 1.5 g | Cholesterol: 85 mg | Sodium: 950 mg | Total carbohydrates: 83 g | Dietary fiber: 5 g | Sugars: 32 g | Protein: 40 g

Classic Macaroni and Cheese (pictured)

Hands-On Time: 10 minutes
Total Time: 10 minutes
Yield: Serves 4

2 tablespoons canola oil
½ medium stalk celery, minced
¼ cup minced onion
3 tablespoons fat-free milk
4 tablespoons all-purpose flour
1 cup low-fat grated Cheddar
   cheese
½ cup low-fat grated Swiss cheese
½ teaspoon ground nutmeg
½ teaspoon salt
¼ teaspoon ground black pepper
16 ounces cooked small pasta

1. Heat oil in a large skillet over medium heat. Sauté celery and onion 5 minutes. Mix in the milk and flour, stirring until smooth.

2. Mix in the cheese, stirring constantly until thick. Remove immediately from heat.

3. Stir in the nutmeg and season with salt and pepper. Pour mixture over pasta. Toss and serve.

Per Serving: Calories: 410 | Fat: 17 g | Saturated fat: 4 g | Cholesterol: 20 mg | Sodium: 530 mg | Total carbohydrates: 44 g | Dietary fiber: 3 g | Sugars: 2 g | Protein: 19 g

Shells with Zucchini

Hands-On Time: 15 minutes
Total Time: 20 minutes
Yield: Serves 4

1 tablespoon butter
2 cloves garlic, minced
3 medium zucchini, sliced
2 teaspoons minced fresh
   rosemary
¼ teaspoon salt
⅛ teaspoon ground white pepper
1 (12-ounce) package medium
   pasta shells
3 tablespoons chopped flat-leaf
   parsley
¼ cup grated Parmesan cheese

1. Bring a large pot of water to a boil. In a large skillet, melt butter over medium heat. Add garlic and zucchini and cook until crisp-tender, about 5–6 minutes. Add rosemary and season with salt and pepper. Cook for 2–3 minutes to blend flavors. Remove from heat.

2. Meanwhile, cook pasta in boiling water until al dente. Drain and add to zucchini mixture. Return to the heat and toss until the shells are coated with sauce, 2–3 minutes. Add the parsley and cheese and toss again. Serve immediately.

Per Serving: Calories: 380 | Fat: 7 g | Saturated fat: 3 g | Cholesterol: 15 mg | Sodium: 400 mg | Total carbohydrates: 67 g | Dietary fiber: 5 g | Sugars: 7 g | Protein: 15 g

Chicken and Orzo

Hands-On Time: 15 minutes
Total Time: 25 minutes
Yield: Serves 4

1 tablespoon olive oil
1 pound chicken tenders, cut into
    1" pieces
½ teaspoon kosher salt
½ teaspoon ground black pepper
1 large red onion, peeled and diced
1 large red bell pepper, seeded
    and diced
1 cup dried orzo
4 cups chicken broth
1 teaspoon dried oregano
1 teaspoon dried basil
2 tablespoons julienned fresh basil
¼ cup shredded Parmesan cheese

1. In a large skillet over medium heat, warm olive oil until it shimmers, about 1 minute. Add chicken tenders, season with salt and black pepper, and sauté for 5 minutes. Add onion and bell pepper and cook until softened, about 7 minutes.

2. Add orzo and stir for 1 minute. Add broth and oregano. Increase heat to medium-high and bring to a light boil. Reduce heat to medium-low and cook until orzo is tender, about 10 minutes, stirring every 2–3 minutes to keep orzo from sticking to the bottom of the pan.

3. Garnish with basil and top with Parmesan before serving.

Per Serving: Calories: 393 | Fat: 7 g | Saturated fat: 2 g | Cholesterol: 72 mg | Sodium: 1,308 mg | Total carbohydrates: 44 g | Dietary fiber: 3 g | Sugars: 5 g | Protein: 36 g

Spaghetti with Chunky Tomato Sauce

Hands-On Time: 15 minutes
Total Time: 30 minutes
Yield: Serves 6

1 pound ground beef

1 small onion, peeled and chopped

3 cloves garlic, minced

2 medium carrots, peeled and diced

2 medium stalks celery, diced

1 teaspoon dried basil leaves

¼ teaspoon salt

1 (28-ounce) can diced tomatoes

1 (16-ounce) package spaghetti, cooked

½ cup grated Parmesan cheese

1. Brown ground beef with onion and garlic in a heavy skillet over medium heat until beef is no longer pink, about 10 minutes. Drain well and then add carrots, celery, basil, salt, and tomatoes.

2. Bring sauce to a boil, then reduce heat to low and simmer for 15 minutes.

3. Serve sauce with hot pasta and grated cheese.

Per Serving: Calories: 490 | Fat: 12 g | Saturated fat: 4.5 g | Cholesterol: 50 mg | Sodium: 670 mg | Total carbohydrates: 66 g | Dietary fiber: 3 g | Sugars: 6 g | Protein: 29 g

Easy Vegetable Pasta

Hands-On Time: 10 minutes
Total Time: 25 minutes
Yield: Serves 6

1 pound gluten-free spaghetti

10 ounces mixed frozen vegetables, thawed

1 teaspoon freshly grated rosemary

2 teaspoons minced onion

2 teaspoons minced garlic

1 teaspoon salt

½ teaspoon ground black pepper

¼ cup grated Parmesan cheese

1. Cook spaghetti according to package directions.

2. In a frying pan over medium heat, toss the mixed vegetables to warm them.

3. Mix rosemary, onion, garlic, salt, and pepper with the vegetables.

4. Pour vegetables over spaghetti and serve, sprinkling with cheese.

Per Serving: Calories: 320 | Fat: 2.5 g | Saturated fat: 0.5 g | Cholesterol: 5 mg | Sodium: 480 mg | Total carbohydrates: 65 g | Dietary fiber: 2 g | Sugars: 2 g | Protein: 7 g

Pasta with Fresh Tomatoes

Hands-On Time: 5 minutes
Total Time: 15 minutes
Yield: Serves 4

6 quarts water
1 tablespoon salt
1 (1-pound) box spaghetti
2 tablespoons olive oil
3 large tomatoes, chopped
2 cloves garlic, minced
2 tablespoons chopped fresh
    basil
⅓ cup shredded Parmesan cheese

1. Add water to a medium stockpot and bring to a boil. Stir in salt and add pasta. Cook, stirring occasionally, 9–10 minutes or until al dente. Immediately drain.

2. Meanwhile, in large bowl combine olive oil, tomatoes, garlic, and basil and mix well. Toss in cooked pasta. Sprinkle with Parmesan cheese.

Per Serving: Calories: 550 | Fat: 11 g | Saturated fat: 2.5 g | Cholesterol: 5 mg | Sodium: 130 mg | Total carbohydrates: 92 g | Dietary fiber: 7 g | Sugars: 5 g | Protein: 19 g

Spaghetti Pancake (pictured)

Hands-On Time: 10 minutes
Total Time: 12 minutes
Yield: Serves 1

1 large egg
⅛ teaspoon garlic powder
⅛ teaspoon ground black pepper
1 tablespoon water
1 cup cooked spaghetti
1 tablespoon olive oil
1 medium scallion, thinly sliced
1 teaspoon fresh thyme

1. In a small bowl, beat together egg, garlic powder, pepper, and one tablespoon water. Toss with spaghetti.

2. Pour olive oil into a medium skillet and heat over medium-high heat. Sauté scallion, stirring frequently for about 1 minute. Add spaghetti mixture, evenly spreading mixture over bottom of skillet.

3. Reduce heat to medium-low and cook for 1–2 minutes until spaghetti is browned. Garnish with fresh thyme and serve immediately.

Per Serving: Calories: 420 | Fat: 20 g | Saturated fat: 3.5 g | Cholesterol: 210 mg | Sodium: 75 mg | Total carbohydrates: 45 g | Dietary fiber: 3 g | Sugars: 2 g | Protein: 15 g

Sun-Dried Tomato Linguine

Hands-On Time: 25 minutes
Total Time: 25 minutes
Yield: Serves 8

20 dry sun-dried tomatoes
1½ cups boiling water
½ cup grated Parmesan cheese
½ cup tightly packed fresh parsley sprigs
2 teaspoons olive oil
⅛ teaspoon salt
6 cloves garlic, minced
1 pound fresh spinach
¼ cup fresh basil
Nonstick cooking spray
12 ounces linguine

1. Combine tomatoes and boiling water in a small bowl. Let stand for 5 minutes. Drain, reserving 1 cup liquid.

2. Combine tomatoes, reserved liquid, cheese, parsley sprigs, olive oil, salt, and garlic; set aside.

3. Prepare spinach by removing stems; wash leaves thoroughly and pat dry. Shred spinach and add basil.

4. Coat a large, heavy saucepan with cooking spray and place over medium heat until hot. Add spinach and basil mixture. Cover and cook until spinach wilts, stirring occasionally. Add tomato mixture and warm through.

5. Cook pasta according to package directions, omitting salt. Drain well. Combine pasta with spinach, basil, and tomato mixture and toss until well combined.

Per Serving: Calories: 300 | Fat: 4 g | Saturated fat: 1 g | Cholesterol: 170 mg | Sodium: 740 mg | Total carbohydrates: 35 g | Dietary fiber: 4 g | Sugars: 8 g | Protein: 29 g

Fusion Lo Mein

Hands-On Time: 20 minutes
Total Time: 20 minutes
Yield: Serves 6

2 tablespoons rice vinegar

2 tablespoons thawed pineapple-orange juice concentrate

2 teaspoons minced shallots

2 teaspoons fresh lemon juice

1 teaspoon arrowroot starch

1 teaspoon Worcestershire sauce

1 teaspoon agave syrup

2 cloves garlic, peeled and minced

1 teaspoon olive oil

½ cup diced onion

1 cup julienned carrots

1 cup julienned yellow bell pepper

1 cup julienned red bell pepper

3 cups small broccoli florets

1 cup chopped savoy cabbage

¾ cup snow peas

1 (13.25-ounce) package whole-grain spaghetti, cooked

1. In a food processor or blender, combine vinegar, juice concentrate, shallots, lemon juice, arrowroot, Worcestershire, agave syrup, and garlic; process until smooth.

2. Heat a wok or large nonstick skillet coated with cooking spray over medium-high heat until hot; add the olive oil. Add onion and stir-fry for 5 minutes. Add carrots, bell peppers, broccoli, and cabbage; stir-fry another minute. Cover pan and cook for 2 more minutes.

3. Add vinegar mixture and snow peas to skillet. Bring mixture to a boil; cook uncovered for 30 seconds, stirring constantly. Add cooked pasta and toss to mix.

Per Serving: Calories: 336 | Fat: 4 g | Saturated fat: 0.6 g | Cholesterol: 0 mg | Sodium: 127 mg | Total carbohydrates: 69 g | Dietary fiber: 10 g | Sugars: 10 g | Protein: 13 g

Italian Pasta Stir-Fry

Hands-On Time: 15 minutes
Total Time: 15 minutes
Yield: Serves 6

8 ounces uncooked linguine
1 tablespoon olive oil
2 large cloves garlic, peeled and pressed
1 medium zucchini, sliced
2 medium tomatoes, peeled and chopped
¼ cup fresh parsley, minced
1 teaspoon dried oregano
⅛ teaspoon salt
⅛ teaspoon ground black pepper
¼ cup grated Parmesan cheese

1. Cook pasta according to package directions. Drain and keep warm.
2. Heat olive oil in a heavy skillet or wok over medium-high heat. Add garlic and stir-fry for 15 seconds.
3. Add zucchini. Stir-fry until crisp-tender, 2–3 minutes.
4. Add tomatoes, parsley, oregano, salt, and pepper to skillet. Gently stir until thoroughly heated, 1–2 minutes. Remove from heat.
5. Stir in warm pasta. Add Parmesan cheese. Serve immediately.

Per Serving: Calories: 190 | Fat: 4.5 g | Saturated fat: 1 g | Cholesterol: 5 mg | Sodium: 170 mg | Total carbohydrates: 31 g | Dietary fiber: 2 g | Sugars: 2 g | Protein: 7 g

Pasta Carbonara

Hands-On Time: 5 minutes
Total Time: 15 minutes
Yield: Serves 6

1 pound spaghetti
½ cup Egg Beaters
½ cup grated Parmesan cheese, divided
¼ cup grated Pecorino Romano cheese
½ teaspoon salt
½ cup diced Canadian bacon
¼ teaspoon black pepper

1. Cook spaghetti according to package directions. While the pasta cooks, whisk the Egg Beaters, ⅓ cup Parmesan, Pecorino, and salt in a medium mixing bowl until smooth and creamy.
2. As soon as the spaghetti is done, fold the egg mixture into the drained hot spaghetti. Add the bacon. Top with pepper and reserved Parmesan.

Per Serving: Calories: 410 | Fat: 4.5 g | Saturated fat: 2 g | Cholesterol: 15 mg | Sodium: 500 mg | Total carbohydrates: 75 g | Dietary fiber: 4 g | Sugars: 4 g | Protein: 14 g

Spaghetti ai Pomodori

Hands-On Time: 10 minutes
Total Time: 20 minutes
Yield: Serves 4

½ **pound spaghetti**
2 **cups halved cherry tomatoes**
2 **tablespoons chopped basil**
3 **tablespoons extra-virgin olive oil**
1 **teaspoon minced garlic**
½ **teaspoon salt**
¼ **teaspoon ground black pepper**

Cook the spaghetti according to the directions on the package; drain. Transfer the hot spaghetti to a large mixing bowl; add all other ingredients. Toss thoroughly.

Per Serving: Calories: 220 | Fat: 1 g | Saturated fat: 0 g | Cholesterol: 0 mg | Sodium: 300 mg | Total carbohydrates: 45 g | Dietary fiber: 3 g | Sugars: 3 g | Protein: 8 g

Apple and Chicken Orzo

Hands-On Time: 20 minutes
Total Time: 20 minutes
Yield: Serves 6

1 **tablespoon butter**
1 **pound boneless, skinless chicken breasts, cubed**
1 **tablespoon garlic powder**
1 **teaspoon ground ginger**
½ **teaspoon salt**
¼ **teaspoon ground black pepper**
1 **medium sweet onion, peeled and diced**
4 **medium carrots, peeled and thinly sliced**
1 **medium sweet apple, peeled, cored, and chopped**
1 **medium bunch asparagus, chopped into 1″–2″ pieces**
½ **cup dried cranberries**
1 **cup apple cider, divided**
1½ **tablespoons cornstarch**
2 **tablespoons soy sauce**
1 **(16-ounce) package orzo, cooked**

1. Add butter to a large wok or skillet. Add chicken and cook over medium heat until browned, about 3–5 minutes. Add garlic powder, ginger, salt, and pepper. Add onion, carrots, apples, asparagus, cranberries, and ¼ cup apple cider. Stir-fry until vegetables are tender, about 5–7 minutes.

2. While vegetables are cooking, combine remaining ¾ cup apple cider, cornstarch, and soy sauce in a small saucepan. Whisk over low heat until smooth and slightly thickened.

3. Add orzo to stir-fry pan and top with the apple and soy sauce. Stir in pan for one minute, remove from heat, and serve hot.

Per Serving: Calories: 500 | Fat: 4.5 g | Saturated fat: 1.5 g | Cholesterol: 50 mg | Sodium: 670 mg | Total carbohydrates: 86 g | Dietary fiber: 7 g | Sugars: 22 g | Protein: 29 g

Asparagus and Bread Crumb Pasta (pictured)

Hands-On Time: 15 minutes
Total Time: 25 minutes
Yield: Serves 4

8 ounces medium pasta shells

2 teaspoons kosher salt, divided

2 tablespoons unsalted butter, divided

1 pound asparagus, trimmed

½ cup panko bread crumbs

¼ cup shredded Parmesan cheese, divided

1 teaspoon dried parsley

1 teaspoon dried dill weed

1 teaspoon lemon pepper

½ teaspoon crushed red pepper

1 tablespoon lemon juice

1. Bring a large pot of water to a boil over high heat. Add pasta and 1 teaspoon salt. Cook for 7–9 minutes until al dente. Drain and toss with 1 tablespoon butter. Set aside.

2. Pour 1½" water into a medium saucepan. Bring to a boil over medium-high heat and place a collapsible steamer basket into the pan. Place asparagus in steamer basket and cook until bright green and crisp-tender, 3–5 minutes.

3. In a small frying pan over medium heat, sauté the bread crumbs with half of the cheese, remaining salt, butter, parsley, dill, lemon pepper, and crushed red pepper. Cook until browned, approximately 3–5 minutes.

4. Top pasta with asparagus, bread crumb topping, and remaining cheese. Serve immediately.

Per Serving: Calories: 535 | Fat: 8 g | Saturated fat: 5 g | Cholesterol: 19 mg | Sodium: 662 mg | Total carbohydrates: 99 g | Dietary fiber: 6 g | Sugars: 4 g | Protein: 16 g

Orecchiette with Peas and Onions

Hands-On Time: 10 minutes
Total Time: 20 minutes
Yield: Serves 6

1 tablespoon olive oil

4 medium onions, cut in half through the stem and thinly sliced (about 4 cups)

4 cups fresh or frozen tiny peas

¼ teaspoon salt

⅛ teaspoon ground black pepper

1 pound orecchiette

1 cup freshly grated pecorino cheese

1. In a large pot, bring at least 4 quarts water to a rolling boil.

2. Meanwhile, in a large skillet, heat the oil over medium heat. Add the onions and sauté 5 minutes, stirring occasionally, until the onions are softened. Add the peas, salt, and pepper, and cook 2 minutes longer. Stir in 2 tablespoons of water from the pot of boiling water. Reduce heat to low and cover skillet.

3. Add the pasta to the boiling water, stir well to separate, and cook 7–9 minutes until al dente. Drain and transfer to a warm serving bowl. Add some of the cheese and toss until melted. Top with the onion mixture and the remaining cheese.

Per Serving: Calories: 505 | Fat: 10 g | Saturated fat: 5 g | Cholesterol: 4 mg | Sodium: 405 mg | Total carbohydrates: 80 g | Dietary fiber: 10 g | Sugars: 10 g | Protein: 25 g

Pasta with Chickpea and Tomato Sauce

Hands-On Time: 15 minutes
Total Time: 45 minutes
Yield: Serves 6

- 2 teaspoons olive oil
- 1 large onion, peeled and chopped
- 1 medium carrot, peeled and diced
- 3 cloves garlic, minced
- 1 (15-ounce) can chickpeas, drained and rinsed
- 3 tablespoons red wine
- 1 teaspoon dried oregano
- ½ teaspoon dried basil
- ½ teaspoon dried thyme
- ½ teaspoon garlic powder
- ½ teaspoon ground paprika
- ¼ teaspoon ground black pepper
- ⅛ teaspoon dried red pepper flakes
- 1 (28-ounce) can crushed tomatoes
- 1 teaspoon salt
- 1 tablespoon agave nectar
- 1 (12-ounce) package orecchiette pasta
- 3 tablespoons chopped fresh parsley

1. Heat oil in a medium sauté pan over medium heat. Add onion and carrot and cook, stirring, 3 minutes. Add garlic and sauté 2 minutes. Add chickpeas, red wine, oregano, dried basil, thyme, garlic powder, paprika, black pepper, and red pepper flakes and cook, stirring, 5 minutes until tender.

2. Stir in tomatoes, salt, and agave and bring to a simmer. Lower the heat to medium-low to low, cover, and simmer 20 minutes.

3. Cook pasta according to package directions, then drain.

4. Toss sauce with pasta and sprinkle with fresh parsley. Serve immediately.

Per Serving: Calories: 420 | Fat: 4.5 g | Saturated fat: 1 g | Cholesterol: 0 mg | Sodium: 730 mg | Total carbohydrates: 82 g | Dietary fiber: 9 g | Sugars: 14 g | Protein: 11 g

Lazy and Hungry Garlic Pasta

Hands-On Time: 10 minutes
Total Time: 10 minutes
Yield: Serves 6

2 cloves garlic, peeled and
   minced
2 tablespoons olive oil
3 cups cooked pasta
2 tablespoons lemon juice
2 tablespoons nutritional yeast
½ teaspoon dried parsley
¼ teaspoon crushed red pepper
½ teaspoon salt
¼ teaspoon ground black pepper
1 tablespoon minced parsley

1. In a medium skillet, heat the garlic in olive oil over medium heat for 1– 2 minutes until almost browned.

2. Toss garlic and olive oil in a large bowl with remaining ingredients. Serve hot.

Per Serving: Calories: 130 | Fat: 5 g | Saturated fat: 1 g | Cholesterol: 0 mg | Sodium: 250 mg | Total carbohydrates: 19 g | Dietary fiber: 1 g | Sugars: 0 g | Protein: 4 g

Fettuccine with Alfredo Sauce

Hands-On Time: 10 minutes
Total Time: 10 minutes
Yield: Serves 4

1 cup evaporated skim milk
½ cup freshly grated Parmesan
   cheese
½ cup finely chopped parsley
1 pound fettuccine, cooked,
   drained, and kept warm
¼ teaspoon ground white pepper

1. Heat the milk in a deep saucepan over medium heat. Simmer but do not boil. Add the Parmesan cheese and parsley.

2. As soon as the cheese has melted and the sauce is thick and creamy, remove from the heat and toss with the pasta in a large bowl. Season with white pepper.

Per Serving: Calories: 532 | Fat: 6 g | Saturated fat: 2 g | Cholesterol: 11 mg | Sodium: 261 mg | Total carbohydrates: 95 g | Dietary fiber: 5 g | Sugars: 9 g | Protein: 24 g

Cheesy Fried Ravioli Skillet with Spring Peas and Asparagus (pictured)

Hands-On Time: 20 minutes
Total Time: 20 minutes
Yield: Serves 4

- 4 tablespoons olive oil
- 4 garlic cloves, peeled and minced
- 3 (9-ounce) packages refrigerated cheese-filled ravioli
- 1 pound asparagus, trimmed
- 1 cup shelled fresh spring peas
- 1 medium bunch scallions, minced
- ½ cup half-and-half
- ¼ cup shredded provolone cheese
- 1 teaspoon salt
- ½ teaspoon ground black pepper
- ½ cup shaved Parmesan cheese
- ¼ cup French-fried onions
- 1 tablespoon fresh chopped dill
- 1 tablespoon fresh chopped chives

1. In a large, deep-sided skillet, heat olive oil over medium-high heat. Add garlic and sauté for 30 seconds until aromatic.

2. Spread ravioli along the bottom of the pan and let it cook for 3–4 minutes, then flip quickly with a metal spatula and fry on the other side until golden brown.

3. Add asparagus, peas, and scallions and sauté just until crisp-tender.

4. Stir in half-and-half and sprinkle with provolone. Cover skillet, reduce heat to medium-low, and cook just until cheese melts, about 2 minutes.

5. Season with salt and pepper and garnish with Parmesan, onions, chives, and dill.

Per Serving: Calories: 753 | Fat: 25 g | Saturated fat: 11 g | Cholesterol: 100 mg | Sodium: 1,604 mg | Total carbohydrates: 100 g | Dietary fiber: 8 g | Sugars: 6 g | Protein: 33 g

Quick Chicken Pancit

Hands-On Time: 20 minutes
Total Time: 30 minutes
Yield: Serves 6

1 (6.75-ounce) package rice stick noodles or pancit noodles

2 tablespoons vegetable oil, divided

2 (5-ounce) boneless, skinless chicken breasts, thinly sliced

1 medium onion, peeled and chopped

3 cloves garlic, peeled and minced

½ small head cabbage, thinly sliced

2 large carrots, peeled and thinly sliced

¼ cup soy sauce

1. Place rice noodles in a large bowl and cover with hot water. Let stand until soft, about 10 minutes. Drain and set aside.

2. Heat 1 tablespoon oil in a large skillet over medium-high heat. Add chicken and cook until browned, about 8 minutes. Remove from the skillet and reserve.

3. Add remaining oil to the skillet and heat over medium-high heat. Add onion and garlic and cook for 1 minute, then add cabbage and carrots and cook until tender, about 2 minutes. Add chicken, noodles, and soy sauce to skillet and toss to combine. Serve hot.

Per Serving: Calories: 261 | Fat: 6 g | Saturated fat: 1 g | Cholesterol: 30 mg | Sodium: 763 mg | Total carbohydrates: 37 g | Dietary fiber: 4 g | Sugars: 2 g | Protein: 14 g

Spaghetti with Eggplant and Peppers

Hands-On Time: 15 minutes
Total Time: 15 minutes
Yield: Serves 6

2 tablespoons olive oil

1 cup chopped eggplant

2 cloves garlic, peeled and minced

1 medium zucchini, sliced

1 medium red bell pepper, seeded and chopped

1 medium yellow bell pepper, seeded and chopped

1 teaspoon fresh rosemary

½ teaspoon salt

¼ teaspoon ground black pepper

1 pound cooked spaghetti

1. Heat oil in a large skillet over medium heat. Add the eggplant and fry until soft and brown. Add the garlic, zucchini, red, and yellow peppers. Sauté for 2 minutes. Stir in rosemary, salt, and pepper.

2. Pour mixture over spaghetti in a large bowl and toss to combine.

Per Serving: Calories: 430 | Fat: 7 g | Saturated fat: 1.5 g | Cholesterol: 0 mg | Sodium: 100 mg | Total carbohydrates: 79 g | Dietary fiber: 5 g | Sugars: 6 g | Protein: 8 g

Linguine with Mushroom Sauce

Hands-On Time: 10 minutes
Total Time: 10 minutes
Yield: Serves 6

1 (16-ounce) package linguine
1 tablespoon olive oil
1 tablespoon butter
1 medium onion, peeled and
    chopped
3 cloves garlic, peeled and minced
1 (4-ounce) can mushroom
    pieces, drained
1 (10.75-ounce) can condensed
    cream of mushroom soup
1¼ cups whole milk
⅛ teaspoon nutmeg
⅓ cup grated Parmesan cheese

1. Cook linguine until al dente according to package directions. Drain. Set aside.

2. Meanwhile, in large saucepan, combine olive oil and butter over medium heat. Add onion and garlic; cook and stir until tender, about 5 minutes. Add mushrooms; cook and stir for about 3 minutes. Add soup, milk, and nutmeg; stir and bring to a simmer. Add cheese and stir to combine.

3. Serve pasta topped with sauce.

Per Serving: Calories: 263 | Fat: 11 g | Saturated fat: 4 g | Cholesterol: 15 mg | Sodium: 581 mg | Total carbohydrates: 33 g | Dietary fiber: 2 g | Sugars: 5 g | Protein: 8 g

Cacio e Pepe with Cauliflower

Hands-On Time: 20 minutes
Total Time: 20 minutes
Yield: Serves 4

12 ounces bucatini pasta
3 cups cauliflower florets
2 tablespoons butter
1 clove garlic, peeled and
    chopped
2 tablespoons water
1 teaspoon ground black pepper
¾ cup shredded Pecorino
    Romano cheese, divided

1. Bring a large pot of water to a boil. Add the bucatini pasta and cook according to the package directions. Drain pasta, reserving 1 cup of the cooking liquid.

2. While the pasta is cooking, combine the cauliflower, butter, garlic, and 2 tablespoons water in a medium-sized microwave-safe bowl. Cover with plastic wrap and poke a small hole in the top. Microwave on high for 6 minutes until very tender.

3. Transfer cauliflower mixture to a blender or food processor along with pepper and ½ cup cheese. Blend until combined. With the blender running, add 1 cup of the pasta cooking water to the mixture. Continue to blend until mixture is smooth.

4. Toss the pasta with the sauce and top with remaining cheese. Serve immediately.

Per Serving: Calories: 451 | Fat: 12 g | Saturated fat: 6 g | Cholesterol: 26 mg | Sodium: 280 mg | Total carbohydrates: 70 g | Dietary fiber: 5 g | Sugars: 5 g | Protein: 16 g

One-Pot Chicken, Pasta, and Broccoli

Hands-On Time: 15 minutes
Total Time: 30 minutes
Yield: Serves 4

12 ounces boneless, skinless chicken breasts, sliced

1½ teaspoons salt, divided

¾ teaspoon ground black pepper, divided

2 tablespoons all-purpose flour, divided

1½ tablespoons olive oil, divided

1 small onion, peeled and diced

6 cloves garlic, minced

2½ cups chicken broth

½ cup whole milk

8 ounces penne, uncooked

1 pound broccoli, cut into small florets

1 cup grated Parmesan cheese, divided

¼ cup chopped parsley

1. Season chicken with ½ teaspoon salt and ¼ teaspoon pepper. Sprinkle the chicken pieces with 1½ tablespoons flour and toss to coat.

2. Heat a large deep skillet or Dutch oven over medium-high heat. Add 1 tablespoon olive oil. When the oil starts to shimmer, add the chicken pieces. Cook until light golden brown on both sides, about 5 minutes. Remove the chicken pieces to a covered dish to keep warm.

3. Add the remaining olive oil and the onion to the skillet. Cook, stirring frequently, until light brown and translucent, about 5 minutes. Add the garlic and remaining flour and cook until fragrant, about 1 minute longer. Add the chicken broth, milk, and remaining salt and pepper and bring just to a simmer. Add the pasta and cook for 8 minutes.

4. Arrange the broccoli on top of the pasta and cover the pan. Cook until the broccoli is crisp-tender and the pasta is al dente, about 6 minutes. Return the chicken and ¾ cup grated Parmesan cheese to the pot and toss until creamy and combined.

5. Top with parsley and remaining cheese and serve immediately.

Per Serving: Calories: 543 | Fat: 14 g | Saturated fat: 6 g | Cholesterol: 89 mg | Sodium: 1,986 mg | Total carbohydrates: 60 g | Dietary fiber: 5 g | Sugars: 6 g | Protein: 38 g

Cajun Chicken Pasta

Hands-On Time: 30 minutes
Total Time: 30 minutes
Yield: Serves 6

1 pound boneless, skinless
   chicken breasts, cut into strips
1 tablespoon Cajun seasoning
2 tablespoons butter
2 cups heavy cream
½ teaspoon dried basil, crumbled
½ teaspoon lemon pepper
½ teaspoon salt
¼ teaspoon ground black pepper
¼ teaspoon garlic powder
8 ounces cooked linguine or
   fettuccine
½ cup grated Parmesan cheese

1. Place chicken and Cajun seasoning in a food storage bag. Rub and shake to coat chicken well.
2. In a large skillet over medium heat, melt butter and sauté chicken. Cook for about 7–9 minutes, then reduce heat to medium-low.
3. Add cream, basil, lemon pepper, salt, black pepper, and garlic powder. Stir for 5 minutes until sauce thickens.
4. Add pasta and toss to coat. Heat for another 5 minutes. Sprinkle with Parmesan cheese.

Per Serving: Calories: 536 | Fat: 43 g | Saturated fat: 24 g | Cholesterol: 170 mg | Sodium: 460 mg | Total carbohydrates: 16 g | Dietary fiber: 1 g | Sugars: 3 g | Protein: 30 g

Sweet and Savory Pepper Penne

Hands-On Time: 15 minutes
Total Time: 15 minutes
Yield: Serves 2

1 medium yellow onion, peeled
   and sliced
2 cloves garlic, minced
1 medium yellow pepper, seeded
   and sliced
1 medium red pepper, seeded and
   sliced
1 medium orange pepper, seeded
   and sliced
3 tablespoons extra-virgin olive
   oil, divided
1 tablespoon balsamic vinegar
2 cups 100 percent whole-wheat
   penne, cooked
1 teaspoon all-natural sea salt
1 teaspoon ground black pepper

1. In a large skillet over medium heat, sauté the onion, garlic, and peppers in 1 tablespoon of the oil until slightly softened but still crisp, about 4–6 minutes.
2. Add the balsamic vinegar to the skillet and toss to coat peppers and onions. Add the penne to the skillet, drizzling remaining olive oil over penne and vegetables until evenly coated. Season with salt and pepper.

Per Serving: Calories: 450 | Fat: 24 g | Saturated fat: 3 g | Cholesterol: 0 mg | Sodium: 1,170 mg | Total carbohydrates: 50 g | Dietary fiber: 8 g | Sugars: 10 g | Protein: 9 g

One-Pot Pesto Farfalle with Spring Vegetables (pictured)

Hands-On Time: 20 minutes
Total Time: 25 minutes
Yield: Serves 4

2 cups chicken stock

8 ounces farfalle pasta, uncooked

2 cups broccoli florets

1 pound asparagus, trimmed and cut into 1" pieces

4 medium cloves garlic, peeled and minced

1 teaspoon kosher salt

½ teaspoon ground black pepper

1 (8.5-ounce) jar sundried tomatoes, drained and chopped

¾ cup frozen peas

¼ cup pesto

½ cup grated Parmesan cheese

1. In a large pot over medium-high heat, bring broth to a boil. Stir in farfalle, broccoli, asparagus, garlic, salt, and pepper, and stir constantly for 12 minutes or until the farfalle and vegetables are tender.

2. Stir in tomatoes, peas, and pesto, and cook for an additional 5 minutes. Spoon into bowls and top with Parmesan to serve.

Per Serving: Calories: 497 | Fat: 18 g | Saturated fat: 4 g | Cholesterol: 14 mg | Sodium: 1,280 mg | Total carbohydrates: 77 g | Dietary fiber: 11 g | Sugars: 7 g | Protein: 23 g

Rotini with Broccoli Basil Pesto

Hands-On Time: 10 minutes
Total Time: 10 minutes
Yield: Serves 8

3 cloves garlic

3½ cups broccoli florets, cooked

3 tablespoons toasted pine nuts

½ cup shaved Parmesan cheese, divided

3 cups fresh basil leaves

3 tablespoons olive oil

1 tablespoon lemon juice

¼ teaspoon salt

½ teaspoon ground black pepper

1 pound cooked rotini pasta

1. In the bowl of a food processor with the motor running, chop garlic. Turn motor off and add the cooked broccoli, pine nuts, ¼ cup grated Parmesan cheese, basil, olive oil, lemon juice, salt, and pepper. Pulse until evenly chunky.

2. Pour pesto over hot or cold pasta and toss well. Sprinkle with the remaining ¼ cup Parmesan cheese.

Per Serving: Calories: 384 | Fat: 15 g | Saturated fat: 5 g | Cholesterol: 18 mg | Sodium: 516 mg | Total carbohydrates: 44 g | Dietary fiber: 3 g | Sugars: 3 g | Protein: 17 g

Spaghetti with Three-Cheese Sauce

Hands-On Time: 15 minutes
Total Time: 15 minutes
Yield: Serves 8

2 tablespoons butter

3 tablespoons all-purpose flour

½ teaspoon salt

1 teaspoon ground black pepper

⅛ teaspoon ground nutmeg

2 cups whole milk

½ cup mascarpone cheese

1 cup finely shredded mozzarella cheese

1 cup grated Parmesan cheese

1 pound cooked spaghetti

1. In large saucepan, melt butter over medium heat. Add flour, salt, pepper, and nutmeg; cook and stir until mixture bubbles, about 3 minutes. Add milk all at once, stirring with wire whisk. Cook over medium heat, stirring constantly, until sauce thickens and bubbles, about 5 minutes.

2. Remove from heat and stir in all three cheeses. Stir until melted and smooth. Serve immediately over cooked pasta.

Per Serving: Calories: 370 | Fat: 24 g | Saturated fat: 13 g | Cholesterol: 65 mg | Sodium: 460 mg | Total carbohydrates: 25 g | Dietary fiber: 1 g | Sugars: 4 g | Protein: 14 g

Fettuccine Carbonara with Peas

Hands-On Time: 25 minutes
Total Time: 25 minutes
Yield: Serves 6

1 (16-ounce) package fettuccine
2 cups frozen peas, thawed
4 ounces bacon, diced
½ cup heavy cream
¼ cup whole milk
4 large eggs
¼ cup grated Parmesan cheese
½ teaspoon salt
⅛ teaspoon ground black pepper
⅓ cup shredded Parmesan cheese

1. Cook fettuccine according to package directions. Place peas in colander and place in sink. Drain cooked pasta over peas in colander and set aside.

2. While pasta is cooking, heat a medium skillet over medium heat. Add the bacon and fry until crispy. Use a slotted spoon to transfer the bacon to a paper towel. Drain fat from the pan.

3. Add cream and milk to large pan and heat over medium until almost simmering. Remove from heat and beat in eggs, cheese, bacon, salt, and pepper and mix with wire whisk. Add cooked pasta to the pan and return to the heat for 2–3 minutes or until sauce forms and mixture is hot. Sprinkle with shredded Parmesan cheese and serve immediately.

Per Serving: Calories: 382 | Fat: 21.1 g | Saturated fat: 10 g | Cholesterol: 167 mg | Sodium: 575 mg | Total carbohydrates: 31 g | Dietary fiber: 3 g | Sugars: 5 g | Protein: 17 g

Greek Macaroni and Cheese

Hands-On Time: 5 minutes
Total Time: 25 minutes
Yield: Serves 3

4 tablespoons unsalted butter
3 tablespoons flour
1 teaspoon bottled minced garlic
1 cup whole milk
⅓ cup crumbled feta cheese
¼ teaspoon ground nutmeg
1 teaspoon dried mint
¼ teaspoon black pepper
1 teaspoon lemon juice
½ pound cooked tubular pasta

1. Melt the butter in a medium pan over very low heat. Add the flour and blend it into the melted butter, stirring continually until it thickens and forms a roux. Stir in the garlic.

2. Turn the heat up to medium-low and slowly add the milk and cheese. Stir in the ground nutmeg and the dried mint. Continue stirring with a whisk until the mixture has thickened. Stir in the pepper and lemon juice.

3. Toss the pasta with the sauce and serve immediately.

Per Serving: Calories: 368 | Fat: 21 g | Saturated fat: 13 g | Cholesterol: 56 mg | Sodium: 158 mg | Total carbohydrates: 34 g | Dietary fiber: 2 g | Sugars: 5 g | Protein: 10 g

Skillet Gnocchi with Brussels Sprouts and Sausage (pictured)

Hands-On Time: 20 minutes
Total Time: 20 minutes
Yield: Serves 4

2 tablespoons olive oil

8 ounces sweet Italian sausage, casings removed

8 ounces Brussels sprouts, trimmed and halved

3 cloves garlic, minced

1 pound fresh gnocchi

½ cup white wine

1 cup chicken broth

½ teaspoon salt

½ teaspoon ground black pepper

½ cup shredded Parmesan cheese

1. Heat oil in a large skillet over medium heat. Add sausage and use spoon to break sausage up as it cooks. Sauté until sausage begins to brown and is cooked through, about 10 minutes.

2. Add Brussels sprouts and continue to cook until sprouts also begin to soften, about 5 minutes. Add garlic and cook 1 minute more.

3. Add gnocchi to pan (do not precook it). Cook 2–3 minutes until gnocchi begins to soften slightly and brown.

4. Add wine, then cook 2 minutes. Add broth, salt, and pepper. Bring to a full boil. Remove from heat and add cheese. Stir until cheese melts and serve hot.

Per Serving: Calories: 320 | Fat: 15 g | Saturated fat: 5 g | Cholesterol: 25 mg | Sodium: 1,380 mg | Total carbohydrates: 26 g | Dietary fiber: 2 g | Sugars: 3 g | Protein: 19 g

Pumpkin Ravioli

Hands-On Time: 25 minutes
Total Time: 25 minutes
Yield: Serves 4

½ cup cooked pumpkin purée

2 large eggs, divided

⅛ teaspoon ground nutmeg

2 tablespoons bread crumbs

2 amaretti cookies, crushed into crumbs

1 tablespoon chopped dried apricot

1 teaspoon honey mustard

1 tablespoon water

12 gyoza wrappers

¼ cup browned butter

1 teaspoon minced sage

2 tablespoons grated Parmesan cheese

1. Combine the pumpkin purée with 1 egg, nutmeg, bread crumbs, amaretti crumbs, dried apricot, and honey mustard.

2. Beat remaining egg with water in a small bowl.

3. Put one spoonful of filling in the middle of each gyoza wrapper. Brush the edges of the wrapper with egg mixture and then fold it over to make a half moon. Press the edges down to seal.

4. Bring a large pot of salted water to a boil, then add the ravioli and cook for about 1 minute. Drain and put the ravioli on a platter.

5. Drizzle the browned butter over the ravioli, sprinkle with sage and Parmesan cheese, and serve hot.

Per Serving: Calories: 270 | Fat: 16 g | Saturated fat: 9 g | Cholesterol: 125 mg | Sodium: 250 mg | Total carbohydrates: 22 g | Dietary fiber: 2 g | Sugars: 7 g | Protein: 7 g

Dan Dan Noodles

Hands-On Time: 10 minutes
Total Time: 30 minutes
Yield: Serves 4

8 ounces fresh egg noodles

2 teaspoons plus 1 tablespoon sesame oil, divided

3 tablespoons peanut butter

2 tablespoons dark soy sauce

1 tablespoon light soy sauce

3 tablespoons rice vinegar

1 teaspoon sugar

1 tablespoon hot chili oil

1½ tablespoons toasted sesame seeds

3 medium green onions, cut into 1″ pieces

1. Bring a large pot of water to boil and cook the noodles al dente, no longer than 5 minutes. Drain thoroughly and toss with 2 teaspoons of sesame oil. Cool.

2. In a blender or food processor, combine the peanut butter, dark soy sauce, light soy sauce, rice vinegar, sugar, 1 tablespoon of sesame oil, and chili oil. Process until smooth.

3. Mix the sauce in with the noodles. Sprinkle the toasted sesame seeds over the noodles. Garnish with the green onion.

Per Serving: Calories: 420 | Fat: 21 g | Saturated fat: 3 g | Cholesterol: 40 mg | Sodium: 640 mg | Total carbohydrates: 47 g | Dietary fiber: 4 g | Sugars: 3 g | Protein: 12 g

Skillet-Baked Spaghetti Pie

Hands-On Time: 15 minutes
Total Time: 35 minutes
Yield: Serves 4

4 cups cooked spaghetti

2 tablespoons olive oil, divided

1 cup grated Parmesan cheese

½ pound lean ground beef

½ teaspoon salt

2 cups jarred marinara sauce

½ cup part-skim shredded mozzarella cheese

1. Preheat oven to 350°F.

2. Place cooked spaghetti in a large bowl and toss with 1 tablespoon of the olive oil. Add Parmesan cheese and toss to combine.

3. Heat a large oven-safe skillet over medium-high heat. Add the remaining tablespoon of olive oil, ground beef, and salt. Cook, breaking up the meat, until the meat is no longer pink and any liquid has cooked off. Add the marinara. Bring to a simmer.

4. Add the spaghetti to the skillet and sprinkle the mozzarella cheese over the top. Move to the oven and bake for 20 minutes or until the cheese is bubbly.

5. Remove from the oven and serve immediately.

Per Serving: Calories: 530 | Fat: 23 g | Saturated fat: 8 g | Cholesterol: 65 mg | Sodium: 1,350 mg | Total carbohydrates: 52 g | Dietary fiber: 2 g | Sugars: 7 g | Protein: 29 g

Chicken Spaghetti

Hands-On Time: 10 minutes
Total Time: 35 minutes
Yield: Serves 4

2 teaspoons lactose-free
    margarine
½ cup minced onion
1 clove garlic, peeled and minced
1 pound ground chicken
1 (15-ounce) can puréed tomatoes
1 (8-ounce) can tomato sauce
1 teaspoon dried basil
¼ teaspoon dried thyme
¼ teaspoon Italian seasoning
½ teaspoon salt
½ teaspoon ground black pepper
4 cups cooked whole-wheat
    spaghetti

1. Melt margarine in a large skillet over medium heat. Add onion and garlic. Sauté until lightly browned, about 5 minutes.

2. Add chicken to skillet with onion and garlic and brown. Add tomatoes and sauce. Bring to a boil.

3. Reduce heat and add basil, thyme, Italian seasoning, salt, and pepper. Cover and simmer until chicken is tender, about 25 minutes. Serve over hot cooked spaghetti.

Per Serving: Calories: 410 | Fat: 11 g | Saturated fat: 3 g | Cholesterol: 95 mg | Sodium: 1,090 mg | Total carbohydrates: 52 g | Dietary fiber: 10 g | Sugars: 9 g | Protein: 30 g

Garlic Noodles with Bacon

Hands-On Time: 5 minutes
Total Time: 15 minutes
Yield: Serves 4

3 slices bacon
3 tablespoons butter
2 tablespoons cream cheese,
    softened
2 teaspoons bottled minced garlic
1 cup half-and-half
⅓ cup grated Parmesan cheese
½ teaspoon dried basil
½ teaspoon dried oregano
⅛ teaspoon ground black pepper
8 ounces cooked spaghetti

1. Place bacon on a plate lined with a paper towel. Lay two more paper towels over the bacon. Microwave on high heat for 2 minutes, and then for 1 minute at a time until the bacon is cooked. Remove and chop.

2. Melt the butter in a medium saucepan over low heat. Whisk in the cream cheese. Stir in the garlic. Turn the heat up and add the half-and-half. Add the Parmesan cheese and continue stirring with a whisk until the mixture has thickened. Stir in the basil, oregano, and pepper.

3. Place the pasta in a large bowl. Toss with the sauce.

Per Serving: Calories: 347 | Fat: 24 g | Saturated fat: 14 g | Cholesterol: 60 mg | Sodium: 344 mg | Total carbohydrates: 21 g | Dietary fiber: 1 g | Sugars: 3 g | Protein: 12 g

Chapter 7

Chicken and Turkey Main Dishes

Chicken Fries

Hands-On Time: 20 minutes
Total Time: 20 minutes
Yield: Serves 4

1 pound boneless, skinless
   chicken breasts
½ cup all-purpose flour
½ cup seasoned fish-fry breading
   mix
1 large egg
1 tablespoon water
2 cups vegetable oil

1. Butterfly the chicken breasts. Cut them down the middle to separate the breast halves. Cut into the shape of French fries with meat scissors or a knife.

2. Put the flour and breading mix into 2 separate zip-top plastic bags. In a small bowl, lightly beat the egg with the water.

3. Place 4 chicken fries at a time into the flour bag. Remove and shake off the excess flour.

4. Dip them into the egg wash, shake off the excess, then shake them in the breading mix. Place each breaded chicken piece on a plate.

5. Heat the oil in a large skillet over medium-high heat. Fry the chicken fries in batches so they do not touch, turning often, until golden brown (about 4–5 minutes). Drain on paper towels.

Per Serving: Calories: 280 | Fat: 8 g | Saturated fat: 1.5 g | Cholesterol: 120 mg | Sodium: 650 mg | Total carbohydrates: 20 g | Dietary fiber: 0 g | Sugars: 0 g | Protein: 28 g

Chicken Veggie Tacos

Hands-On Time: 10 minutes
Total Time: 30 minutes
Yield: Serves 8

1 tablespoon olive oil

1 small red onion, peeled and chopped

3 cloves garlic, minced

1 medium jalapeño pepper, seeded and minced

1 pound boneless, skinless chicken breasts, cubed

½ teaspoon salt

⅛ teaspoon ground black pepper

1 teaspoon dried oregano leaves

2 tablespoons lime juice

8 crisp corn taco shells

2 cups shredded lettuce

2 medium tomatoes, chopped

1 cup shredded Monterey jack cheese

1. In large skillet, heat olive oil over medium heat. Add onion, garlic, and jalapeño pepper; cook and stir for 4 minutes. Add chicken and sprinkle with salt, pepper, and oregano. Cook and stir for 8–10 minutes until chicken is almost cooked.

2. Add lime juice; cook and stir for 3–4 minutes longer until chicken is tender. Remove from heat. Heat taco shells as directed on package. Fill taco shells with chicken mixture; top with lettuce, tomatoes, and cheese.

Per Serving: Calories: 210 | Fat: 10 g | Saturated fat: 4 g | Cholesterol: 55 mg | Sodium: 300 mg | Total carbohydrates: 12 g | Dietary fiber: 2 g | Sugars: 2 g | Protein: 18 g

Oven-Baked Chicken Tenders (pictured)

Hands-On Time: 15 minutes
Total Time: 30 minutes
Yield: Serves 12

3 pounds boneless, skinless chicken breasts, cut into strips
½ cup unbleached all-purpose flour
½ cup white whole-wheat flour
½ cup bread crumbs
2 teaspoons garlic powder
2 teaspoons onion powder
1 teaspoon ground black pepper
½ cup low-fat milk
1 large egg white

1. Preheat oven to 375°F. Cover a large baking sheet with aluminum foil, spray lightly with oil, and set aside.
2. Wash the chicken and pat dry.
3. Combine the flours, bread crumbs, and seasonings in a large zip-top plastic bag. Seal and shake well to combine.
4. Whisk together the milk and egg white in a shallow bowl. One piece at a time, dip the chicken into the milk mixture, then place in the flour bag, seal, and shake vigorously to coat. Place breaded tenders on the prepared baking sheet.
5. Place baking sheet on middle rack in oven and bake for 10–15 minutes, until golden brown.
6. Remove from oven and serve immediately.

Per Serving: Calories: 180 | Fat: 3 g | Saturated fat: 1 g | Cholesterol: 75 mg | Sodium: 120 mg | Total carbohydrates: 11 g | Dietary fiber: 1 g | Sugars: 1 g | Protein: 29 g

Parmesan-Crusted Chicken Breast

Hands-On Time: 5 minutes
Total Time: 25 minutes
Yield: Serves 1

1 (5-ounce) skinless, boneless chicken breast
⅛ teaspoon seasoned salt
⅛ teaspoon ground black pepper
1 tablespoon grated Parmesan
1 tablespoon dry white wine

1. Preheat oven to 375°F. Line a small baking pan with foil.
2. Rinse the chicken under cold running water and pat dry with paper towels. Season the chicken with seasoned salt and pepper and place in the center of the baking pan.
3. Combine the Parmesan and wine in a small bowl and mix to a paste-like consistency. Spread the mixture on top of the chicken breast. Bake the chicken uncovered until cooked through and juices run clear, about 17–20 minutes. Serve hot.

Per Serving: Calories: 160 | Fat: 3 g | Saturated fat: 1 g | Cholesterol: 80 mg | Sodium: 230 mg | Total carbohydrates: 0 g | Dietary fiber: 0 g | Sugars: 0 g | Protein: 29 g

Yogurt "Fried" Chicken

Hands-On Time: 20 minutes
Total Time: 30 minutes
Yield: Serves 4

Spectrum Naturals Extra Virgin Olive Spray Oil with Garlic Flavor

4 (1-ounce) slices French bread

1 pound boneless, skinless chicken breasts (trimmed of fat)

1 teaspoon garlic powder

1 teaspoon paprika

¼ teaspoon mustard powder

¼ teaspoon dried thyme

2 teaspoons salt-free lemon pepper

1 cup nonfat plain yogurt

1. Preheat oven to 350°. Treat a baking pan with the spray oil.

2. Place the bread in the bowl of a food processor or in a blender; process to make bread crumbs.

3. Cut the chicken breasts into 8 equal-sized strips. In a medium-sized bowl, combine the garlic powder, paprika, mustard powder, thyme, and lemon pepper with the yogurt and mix well. Add the chicken to the yogurt mixture, stirring to make sure all sides of the strips are covered. Lift the chicken strips out of the yogurt mixture and dredge all sides in the bread crumbs. Lightly mist the breaded chicken pieces with the spray oil and arrange in the pan.

4. Bake for 10 minutes, using a spatula or tongs to turn the chicken pieces halfway through.

Per Serving: Calories: 240 | Fat: 3.5 g | Saturated fat: 1 g | Cholesterol: 65 mg | Sodium: 270 mg | Total carbohydrates: 21 g | Dietary fiber: 1 g | Sugars: 5 g | Protein: 29 g

Grilled Jerk Chicken

Hands-On Time: 20 minutes
Total Time: 20 minutes
Yield: Serves 4

1 teaspoon salt-free jerk spice blend

1 teaspoon Bragg Liquid Aminos

2 teaspoons fresh lime juice

1 teaspoon olive or canola oil

1 medium jalapeño pepper, seeded and chopped

2 medium scallions, white and green parts chopped

1 teaspoon granulated sugar

Pinch mustard powder

4 (4-ounce) boneless, skinless chicken breasts

1. Preheat an indoor grill or grill pan on high heat.

2. Add all the ingredients except the chicken to a small food processor or blender and purée.

3. Rinse the chicken in cold water and pat dry between paper towels. Rub both sides with the spice mixture. Grill for 3–4 minutes, until the chicken is cooked through and the juices run clear. Serve immediately.

Per Serving: Calories: 140 | Fat: 4 g | Saturated fat: 1 g | Cholesterol: 65 mg | Sodium: 135 mg | Total carbohydrates: 2 g | Dietary fiber: 0 g | Sugars: 1 g | Protein: 23 g

Sweet Crusted Chicken Nuggets

Hands-On Time: 5 minutes
Total Time: 25 minutes
Yield: Serves 4

4 (5-ounce) boneless, skinless
   chicken breasts, cut into
   chunks
1 cup Egg Beaters
2 cups crushed Frosted Flakes
   cereal
1 tablespoon Splenda

1. Preheat oven to 400°F.
2. Coat chicken chunks in Egg Beaters. Roll coated chicken in cereal crumbs until covered.
3. Place chicken on 2 large baking sheets and sprinkle with Splenda.
4. Bake for 20 minutes or until internal temperature reaches 165°F.

Per Serving: Calories: 250 | Fat: 4 g | Saturated fat: 1 g | Cholesterol: 70 mg | Sodium: 500 mg | Total carbohydrates: 20 g | Dietary fiber: 1 g | Sugars: 7 g | Protein: 35 g

Sweet Chicken Curry

Hands-On Time: 20 minutes
Total Time: 30 minutes
Yield: Serves 4

1 (10-ounce) package frozen
   green beans
1½ cups julienned carrots
1 tablespoon olive oil
1 medium onion, diced
2 medium cloves garlic, minced
1 cup chicken broth
⅓ cup peach preserves, no sugar
   added
1 tablespoon arrowroot or tapioca
   powder
1 tablespoon filtered water
3 cups chopped cooked chicken
2 medium scallions, chopped
2 teaspoons grated gingerroot or
   1 teaspoon ground ginger
1 teaspoon curry powder

1. Place green beans and carrots in a medium glass bowl; cover and microwave on high for about 6 minutes or until veggies are slightly softened. Set aside.
2. Heat olive oil over medium-high heat in a large skillet. Add onion and garlic. Sauté for 5 minutes or until onion is translucent.
3. Add chicken broth and peach preserves to skillet and bring to a boil.
4. In a small bowl, combine arrowroot or tapioca powder with water. Whisk mixture into skillet and cook for 1 minute. Reduce heat to medium-low, add green beans and carrots, chicken, scallions, ginger, and curry powder. Heat through, about 3–5 minutes.

Per Serving: Calories: 300 | Fat: 7 g | Saturated fat: 1.5 g | Cholesterol: 110 mg | Sodium: 300 mg | Total carbohydrates: 34 g | Dietary fiber: 4 g | Sugars: 7 g | Protein: 33 g

Orange Chicken and Broccoli Stir-Fry (pictured)

Hands-On Time: 20 minutes
Total Time: 20 minutes
Yield: Serves 4

2 tablespoons fresh orange juice

2 tablespoons fresh lemon juice

2 tablespoons gluten-free soy sauce (tamari)

2 tablespoons orange marmalade (without high-fructose corn syrup)

2 teaspoons cornstarch

2 tablespoons safflower oil

2 pounds chicken tenders, cut into 1" pieces

1 pound broccoli, cut into florets

1 small red bell pepper, seeded and chopped

1 small yellow bell pepper, seeded and chopped

6 ounces fresh green beans, trimmed

2 teaspoons chopped fresh gingerroot

1. In a small bowl, combine orange juice, lemon juice, soy sauce, marmalade, and cornstarch. Set aside.

2. Heat oil over medium-high heat in a medium-sized wok or 9" nonstick skillet. Add chicken and stir until cooked through, 2–3 minutes. Transfer chicken to a plate.

3. Add broccoli to wok and cook 3 minutes. Increase heat to high, add bell peppers and green beans, and cook 4 minutes, stirring frequently. Transfer vegetables to plate with chicken.

4. Reduce heat to medium-high and add ginger. Cook until fragrant, about 30 seconds.

5. Add orange sauce to pan and cook until slightly thickened, about 30 seconds. Add chicken and vegetables to wok and toss to coat.

Per Serving: Calories: 515 | Fat: 18 g | Saturated fat: 1 g | Cholesterol: 0 mg | Sodium: 140 mg | Total carbohydrates: 25 g | Dietary fiber: 3 g | Sugars: 17 g | Protein: 65 g

Sweet and Sour Chicken with Vegetables

Hands-On Time: 20 minutes
Total Time: 20 minutes
Yield: Serves 4

¾ cup pineapple juice

2 tablespoons rice vinegar

1 teaspoon black rice vinegar

1 tablespoon soy sauce

2 tablespoons oil for stir-frying

1½ cups bite-sized pieces of chicken

2 tablespoons plus 1 teaspoon sugar, divided

½ medium green bell pepper, seeded and cut into bite-sized cubes

½ medium red bell pepper, seeded and cut into bite-sized cubes

¼ cup pineapple chunks

1 tablespoon cornstarch mixed with 4 tablespoons water

1. In a large bowl, mix pineapple juice, rice vinegar, black rice vinegar, and soy sauce, and set aside.

2. Add oil to a wok or medium skillet over medium-high heat. When oil is hot, add the chicken. Stir-fry until it changes color and is nearly cooked through, about 5–6 minutes.

3. In a medium saucepan, bring the pineapple juice mixture to a boil. Stir in the sugar until it dissolves. Add green and red peppers and pineapple chunks. Bring back to a boil and add cornstarch and water mixture, stirring quickly to thicken.

4. Pour the sauce over the stir-fried chicken and heat through.

Per Serving: Calories: 220 | Fat: 10 g | Saturated fat: 2 g | Cholesterol: 35 mg | Sodium: 290 mg | Total carbohydrates: 18 g | Dietary fiber: 1 g | Sugars: 14 g | Protein: 13 g

Blackberry Chicken

Hands-On Time: 10 minutes
Total Time: 30 minutes
Yield: Serves 4

¼ cup apple cider vinegar
¼ cup honey
¼ cup fresh mint
¼ teaspoon salt
¼ teaspoon ground black pepper
4 (4-ounce) boneless, skinless chicken breasts
2 tablespoons coconut oil
⅓ cup finely diced sweet onion
2 cups blackberries

1. In a large bowl, whisk together vinegar, honey, and half the mint. Add salt and pepper. Pour ¼ cup marinade into a small bowl and reserve. Marinate chicken in bowl 10 minutes.

2. Add coconut oil to a large skillet over medium heat. Add chicken and cook. Flip chicken after 4–5 minutes and cook another 4–5 minutes or until chicken is cooked through. Remove chicken from skillet and drizzle with the reserved marinade.

3. Add onion into the skillet and cook until softened, about 1 minute. Add remaining blackberries and honey mixture into the skillet and cook for 2–3 minutes.

4. When the blackberries are bright purple, spoon over chicken.

Per Serving: Calories: 280 | Fat: 9 g | Saturated fat: 6 g | Cholesterol: 65 mg | Sodium: 220 mg | Total carbohydrates: 25 g | Dietary fiber: 4 g | Sugars: 20 g | Protein: 27 g

Chicken and Vegetable Stir-Fry

Hands-On Time: 20 minutes
Total Time: 20 minutes
Yield: Serves 4

½ cup water
2 tablespoons soy sauce
2 tablespoons hoisin sauce
2 teaspoons cornstarch
1 teaspoon grated fresh ginger
1 teaspoon toasted sesame oil
2 tablespoons peanut oil
12 ounces skinless, boneless chicken breasts, cut into bite-sized pieces
1 (1-pound) package frozen broccoli stir-fry mix, thawed
1 medium yellow sweet pepper, seeded and cut into strips
2 cups hot cooked rice

1. In a small bowl, make the sauce by stirring together the water, soy sauce, hoisin sauce, cornstarch, ginger, and sesame oil. Set aside.

2. Add the peanut oil to a wok or large skillet and bring to temperature over medium-high heat. Add the chicken pieces and stir-fry for 5 minutes or until the chicken is cooked through. Push the chicken to the edges of the pan; add the stir-fry mix and pepper strips and stir-fry for 3 minutes or until the vegetables are crisp-tender.

3. Push the vegetables away from the center of pan. Pour the sauce mixture into the center of pan; cook and stir until thickened and bubbly. Stir the sauce into the chicken and vegetables. Serve over rice.

Per Serving: Calories: 300 | Fat: 10 g | Saturated fat: 1.5 g | Cholesterol: 30 mg | Sodium: 690 mg | Total carbohydrates: 37 g | Dietary fiber: 3 g | Sugars: 7 g | Protein: 14 g

Sheet Pan Chicken, Sausage, and Mushrooms (pictured)

Hands-On Time: 10 minutes
Total Time: 35 minutes
Yield: Serves 4

2 tablespoons olive oil
1 teaspoon salt
1 teaspoon ground black pepper
½ teaspoon smoked paprika
1 medium red onion, peeled and thinly sliced
2 cups sliced mushrooms
12 ounces smoked beef sausage, cut into 1" pieces
1 pound chicken legs

1. Preheat oven to 450°F. Line a rimmed baking sheet with foil and spray with nonstick cooking spray.

2. In a large bowl combine all ingredients and mix well to coat. Transfer to the baking sheet, making sure chicken legs are resting on top of the other ingredients.

3. Bake for 25 minutes or until chicken reaches an internal temperature of 160°F and the vegetables are tender. Serve warm.

Per Serving: Calories: 605 | Fat: 43 g | Saturated fat: 15 g | Cholesterol: 174 mg | Sodium: 1,370 mg | Total carbohydrates: 5.13 g | Dietary fiber: 1 g | Sugars: 2 g | Protein: 35 g

Turkey Piccata

Hands-On Time: 20 minutes
Total Time: 30 minutes
Yield: Serves 10

2 tablespoons olive oil
4 pounds boneless turkey cutlets
½ cup all-purpose flour
2 tablespoons capers, rinsed
1½ tablespoons grated lemon zest
6 tablespoons lemon juice
1 cup chicken stock
½ teaspoon ground black pepper

1. Heat the oil over medium heat in a large sauté pan. Dust the turkey with the flour and shake off excess. Add the turkey to the pan and brown the turkey pieces on one side, then turn.

2. Add the capers, lemon zest, lemon juice, stock, and pepper. Cook for 6–10 minutes longer until browned and cooked through.

3. Serve hot.

Per Serving: Calories: 250 | Fat: 4 g | Saturated fat: 0 g | Cholesterol: 70 mg | Sodium: 240 mg | Total carbohydrates: 6 g | Dietary fiber: 0 g | Sugars: 0 g | Protein: 46 g

Chicken and Bean Tacos

Hands-On Time: 20 minutes
Total Time: 25 minutes
Yield: Serves 8

1 pound boneless, skinless
    chicken breasts
½ teaspoon salt
⅛ teaspoon black pepper
1 tablespoon arrowroot
2 tablespoons olive oil
1 medium onion, chopped
1 medium yellow bell pepper,
    chopped
1 (15-ounce) can Great Northern
    beans, drained
1 cup salsa
8 crisp corn taco shells
2 cups shredded lettuce
1 cup grape tomatoes
½ cup sour cream
1 cup shredded Cheddar cheese

1. Heat oven to 350°F.

2. Cut chicken into 1" cubes and sprinkle with salt, pepper, and arrowroot.

3. Heat olive oil in large skillet and add chicken. Cook and stir until almost cooked, about 4 minutes; remove from skillet. Add onion and bell pepper to skillet; cook and stir 4–5 minutes or until crisp-tender.

4. Return chicken to skillet along with beans and salsa; bring to a simmer. Simmer until chicken is cooked, about 3–5 minutes longer.

5. Meanwhile, heat taco shells as directed on package. When shells are hot, fill with chicken mixture and top with lettuce, tomatoes, sour cream, and cheese. Serve immediately.

Per Serving: Calories: 314 | Fat: 13 g | Saturated fat: 5 g | Cholesterol: 52 mg | Sodium: 710 mg | Total carbohydrates: 31 g | Dietary fiber: 6 g | Sugars: 4 g | Protein: 21 g

Lemon Poppy Seed Chicken

Hands-On Time: 15 minutes
Total Time: 25 minutes
Yield: Serves 4

3 tablespoons coconut oil
4 (4-ounce) boneless, skinless chicken breasts, cubed
3 medium lemons, juiced and zested
1½ cups vegetable broth
1 tablespoon coconut aminos
1 tablespoon tapioca starch
4 tablespoons honey
½ teaspoon poppy seeds
¼ cup diced green onions

1. In a large skillet over medium-high heat, melt coconut oil. Add chicken; cook until golden brown, about 6 minutes per side.

2. In a small bowl, whisk together lemon juice and zest, broth, aminos, tapioca, and honey. Add mixture to skillet with chicken. Turn heat to medium, cover, and cook until the sauce thickens, about 10 minutes. Garnish with poppy seeds and green onions.

Per Serving: Calories: 320 | Fat: 13 g | Saturated fat: 9 g | Cholesterol: 85 mg | Sodium: 390 mg | Total carbohydrates: 23 g | Dietary fiber: 1 g | Sugars: 18 g | Protein: 26 g

Skillet Chicken Parmesan

Hands-On Time: 25 minutes
Total Time: 30 minutes
Yield: Serves 8

8 (4-ounce) chicken breast cutlets, pounded to ¼"–⅛" thickness
1 tablespoon Italian seasoning
½ teaspoon ground black pepper
1 tablespoon kosher salt
½ cup grated Parmesan cheese
¾ cup all-purpose flour
3 large eggs, beaten
1 cup panko bread crumbs
4 tablespoons vegetable oil
2 cups jarred marinara sauce
8 slices mozzarella cheese

1. Preheat the oven broiler. Season the chicken with Italian seasoning, pepper, and salt. In a shallow dish, mix together the Parmesan cheese and flour. In a second shallow dish, place the beaten eggs. In a third dish, place the bread crumbs.

2. Working with 1 piece of chicken at a time, dredge the cutlet into the flour mixture, then the beaten eggs, and finally the bread crumbs. Use fingers to gently adhere the bread crumbs to the cutlet and place on a baking sheet. Repeat with the remaining cutlets.

3. Heat large wok over medium heat and add 2 tablespoons vegetable oil. Once the oil is hot, cook 2 cutlets at a time for 2 minutes on each side or until golden. Transfer the cooked chicken to a plate and tent with aluminum foil. Repeat with the remaining cutlets.

4. Place the cutlets in a baking dish. Cover the tops with the marinara sauce and place 1 piece of cheese on top of each cutlet. Broil until the cheese has bubbled and browned. Serve immediately.

Per Serving: Calories: 320 | Fat: 13 g | Saturated fat: 6 g | Cholesterol: 145 mg | Sodium: 1,380 mg | Total carbohydrates: 15 g | Dietary fiber: 1 g | Sugars: 0 g | Protein: 36 g

Sautéed Chicken with Asparagus

Hands-On Time: 15 minutes
Total Time: 25 minutes
Yield: Serves 1

1 (5-ounce) skinless, boneless
    chicken breast
⅛ teaspoon salt
⅛ teaspoon ground black pepper
1 tablespoon all-purpose flour
1 tablespoon olive oil
1 teaspoon lemon zest
4 ounces asparagus spears,
    trimmed and cut into 1½"
    pieces
1 teaspoon chopped tarragon
1 teaspoon chopped chives
⅓ cup chicken stock

1. Season chicken breast with salt and pepper and coat with flour.

2. Heat the oil in a medium-sized nonstick skillet over medium-high heat. Add the chicken and cook for about 4 minutes until golden brown. Turn the chicken and add the lemon zest, asparagus, tarragon, chives, and stock; bring to a simmer. Simmer until the chicken is tender and cooked through, about 8 minutes.

Per Serving: Calories: 370 | Fat: 17 g | Saturated fat: 3 g | Cholesterol: 80 mg | Sodium: 210 mg | Total carbohydrates: 17 g | Dietary fiber: 1 g | Sugars: 0 g | Protein: 35 g

Honey Mustard BBQ Chicken Sandwiches

Hands-On Time: 15 minutes
Total Time: 15 minutes
Yield: Serves 8

1 (3-pound) rotisserie chicken
1½ cups bottled barbecue sauce
¼ cup honey
2 teaspoons yellow mustard
1½ teaspoons Worcestershire
    sauce
8 hamburger buns

Remove and discard the skin from the chicken; remove the meat from the bones and shred it. Add the chicken to a large nonstick saucepan or skillet along with the barbecue sauce, honey, mustard, and Worcestershire sauce. Cook and stir over medium heat until heated through. Divide between the buns.

Per Serving: Calories: 330 | Fat: 6 g | Saturated fat: 1.5 g | Cholesterol: 45 mg | Sodium: 760 mg | Total carbohydrates: 50 g | Dietary fiber: 1 g | Sugars: 28 g | Protein: 20 g

Pesto Chicken Pasta

Hands-On Time: 30 minutes
Total Time: 30 minutes
Yield: Serves 8

2 tablespoons olive oil

3 shallots, chopped

4 (5-ounce) boneless, skinless
   chicken breasts, cubed

¼ cup all-purpose flour

¼ teaspoon salt

¼ teaspoon ground black pepper

1½ cups chicken broth

½ cup light cream

1 (16-ounce) package linguine

¾ cup pesto

¼ cup grated Parmesan cheese

1. Bring a large pot of salted water to a boil. Meanwhile, heat olive oil in large saucepan over medium heat. Add shallots; cook and stir until tender, about 4 minutes.

2. Toss chicken with flour, salt, and pepper and add to saucepan. Cook and stir until chicken is almost cooked. Add broth and cream; bring to a simmer. Cook and stir until sauce begins to thicken.

3. Cook pasta until al dente according to package directions. Drain pasta and add to chicken mixture along with pesto and cheese. Cook and stir over medium heat until heated through, then serve immediately.

Per Serving: Calories: 503 | Fat: 20 g | Saturated fat: 5 g | Cholesterol: 63 mg | Sodium: 648 mg | Total carbohydrates: 50.2 g | Dietary fiber: 4 g | Sugars: 3 g | Protein: 29 g

Broiled Chicken Skewers

Hands-On Time: 10 minutes
Total Time: 20 minutes
Yield: Serves 4

1 pound chicken tenders

¼ cup olive oil

½ teaspoon salt

¼ teaspoon ground black pepper

8 skewers (if wooden, soak
   skewers)

2 cups cooked rice

1 cup tzatziki

1. Preheat broiler.

2. Rinse the chicken tenders and pat dry. Mix the olive oil, salt, and pepper in a shallow dish. Dip the chicken tenders in this mixture.

3. Skewer each piece of chicken tender and broil on a baking sheet for 3 minutes per side. Serve with rice and tzatziki.

Per Serving: Calories: 440 | Fat: 21 g | Saturated fat: 4.5 g | Cholesterol: 95 mg | Sodium: 340 mg | Total carbohydrates: 31 g | Dietary fiber: 0 g | Sugars: 2 g | Protein: 30 g

Chicken with Lime Sauce

Hands-On Time: 10 minutes
Total Time: 25 minutes
Yield: Serves 6

6 (6-ounce) boneless, skinless chicken breasts

½ tablespoon olive oil

1 clove fresh garlic, minced

½ teaspoon all-purpose seasoning

1 cup chicken broth

1½ tablespoons brown sugar

¼ cup lemon juice

2 teaspoons mustard

3 tablespoons water

1 teaspoon cornstarch

1½ tablespoons low-fat buttery spread

½ cup limes, sliced

Spray large skillet with nonstick spray. Add chicken to skillet. Sear one side, 5 minutes, then flip. In a small bowl, mix remaining ingredients except lime slices. Pour mixture over chicken and cook over medium heat for 10 minutes more. Serve with sliced limes.

Per Serving: Calories: 250 | Fat: 7 g | Saturated fat: 1.5 g | Cholesterol: 125 mg | Sodium: 260 mg | Total carbohydrates: 5 g | Dietary fiber: 0 g | Sugars: 4 g | Protein: 39 g

Balsamic Strawberry Chicken (pictured)

Hands-On Time: 15 minutes
Total Time: 25 minutes
Yield: Serves 2

2 (6-ounce) boneless, skinless chicken breasts

5 medium strawberries, trimmed and thinly sliced

2 tablespoons balsamic vinegar

1 tablespoon honey

¼ teaspoon kosher salt

2 tablespoons chopped fresh basil

1. Preheat grill to medium-high heat.

2. Grill chicken 5 minutes per side or until it registers 165°F internally with a meat thermometer.

3. Bring strawberries, vinegar, honey, salt, and basil to a simmer over medium heat in a small saucepan. Reduce heat to medium-low and simmer until the mixture is thickened and can coat the back of a spoon, about 10 minutes.

4. Pour strawberry balsamic sauce over chicken and serve.

Per Serving: Calories: 240 | Fat: 4.5 g | Saturated fat: 1 g | Cholesterol: 109 mg | Sodium: 387 mg | Total carbohydrates: 11 g | Dietary fiber: 1 g | Sugars: 10 g | Protein: 37 g

Easy Chicken Lo Mein

Hands-On Time: 10 minutes
Total Time: 25 minutes
Yield: Serves 12

⅛ teaspoon Minor's Low Sodium
   Chicken Base
2 (10-ounce) packages frozen
   stir-fry vegetables
1 tablespoon freeze-dried shallots
1 pound cooked dark and light
   meat chicken
⅛ cup ginger stir-fry sauce
1 pound spaghetti
1 teaspoon lemon juice
⅛ teaspoon mustard powder
1 teaspoon cornstarch
¼ teaspoon toasted sesame oil

1. Add the chicken base and ½ cup water to a large microwave-safe bowl; microwave on high for 30 seconds. Stir to dissolve the base into the water. Add the vegetables and freeze-dried shallots; microwave on high for 3–5 minutes. Drain some of the broth into a small nonstick sauté pan and set aside. Add the chicken and stir-fry sauce to the vegetables; stir well. Cover and set aside.

2. Consult the package for the spaghetti. In a large pot, bring the noted amount of water to a boil, but omit any salt, if required. Add the pasta, lemon juice, and mustard powder.

3. While the pasta cooks, in a small cup or bowl, add a tablespoon of water to the cornstarch and whisk to make a slurry. Bring the reserved broth in the sauté pan to a boil over medium-high heat. Whisk in the slurry; cook for at least 1 minute, stirring constantly.

4. Once the mixture thickens, remove from heat; add the toasted sesame oil to the broth mixture, then whisk again. Pour the thickened broth mixture over the vegetables and chicken; toss to mix. Cover and microwave the chicken mixture at 70 percent power for 2 minutes or until the chicken is heated through.

5. Drain the pasta; add it to the chicken mixture and stir to combine. Divide among 4 plates.

Per Serving: Calories: 226 | Fat: 3 g | Saturated fat: 1 g | Cholesterol: 28 mg | Sodium: 145 mg | Total carbohydrates: 33 g | Dietary fiber: 2 g | Sugars: 3 g | Protein: 16 g

Chicken and Chili Jam

Hands-On Time: 15 minutes
Total Time: 25 minutes
Yield: Serves 2

2 tablespoons whole milk

3 tablespoons jarred chili jam

8 ounces boneless, skinless chicken breasts, thinly sliced

½ cup sliced red bell pepper

1 teaspoon sugar

1 teaspoon fish sauce

1 tablespoon chopped cilantro

2 cups cooked white rice

Heat a large, deep sauté pan on high and, when hot, turn the heat down to medium-low. Add milk and chili jam and simmer. Add chicken and stir-fry about 1–2 minutes until it is no longer pink. Add bell pepper, sugar, and fish sauce. Garnish with cilantro and serve with rice.

Per Serving: Calories: 440 | Fat: 4 g | Saturated fat: 1 g | Cholesterol: 85 mg | Sodium: 320 mg | Total carbohydrates: 70 g | Dietary fiber: 1 g | Sugars: 25 g | Protein: 31 g

Simple Skillet Chicken Breasts

Hands-On Time: 20 minutes
Total Time: 20 minutes
Yield: Serves 6

6 (5-ounce) boneless, skinless chicken breasts

½ teaspoon all-purpose seasoning

1. Trim visible fat from chicken breasts. Sprinkle chicken with all-purpose seasoning.

2. Coat grill pan with nonstick spray. Place chicken in pan and cook over medium heat for 12–15 minutes or until internal temperature of chicken is 165°F or juices run clear when pricked.

Per Serving: Calories: 140 | Fat: 4 g | Saturated fat: 1 g | Cholesterol: 70 mg | Sodium: 320 mg | Total carbohydrates: 0 g | Dietary fiber: 0 g | Sugars: 0 g | Protein: 28 g

All-American Barbecued Chicken Breasts

Hands-On Time: 30 minutes
Total Time: 30 minutes
Yield: Serves 8

2 tablespoons vegetable oil

1 medium onion, peeled and sliced

2 (15-ounce) cans tomato sauce

1 cup red wine vinegar

1 teaspoon prepared mustard

½ cup dark molasses

¼ cup Worcestershire sauce

⅓ packed cup brown sugar

¾ teaspoon cayenne pepper

6 (6-ounce) boneless, skinless chicken breasts

1. Heat the oil in a large skillet over medium heat. Add the onion and sauté until tender, about 10 minutes.

2. Mix in the tomato sauce, vinegar, mustard, molasses, Worcestershire sauce, brown sugar, and cayenne. Heat to boiling over high heat, stirring frequently. Reduce heat and simmer, uncovered, for 30–45 minutes or until the sauce thickens slightly. Use a blender to purée sauce until smooth. Reserve 1½ cups of the mixture to serve as a sauce.

3. Preheat grill to medium temperature.

4. Place the chicken on the grill over medium heat. Cook for 8 minutes. Turn and baste generously with sauce. Cook for 8 minutes more, turning the pieces often and basting frequently. To test for doneness, pierce the chicken with a fork. The juices will run clear when the chicken is fully cooked.

Per Serving: Calories: 324 | Fat: 7 g | Saturated fat: 4 g | Cholesterol: 93 mg | Sodium: 175 mg | Total carbohydrates: 34 g | Dietary fiber: 2 g | Sugars: 30 g | Protein: 30 g

Pizza with Chicken and Onion

Hands-On Time: 10 minutes
Total Time: 25 minutes
Yield: Serves 8

¼ cup all-purpose flour

1 (16-ounce) package ready-made pizza dough, unbaked

¼ cup pizza sauce

1 small white onion, peeled and sliced

2 cups shredded Italian-mix cheese

1 cup chopped cooked chicken breast

1 teaspoon salt

⅛ teaspoon cayenne pepper

1 teaspoon chopped scallions, green parts only

1. Preheat oven to 425°F. Grease a large baking sheet with nonstick cooking spray.

2. Sprinkle flour lightly over work surface; roll pizza dough out into a circle. Transfer to the prepared baking sheet. Spread with pizza sauce and sprinkle all over with onion, cheese, and chicken.

3. Bake for 15 minutes or until crust is golden brown, sauce is bubbling, and cheese is melted and beginning to brown. Sprinkle with salt, cayenne pepper, and scallions and serve immediately.

Per Serving: Calories: 260 | Fat: 9 g | Saturated fat: 4.5 g | Cholesterol: 30 mg | Sodium: 860 mg | Total carbohydrates: 29 g | Dietary fiber: 0 g | Sugars: 4 g | Protein: 15 g

Chicken and Pepper Fajitas

Hands-On Time: 15 minutes
Total Time: 15 minutes
Yield: Serves 4

2 tablespoons canola oil

1 pound skinless, boneless chicken breasts

1 medium red bell pepper, seeded and sliced

1 medium green bell pepper, seeded and sliced

1 medium scallion, thinly sliced

4 (6") flour tortillas

¼ teaspoon salt

⅛ teaspoon ground black pepper

1. Heat canola oil in large frying pan on medium-high heat and fry chicken breasts on both sides. Remove chicken to work surface and allow to cool slightly. Cut fried chicken into long 1" strips and place on large plate.

2. In the same pan, stir-fry pepper slices and scallions in canola oil until tender. Pour over chicken strips.

3. Place tortillas flat on a plate and spoon chicken mixture into center of tortillas. Season each fajita with equal amounts salt and pepper and roll up burrito-style.

Per Serving: Calories: 250 | Fat: 10 g | Saturated fat: 1.5 g | Cholesterol: 65 mg | Sodium: 210 mg | Total carbohydrates: 14 g | Dietary fiber: 1 g | Sugars: 2 g | Protein: 25 g

Healthy Mexican Casserole (pictured)

Hands-On Time: 10 minutes
Total Time: 30 minutes
Yield: Serves 8

1 tablespoon extra-virgin olive oil

1 pound lean ground turkey

½ teaspoon cumin

¼ teaspoon chili powder

¼ teaspoon red pepper flakes

⅛ teaspoon coriander

2 tablespoons water

1 (15-ounce) can black beans, rinsed and drained

1 (15-ounce) can pinto beans, rinsed and drained

4–5 medium plum tomatoes, chopped and seeds removed

1 teaspoon chopped chili peppers

½ cup frozen corn

¼ cup Mexican-blend shredded cheese

1. Preheat the oven to 350°F.

2. Heat the oil in a large skillet over medium-high heat. Cook turkey in hot oil for 5–8 minutes, until the meat is browned. Stir in cumin, chili powder, red pepper flakes, coriander, and water. Add black and pinto beans, tomatoes, chili peppers, and corn. Stir well.

3. Place the meat mixture in a 9" x 13" casserole dish and add cheese on top. Bake for 20 minutes until cheese is melted.

Per Serving: Calories: 240 | Fat: 8 g | Saturated fat: 2 g | Cholesterol: 45 mg | Sodium: 230 mg | Total carbohydrates: 22 g | Dietary fiber: 4 g | Sugars: 3 g | Protein: 19 g

Grilled Turkey Tenderloin

Hands-On Time: 10 minutes
Total Time: 30 minutes
Yield: Serves 4

1 pound turkey tenderloin
½ cup orange juice
2 tablespoons Dijon mustard
¼ cup honey
2 garlic cloves, minced
½ teaspoon salt
⅛ teaspoon ground black pepper

1. Prepare and preheat grill. Butterfly the tenderloin by cutting it in half lengthwise, being careful not to cut all the way through. Stop about 1" from the other side. Spread the tenderloin open, cover it with plastic wrap, and pound gently with a meat mallet or rolling pin to flatten.

2. For marinade, combine remaining ingredients in a large resealable plastic bag. Add the turkey, close the bag, and knead the bag, pressing the marinade into the turkey. Let stand at room temperature for 10 minutes.

3. Cook turkey about 6" above medium-hot coals for 5 minutes; brush with any leftover marinade. Turn turkey and cook for 4–6 minutes on second side, until thoroughly cooked. Discard any remaining marinade. Serve immediately.

Per Serving: Calories: 320 | Fat: 4 g | Saturated fat: 1 g | Cholesterol: 100 mg | Sodium: 1,010 mg | Total carbohydrates: 39 g | Dietary fiber: 0 g | Sugars: 38 g | Protein: 35 g

Too-Good Turkey Burgers

Hands-On Time: 25 minutes
Total Time: 25 minutes
Yield: Serves 4

½ cup chopped onions
1 pound ground turkey breast
1 teaspoon minced garlic
1 teaspoon sea salt
1 teaspoon ground black pepper
4 whole-wheat hamburger buns
4 slices medium beefsteak
    tomato
1 cup shredded romaine hearts

1. Prepare a grill with olive oil spray and heat to medium heat. Prepare a small sauté pan with olive oil spray over medium heat and add onions. Sauté until soft and translucent.

2. In a large mixing bowl, add the ground turkey breast, minced garlic, sautéed onions, salt, and pepper, and combine thoroughly. Form into 4 patties of the same size. Place patties on the grill and cook for 5 minutes undisturbed.

3. Flip the patties and continue cooking for 5 more minutes or until juices run clear. Open the buns and move each patty to the bottom half of each bun. Top burgers with the sliced tomato, shredded lettuce, and bun top, and enjoy!

Per Serving: Calories: 300 | Fat: 11 g | Saturated fat: 3 g | Cholesterol: 85 mg | Sodium: 750 mg | Total carbohydrates: 23 g | Dietary fiber: 3 g | Sugars: 4 g | Protein: 26 g

Turkey Meatloaf

Hands-On Time: 10 minutes
Total Time: 30 minutes
Yield: Serves 4

1 pound lean ground turkey

1 small onion, peeled and chopped

2 medium stalks celery, minced

1 large egg

¼ cup water

¼ teaspoon hot sauce

¼ teaspoon salt

½ teaspoon ground black pepper

¾ cup bread crumbs

1. Combine ground turkey, onion, celery, egg, and water in a large bowl. Using your hands or a wooden spoon, mix together. Fold in hot sauce, salt, pepper, and bread crumbs.

2. Transfer mixture to a glass loaf pan. Microwave on high heat for 10 minutes, and then for 5 minutes, or as needed until the turkey is cooked and the juices run clear (total cooking time should be about 15 minutes).

3. Let stand for 5 minutes. Pour any fat off the dish and serve.

Per Serving: Calories: 193 | Fat: 9 g | Saturated fat: 2 g | Cholesterol: 92 mg | Sodium: 294 mg | Total carbohydrates: 9 g | Dietary fiber: 1 g | Sugars: 2 g | Protein: 25 g

Microwave Turkey Pasta Casserole

Hands-On Time: 20 minutes
Total Time: 20 minutes
Yield: Serves 4

1 pound ground turkey

½ teaspoon salt

¼ teaspoon ground black pepper

1 tablespoon light brown sugar

1 small yellow onion, peeled and chopped

1 clove garlic, peeled and minced

1 (8-ounce) can tomato sauce

1 medium green bell pepper, seeded and chopped

4 cups cooked ziti

1. Place turkey in a large microwave-safe bowl and season with salt and black pepper. Cover and microwave on high for 8 minutes, stirring and breaking up meat occasionally. Uncover and stir in the brown sugar, onion, garlic, tomato sauce, and bell pepper. Cover and microwave on high for an additional 3 minutes, stirring occasionally.

2. In another large microwave-safe bowl, heat the cooked pasta in the microwave on high for 1 minute. Toss the pasta with the sauce and serve immediately.

Per Serving: Calories: 410 | Fat: 11 g | Saturated fat: 2.5 g | Cholesterol: 90 mg | Sodium: 640 mg | Total carbohydrates: 48 g | Dietary fiber: 4 g | Sugars: 9 g | Protein: 31 g

Turkey Sloppy Joes

Hands-On Time: 15 minutes
Total Time: 30 minutes
Yield: Serves 4

1½ pounds ground turkey
1 medium onion, chopped
1 medium green bell pepper, seeded
    and chopped into chunks
½ cup water
1 cup ketchup
3 tablespoons brown sugar
3 tablespoons red wine vinegar
¾ teaspoon ground cumin
¼ teaspoon ground black pepper
4 hamburger buns
⅓ cup crumbled Havarti cheese

1. Brown the ground turkey in a large skillet over medium-high heat. Add the onion and bell peppers. Cook for 4–5 more minutes until the onion is softened. Drain the fat out of the pan.

2. Add the water, ketchup, brown sugar, and red wine vinegar to the pan. Stir in the cumin and pepper. Turn the heat down to low and simmer uncovered for 15 minutes.

3. Spoon the turkey mixture over the hamburger buns. Sprinkle the crumbled cheese on top.

Per Serving: Calories: 459 | Fat: 15 g | Saturated fat: 4 g | Cholesterol: 60 mg | Sodium: 1,135 mg | Total carbohydrates: 55 g | Dietary fiber: 2 g | Sugars: 32 g | Protein: 34 g

Turkey Stroganoff (pictured)

Hands-On Time: 15 minutes
Total Time: 25 minutes
Yield: Serves 4

1 tablespoon olive oil
1 pound ground turkey
½ teaspoon kosher salt
½ teaspoon ground black pepper
1 large yellow onion, peeled and
    diced
8 ounces sliced cremini
    mushrooms
2 teaspoons dried dill weed
1 teaspoon hot smoked paprika
1 teaspoon sweet paprika
4 cups chicken broth
8 ounces dried medium egg
    noodles
½ cup full-fat Greek yogurt
1 tablespoon chopped parsley

1. In a large skillet, heat olive oil over medium heat until it shimmers, about 1 minute. Add turkey to the pan and break up with a spatula. Season with salt and pepper. Sauté until turkey is cooked through, about 8 minutes. Stir in onion and mushrooms. Sauté until softened, about 5 minutes.

2. Add dill and both types of paprika. Stir for 1 minute. Pour in the broth and add the noodles. Bring to a light boil, and then reduce heat to medium-low and simmer until noodles are cooked through, about 10 minutes.

3. Stir in yogurt and garnish with parsley.

Per Serving: Calories: 491 | Fat: 16 g | Saturated fat: 5 g | Cholesterol: 139 mg | Sodium: 1,270 mg | Total carbohydrates: 50 g | Dietary fiber: 3 g | Sugars: 6 g | Protein: 36 g

Chicken Cauliflower Fried Rice

Hands-On Time: 20 minutes
Total Time: 20 minutes
Yield: Serves 2

1 tablespoon coconut oil
1 (4-ounce) boneless, skinless chicken breast, cut into small cubes
2 cloves garlic, finely chopped
1" piece fresh ginger, grated
2 cups frozen cauliflower rice
1 cup frozen peas and carrots
3 medium scallions, diced
2 tablespoons Bragg Liquid Aminos

1. In a large wok or skillet, heat coconut oil over medium-high heat. Toss in chicken, garlic, and ginger. Stir-fry 8 minutes until chicken is cooked through.

2. Add cauliflower rice and frozen vegetables. Stir-fry 10 minutes more. Remove from heat, stir in scallions and aminos, and serve.

Per Serving: Calories: 220 | Fat: 10 g | Saturated fat: 6 g | Cholesterol: 40 mg | Sodium: 1110 mg | Total carbohydrates: 16 g | Dietary fiber: 4 g | Sugars: 5 g | Protein: 18 g

Chicken à la King on Toast

Hands-On Time: 20 minutes
Total Time: 20 minutes
Yield: Serves 4

1 (10.5-ounce) can condensed cream of chicken soup
¼ cup skim milk
½ teaspoon Worcestershire sauce
1 tablespoon mayonnaise
¼ teaspoon ground black pepper
1 cup sliced and stemmed mushrooms
½ pound cooked, chopped chicken breast
2 tablespoons chopped red bell pepper
4 slices whole-wheat bread, toasted

1. Combine the soup, milk, Worcestershire, mayonnaise, and pepper in a large saucepan and bring to a boil.

2. Reduce heat and add mushrooms and chicken. Simmer until the vegetables and chicken are heated through. Add the chopped red pepper and serve over toast.

Per Serving: Calories: 300 | Fat: 14 g | Saturated fat: 3 g | Cholesterol: 65 mg | Sodium: 790 mg | Total carbohydrates: 21 g | Dietary fiber: 2 g | Sugars: 7 g | Protein: 21 g

Stir-Fried Chicken Cacciatore

Hands-On Time: 25 minutes
Total Time: 25 minutes
Yield: Serves 4

1 pound boneless, skinless
    chicken thighs

3½ tablespoons dry white wine,
    divided

1 teaspoon dried oregano

⅛ teaspoon ground black pepper

2 teaspoons cornstarch

3 tablespoons low-sodium
    chicken broth

3 tablespoons diced tomatoes
    with juice

½ teaspoon granulated sugar

1 shallot, peeled and chopped

¼ pound sliced fresh mushrooms

1 medium red bell pepper, seeded
    and cut into thin strips

3 tablespoons olive oil, divided

1 tablespoon chopped fresh
    oregano

1. Cut the chicken into thin strips about 2"–3" long. Place the chicken strips in a medium bowl and add 2½ tablespoons white wine, oregano, pepper, and cornstarch, adding the cornstarch last. Let the chicken stand while preparing the other ingredients.

2. In a small bowl, combine the chicken broth, diced tomatoes, and sugar. Set aside.

3. Heat 1 tablespoon oil in a large preheated wok or heavy skillet. When the oil is hot, add the chopped shallot. Stir-fry for a minute until it begins to soften, then add the sliced mushrooms. Stir-fry for a minute, then add the red bell pepper. Stir-fry for another minute, adding a bit of water if the vegetables begin to dry out. Remove the vegetables from the pan.

4. Heat the remaining 2 tablespoons oil in the hot pan. When the oil is hot, add the chicken. Let the chicken brown for a minute, then stir-fry for about 5 minutes until it turns white and is nearly cooked through. Splash 1 tablespoon of the white wine on the chicken while stir-frying. Add the chicken broth and tomato mixture to the middle of the pan. Bring to a boil. Return the vegetables to the pan. Stir in the fresh oregano. Cook, stirring, for another couple of minutes to mix everything together. Serve immediately.

Per Serving: Calories: 277 | Fat: 17 g | Saturated fat: 3.5 g | Cholesterol: 104 mg | Sodium: 196 mg | Total carbohydrates: 8 g | Dietary fiber: 2 g | Sugars: 371 g | Protein: 22 g

Chapter 8

Beef Main Dishes

Ground Beef Tacos

Hands-On Time: 20 minutes
Total Time: 20 minutes
Yield: Serves 6

1 pound extra-lean ground beef

1 large onion, peeled and chopped

2 cloves garlic, minced

1 (8-ounce) can no-salt-added tomato sauce

2 teaspoons low-sodium Worcestershire sauce

1 tablespoon molasses

1 tablespoon apple cider vinegar

1 tablespoon ground cumin

1 tablespoon ground sweet paprika

½ teaspoon dried red pepper flakes

½ teaspoon ground black pepper

¼ cup chopped fresh cilantro

6 (6") low-sodium flour tortillas, warmed

1 medium tomato, diced

1 medium jalapeño pepper, seeded and chopped

2 medium limes, cut into wedges

1. Place the ground beef, onion, and garlic into a large sauté pan over medium heat and cook, stirring, until the beef is browned, roughly 3–5 minutes.

2. Once beef is cooked, lower heat to medium-low and add the tomato sauce, Worcestershire sauce, molasses, vinegar, cumin, paprika, red pepper flakes, and black pepper. Simmer, stirring frequently, about 10 minutes.

3. Remove sauté pan from heat. Stir in cilantro, then divide beef mixture evenly between the tortillas.

4. Garnish with tomato and jalapeño. Serve with lime wedges.

Per Serving: Calories: 220 | Fat: 5 g | Saturated fat: 2 g | Cholesterol: 40 mg | Sodium: 250 mg | Total carbohydrates: 27 g | Dietary fiber: 5 g | Sugars: 7 g | Protein: 17 g

Orange Beef and Broccoli Stir-Fry

Hands-On Time: 25 minutes
Total Time: 25 minutes
Yield: Serves 6

2 oranges
3 tablespoons soy sauce
1 tablespoon rice wine vinegar
1 tablespoon arrowroot
1 teaspoon agave syrup
1 pound beef sirloin
1 tablespoon sesame oil, divided
6 cloves garlic, minced
2 tablespoons minced gingerroot
2 pounds broccoli, broken into
    small florets
⅓ cup water
½ cup chopped green onion

1. Thinly peel skin from oranges in wide strips, taking care not to include white pith. Julienne zest into thin strips. Squeeze orange juice and combine with soy sauce, vinegar, arrowroot, and agave syrup in small bowl. Trim excess fat from beef and cut across the grain into ⅛" x 3" slices.

2. Heat half of the sesame oil in large wok or skillet over medium-high heat. Add garlic and gingerroot; stir-fry for 2 minutes. Add beef; stir-fry for 3–4 minutes until browned. Remove beef from wok with slotted spoon and set aside.

3. Add remaining oil to wok and add broccoli. Stir-fry for 1 minute, then add water. Cover and simmer, stirring occasionally, until water evaporates and broccoli is tender.

4. Return beef to skillet along with orange juice mixture. Stir-fry until sauce has thickened, about 2–3 minutes. Top with green onion and serve immediately.

Per Serving: Calories: 213 | Fat: 6 g | Saturated fat: 1 g | Cholesterol: 48 mg | Sodium: 596 mg | Total carbohydrates: 21 g | Dietary fiber: 7 g | Sugars: 8 g | Protein: 22 g

Sloppy Joe Sandwiches

Hands-On Time: 15 minutes
Total Time: 25 minutes
Yield: Serves 6

1 pound lean ground beef
1 medium onion, peeled and
    chopped
½ cup chopped celery
1 (14.5-ounce) can chili-style
    diced tomatoes
2 teaspoons Worcestershire sauce
⅛ teaspoon hot pepper sauce
¼ teaspoon salt
¼ teaspoon ground black pepper
6 hamburger buns

1. In a large skillet over medium heat brown the ground beef together with the onion and celery, breaking up the beef until it is browned.

2. Stir in the tomatoes, Worcestershire sauce, hot pepper sauce, salt, and pepper, and simmer at least 15 minutes, stirring occasionally. Skillet can be partially, but not tightly, covered to prevent splattering. Serve on buns.

Per Serving: Calories: 250 | Fat: 7 g | Saturated fat: 3 g | Cholesterol: 40 mg | Sodium: 620 mg | Total carbohydrates: 26 g | Dietary fiber: 3 g | Sugars: 6 g | Protein: 18 g

Diner-Style Country Fried Steak (pictured)

Hands-On Time: 30 minutes
Total Time: 30 minutes
Yield: Serves 4

1 pound beef cube steak, cut into 4 pieces
1 cup all-purpose flour
1 teaspoon salt
½ teaspoon paprika
½ teaspoon ground black pepper
½ cup buttermilk
¼ cup vegetable oil

1. Tenderize the meat by pounding it with a mallet or the bottom of a heavy skillet.
2. Stir together the flour, salt, paprika, and pepper in a shallow dish. Put the buttermilk in a separate, small dish.
3. Dredge steaks in the flour mixture, dip into the buttermilk, and dip again into the flour mixture.
4. Heat the oil in a large skillet over medium-high heat. Cook the steaks 5 minutes on each side.

Per Serving: Calories: 450 | Fat: 28 g | Saturated fat: 7 g | Cholesterol: 85 mg | Sodium: 680 mg | Total carbohydrates: 20 g | Dietary fiber: 1 g | Sugars: 2 g | Protein: 27 g

Beef with Peppers

Hands-On Time: 20 minutes
Total Time: 20 minutes
Yield: Serves 8

1½ pounds flank steak
2 tablespoons olive oil
1 medium onion, peeled and chopped
1 medium red bell pepper, seeded and sliced
1 medium green bell pepper, seeded and sliced
1 medium yellow bell pepper, seeded and sliced
1 medium orange bell pepper, seeded and sliced
½ teaspoon salt
⅛ teaspoon ground black pepper
½ cup beef broth

1. Trim flank steak and cut across the grain into ½" slices. In large skillet, heat olive oil over medium heat. Add steak strips; brown on all sides, about 5 minutes, then remove with slotted spoon and set aside.
2. Add onion to skillet; cook and stir for 2 minutes. Then add all the bell peppers. Sprinkle with salt and black pepper; cook and stir for 4–5 minutes or until crisp-tender.
3. Return beef to skillet and add broth. Bring to a simmer, then cover and cook for 4–5 minutes. Serve immediately.

Per Serving: Calories: 170 | Fat: 8 g | Saturated fat: 2.5 g | Cholesterol: 50 mg | Sodium: 250 mg | Total carbohydrates: 5 g | Dietary fiber: 2 g | Sugars: 3 g | Protein: 19 g

Steak Stir-Fry

Hands-On Time: 15 minutes
Total Time: 25 minutes
Yield: Serves 4

¾ pound round steak, trimmed
    and cut in thin strips
2 tablespoons red wine vinegar
2 tablespoons olive oil, divided
1 tablespoon minced fresh ginger
2 cups broccoli florets
8 ounces fresh mushrooms, sliced
1 large carrot, peeled and sliced
1 cup beef broth
2 tablespoons cornstarch
1 tablespoon soy sauce
⅛ teaspoon ground black pepper

1. Sprinkle steak with vinegar and 1 tablespoon olive oil. Marinate for 10 minutes.

2. In a large skillet or wok, heat 1 tablespoon olive oil over medium-high heat. Drain meat, reserving marinade. Add meat to skillet; stir-fry for 4 minutes until browned. Remove steak from saucepan.

3. Add ginger to skillet; stir-fry 1 minute. Add broccoli, mushrooms, and carrots. Stir-fry for 5 minutes. Return beef to pan.

4. Add broth, cornstarch, soy sauce, and pepper to reserved marinade and stir well. Add to skillet and bring to a boil. Cook for 1–2 minutes until sauce is thickened and beef and vegetables are tender. Serve immediately.

Per Serving: Calories: 249 | Fat: 11 g | Saturated fat: 2.1 g | Cholesterol: 53 mg | Sodium: 347 mg | Total carbohydrates: 15 g | Dietary fiber: 3 g | Sugars: 3.5 g | Protein: 24 g

Beef with Pea Pods

Hands-On Time: 20 minutes
Total Time: 20 minutes
Yield: Serves 4

¾ pound flank steak
1 tablespoon peanut oil
1 small red bell pepper, seeded
    and sliced
8 ounces sliced button
    mushrooms
3 medium scallions, sliced
2 cloves garlic, peeled and
    minced
2 teaspoons minced fresh ginger
4 cups fresh trimmed peapods
3 tablespoons low-sodium soy
    sauce
4 cups cooked rice

1. Slice the steak into thin ½" x 3" strips and set aside.

2. Heat the oil in a large wok over medium heat. Stir-fry bell pepper and mushrooms 3 minutes. Add the scallions, garlic, and ginger and stir-fry for 30 seconds. Add the sliced steak and stir-fry for 5 minutes, until beef has browned.

3. Add the peapods and soy sauce and stir-fry for 3 minutes.

4. Remove from heat. Spoon over cooked rice and serve immediately.

Per Serving: Calories: 460 | Fat: 11 g | Saturated fat: 3.5 g | Cholesterol: 65 mg | Sodium: 490 mg | Total carbohydrates: 55 g | Dietary fiber: 3 g | Sugars: 4 g | Protein: 33 g

Skillet Ziti with Ground Beef and Spinach

Hands-On Time: 25 minutes
Total Time: 25 minutes
Yield: Serves 6

1 tablespoon olive oil
½ cup diced onion
¼ cup diced celery
¼ cup diced carrots
1 teaspoon minced garlic
1 pound ground beef
1 (5-ounce) bag baby spinach
1 teaspoon salt
½ teaspoon ground black pepper
16 ounces ziti, cooked and
  drained

In a large skillet over medium-high heat, heat oil. Add onion, celery, and carrots; cook, stirring often, until translucent, about 5 minutes. Add garlic; sauté for 30 seconds. Add the ground beef; cook, breaking up clumps with a wooden spoon, until no longer pink, about 5 minutes. Stir in the spinach, salt, and pepper; cook until wilted, about 2 minutes. Stir in the cooked ziti; stir over low heat to evenly heat the mixture.

Per Serving: Calories: 452 | Fat: 13 g | Saturated fat: 4 g | Cholesterol: 55 mg | Sodium: 460 mg | Total carbohydrates: 54 g | Dietary fiber: 4 g | Sugars: 2 g | Protein: 27 g

All-American Fajitas

Hands-On Time: 30 minutes
Total Time: 30 minutes
Yield: Serves 4

2 tablespoons vegetable oil,
  divided
1 (24-ounce) package ready-to-
  cook beef for fajitas, thawed
1 large red onion, peeled and
  sliced
1 medium red bell pepper, seeded
  and sliced
1 medium green bell pepper,
  seeded and sliced
1 medium yellow bell pepper,
  seeded and sliced
4 (10″) flour tortillas, warmed

1. In a cast-iron skillet over medium-high heat, heat 1 tablespoon oil until shimmering. Add beef strips and cook for 2–3 minutes per side or until browned and cooked through. Remove from skillet and keep warm.

2. Add remaining oil to skillet and sauté onion and peppers for 8 minutes until crisp-tender. Return beef to skillet and heat, stirring constantly, for 1 minute.

3. Serve immediately with tortillas.

Per Serving: Calories: 470 | Fat: 13 g | Saturated fat: 4 g | Cholesterol: 90 mg | Sodium: 560 mg | Total carbohydrates: 44 g | Dietary fiber: 4 g | Sugars: 7 g | Protein: 41 g

Shredded Beef and Slaw Sandwiches

Hands-On Time: 15 minutes
Total Time: 15 minutes
Yield: Serves 6

3 cups chopped red cabbage
1 cup shredded carrot
⅔ cup mayonnaise
1 teaspoon dried dill weed
1 (17-ounce) package prepared roast beef au jus, cooked according to package directions
¼ cup mustard-mayonnaise blend
6 hoagie buns, split and toasted

1. In large bowl, combine cabbage, carrots, mayonnaise, and dill weed; mix well.
2. Shred beef and stir to mix with gravy.
3. Spread mustard blend on hoagie buns. Top with beef mixture and then coleslaw mixture; top with top half of buns and press down. Serve immediately.

Per Serving: Calories: 565 | Fat: 34 g | Saturated fat: 8 g | Cholesterol: 65 mg | Sodium: 580 mg | Total carbohydrates: 40 g | Dietary fiber: 3 g | Sugars: 6 g | Protein: 24 g

Sweet and Sour Meatloaf (pictured)

Hands-On Time: 10 minutes
Total Time: 25 minutes
Yield: Serves 4

1½ pounds ground beef
1 (5.5-ounce) can tomato paste
¼ cup whole milk
3 tablespoons brown sugar
3 tablespoons vinegar
2 teaspoons soy sauce
1 large egg, beaten
½ cup bread crumbs
2 tablespoons minced onion
¼ teaspoon salt
¼ teaspoon ground black pepper

1. In a large bowl, combine all the ingredients.
2. Shape into a loaf and place in a microwave-safe casserole dish. Cover with microwave-safe wax paper.
3. Microwave on high heat for 15 minutes, 5 minutes at a time, rotating the dish a quarter turn between each period. If the meatloaf is not cooked after 15 minutes, continue to cook for 1 minute at a time until done (total cooking should be about 15 minutes). The meatloaf is cooked when the internal temperature reaches 160°F.
4. Let stand for 5 minutes.
5. Pour any fat off the dish and serve.

Per Serving: Calories: 517 | Fat: 23 g | Saturated fat: 9 g | Cholesterol: 176 mg | Sodium: 683 mg | Total carbohydrates: 31 g | Dietary fiber: 3 g | Sugars: 18 g | Protein: 43 g

Pan-Fried Flank Steak with Swiss Chard

Hands-On Time: 15 minutes
Total Time: 30 minutes
Yield: Serves 8

2 pounds flank steak
1½ teaspoons salt, divided
1½ teaspoons ground black
    pepper, divided
1 tablespoon olive oil
2 cloves garlic, crushed
½ teaspoon crushed red pepper
2 pounds Swiss chard, stems
    trimmed
1 tablespoon butter
1 tablespoon vegetable oil

1. Pat steak dry with paper towels. Rub all sides with 1 teaspoon salt and 1 teaspoon black pepper. Set aside.

2. In a large nonstick skillet over medium heat, heat olive oil until shimmering. Add garlic and crushed red pepper and cook, stirring constantly, for 30 seconds, being careful not to burn garlic. Using tongs, add Swiss chard and stir into oil and garlic. Cover and cook for 5 minutes. Stir in butter, the remaining ½ teaspoon salt and the remaining ½ teaspoon black pepper. Remove to a medium bowl and keep warm.

3. Wipe out skillet and place over medium-high heat until very hot, about 5 minutes. Add vegetable oil and heat until shimmering. Carefully add steak and sear for 3–5 minutes on each side.

4. Remove to a platter. Tent with foil and let it rest for 10 minutes before slicing.

5. Serve sliced beef with pan juices and Swiss chard.

Per Serving: Calories: 245 | Fat: 14 g | Saturated fat: 5 g | Cholesterol: 79 mg | Sodium: 748 mg | Total carbohydrates: 5 g | Dietary fiber: 2 g | Sugars: 1 g | Protein: 26 g

Beefy Fried Rice

Hands-On Time: 15 minutes
Total Time: 15 minutes
Yield: Serves 4

½ cup 80 percent lean ground beef

1 medium onion, peeled and chopped

4 cloves garlic, peeled and minced

2 tablespoons olive oil

1 (8.5-ounce) package ready rice

2 tablespoons soy sauce

2 medium scallions, sliced

1. In large saucepan or wok, combine ground beef with onion and garlic. Cook and stir over medium heat, stirring frequently, until beef is almost cooked. Remove from heat and drain thoroughly; wipe out saucepan or wok.

2. Return wok to heat and add olive oil. Heat over medium-high heat. Then add rice; stir-fry for 1 minute. Sprinkle with soy sauce; stir-fry for 2–3 minutes longer.

3. Return ground beef mixture to saucepan; stir-fry for 1–3 minutes until hot. Top with scallions and serve immediately.

Per Serving: Calories: 153 | Fat: 8 g | Saturated fat: 1 g | Cholesterol: 3 mg | Sodium: 222 mg | Total carbohydrates: 18 g | Dietary fiber: 1 g | Sugars: 2 g | Protein: 3 g

Thai Beef with Rice Noodles

Hands-On Time: 20 minutes
Total Time: 20 minutes
Yield: Serves 4

¾ **pound sirloin, trimmed of all fat, rinsed, and patted dry**
½ **pound dried rice noodles**
¼ **cup soy sauce**
2 **tablespoons fish sauce**
2 **tablespoons dark brown sugar**
¼ **teaspoon ground black pepper**
5 **tablespoons vegetable oil, divided**
2 **tablespoons minced garlic**
1 **pound greens (such as spinach or bok choy), cut into ½" strips**
2 **large eggs, beaten**
⅛ **teaspoon crushed dried red pepper flakes**

1. Slice the meat into 2"-long, ½"-wide strips. Place the noodles in a medium bowl and cover with warm water for 5 minutes, then drain. In a small bowl, combine the soy sauce, fish sauce, brown sugar, and black pepper; set aside.

2. Heat a large wok or heavy skillet over high heat. Add approximately 2 tablespoons of the vegetable oil. When the oil is hot but not smoking add the garlic. After stirring for 5 seconds, add the greens and stir-fry for approximately 2 minutes; set aside.

3. Add 2 more tablespoons of oil to the wok. Add the beef and stir-fry until browned on all sides, about 2 minutes; set aside.

4. Heat 1 tablespoon of oil in the wok and add the noodles. Toss until warmed through, approximately 2 minutes; set aside.

5. Add the eggs and cook without stirring until they are set, about 30 seconds. Break up the eggs slightly and stir in the noodles, beef, greens, and the red pepper flakes. Stir the soy mixture and then add it to the wok. Toss to coat and heat through.

Per Serving: Calories: 450 | Fat: 28 g | Saturated fat: 8 g | Cholesterol: 155 mg | Sodium: 300 mg | Total carbohydrates: 20 g | Dietary fiber: 3 g | Sugars: 1 g | Protein: 25 g

Yummy Meatballs

Hands-On Time: 15 minutes
Total Time: 30 minutes
Yield: Serves 6

2 tablespoons olive oil, divided
1 medium yellow onion, minced
1 medium green bell pepper,
    seeded and minced
2 teaspoons minced garlic
1 pound lean ground beef
1 teaspoon all-natural sea salt
1 teaspoon ground black pepper
1 large egg

1. Preheat oven to 350°F. Add 1 teaspoon olive oil to a large skillet over medium heat.

2. Add onion, pepper, and garlic to skillet; sauté until soft. Remove from heat and let cool.

3. In a large mixing bowl, combine ground beef, sautéed onion and peppers, salt, pepper, and egg; use your hands to mix well. Form mixture into 24 (1½") balls.

4. Brush the rack of a roasting pan with remaining olive oil to coat lightly and place over the roasting pan. Place meatballs 1" apart on rack.

5. Bake for 10 minutes. Turn and bake for another 10 minutes or until completely cooked through.

Per Serving: Calories: 230 | Fat: 17 g | Saturated fat: 5 g | Cholesterol: 80 mg | Sodium: 450 mg | Total carbohydrates: 3 g | Dietary fiber: 1 g | Sugars: 1 g | Protein: 16 g

Kung Pao Chili con Carne

Hands-On Time: 20 minutes
Total Time: 20 minutes
Yield: Serves 3

¾ pound ground beef
½ teaspoon salt
½ teaspoon black pepper
5 teaspoons vegetable oil,
    divided
2 cloves garlic, chopped
1 medium onion, chopped
2 teaspoons Sichuan peppercorns
1 tablespoon chopped jalapeño
    peppers
1 medium tomato, diced
1 cup drained canned kidney
    beans
¾ cup tomato sauce
¼ cup roasted cashews

1. In a medium bowl, combine the ground beef with the salt and pepper.

2. Heat 3 teaspoons oil in a large, heavy saucepan over medium-high heat. Add ground beef and stir-fry until the pinkness is gone. Remove ground beef from the pan. Drain the fat and wipe pan clean with paper towels.

3. Heat 2 tablespoons oil in the pan. Add the garlic and onion. Stir in the Sichuan peppercorns and chopped peppers. Cook, stirring, until the onion begins to soften. Stir in the diced tomato. Stir in the kidney beans and tomato sauce. Bring to a boil.

4. Return the ground beef to the pan. Stir-fry for 1–2 more minutes to mix the flavors together. Stir in the cashews. Serve hot.

Per Serving: Calories: 496 | Fat: 28 g | Saturated fat: 7 g | Cholesterol: 87 mg | Sodium: 901 mg | Total carbohydrates: 27 g | Dietary fiber: 6 g | Sugars: 8 g | Protein: 34 g

Thai-Inspired Spicy Beef Lettuce Wraps

Hands-On Time: 20 minutes
Total Time: 20 minutes
Yield: Serves 4

2 tablespoons vegetable oil
1½ pounds lean ground sirloin
¼ cup diced red pepper
¼ cup sliced scallions
¼ cup chopped cilantro
½ cup peanut sauce
1 tablespoon Asian chili sauce
½ teaspoon salt
12 Boston lettuce leaves

1. Heat the oil in a large nonstick skillet over medium-high heat. Add the sirloin, stirring to break up the meat into small pieces. Cook, stirring frequently, until the meat starts to brown, about 5 minutes. Use a small ladle to remove and discard excess fat.

2. Add the red pepper and stir to incorporate; cook for about 3 minutes. Add the scallions, cilantro, peanut sauce, chili sauce, and salt; stir to blend. Cook until heated through, about 3–4 minutes.

3. To serve, arrange the lettuce leaves on a serving platter. Spoon the beef mixture into the center of each leaf.

Per Serving: Calories: 180 | Fat: 11 g | Saturated fat: 2 g | Cholesterol: 5 mg | Sodium: 890 mg | Total carbohydrates: 13 g | Dietary fiber: 1 g | Sugars: 10 g | Protein: 7 g

Beef and Noodles in Mushroom Sauce (pictured)

Hands-On Time: 20 minutes
Total Time: 20 minutes
Yield: Serves 6

1 pound boneless round steak
2 tablespoons olive oil
1 medium onion, chopped
1 (8-ounce) package sliced mushrooms
3 tablespoons tomato paste
3 tablespoons water
½ teaspoon basil leaves
1 tablespoon arrowroot
1 cup plain low-fat yogurt
¼ cup beef stock
3 cups hot cooked noodles

1. Trim excess fat from the steak and slice against the grain into ¼″ strips.

2. In a large skillet, heat olive oil over medium heat. Add onion and mushrooms; cook and stir until tender, about 5 minutes. Add beef and cook, stirring frequently, until browned, about 4 minutes longer.

3. Meanwhile, in small bowl combine tomato paste, water, basil, arrowroot, yogurt, and stock and mix with wire whisk until blended. Add to skillet and bring to a simmer. Simmer for 3–4 minutes or until sauce thickens. Serve immediately over hot cooked noodles.

Per Serving: Calories: 312 | Fat: 11 g | Saturated fat: 3 g | Cholesterol: 51 mg | Sodium: 109 mg | Total carbohydrates: 28 g | Dietary fiber: 3 g | Sugars: 6 g | Protein: 23 g

Barbecue Onion Burgers

Hands-On Time: 25 minutes
Total Time: 25 minutes
Yield: Serves 6

2 pounds ground beef
½ cup barbecue sauce
2 teaspoons onion powder
6 hamburger buns
2 large tomatoes, sliced
6 lettuce leaves
1 (6-ounce) can French-fried
   onions

1. Preheat grill. Combine the ground beef with the barbecue sauce and onion powder. Mix well. Shape into patties.
2. Grill burgers for 4 minutes per side or until they reach desired level of doneness. Remove from grill and serve on buns with tomatoes, lettuce, and onions.

Per Serving: Calories: 485 | Fat: 21 g | Saturated fat: 8 g | Cholesterol: 94 mg | Sodium: 587 mg | Total carbohydrates: 38 g | Dietary fiber: 2 g | Sugars: 12 g | Protein: 36 g

Steak Salad with Gorgonzola and Walnuts

Hands-On Time: 10 minutes
Total Time: 20 minutes
Yield: Serves 8

1 teaspoon oregano
1 clove garlic, peeled and crushed
¼ teaspoon ground black pepper
1¼ pounds beef sirloin steak, 1"
   thick
¼ teaspoon salt
1 large head romaine lettuce
½ cup crumbled blue cheese
¼ cup chopped red onion
¼ cup toasted chopped walnuts
1 cup prepared Italian dressing
   with balsamic vinegar

1. Preheat the broiler.
2. Combine the oregano, garlic, and pepper, and press into both sides of the meat, distributing mixture evenly.
3. Broil steak to desired degree of doneness. When done, season with salt and slice across the grain into strips ⅛"–¼" thick.
4. Slice the lettuce across the rib into 1"-thick slices. Toss lettuce with meat, cheese, onion, and nuts. Lightly coat with dressing.

Per Serving: Calories: 270 | Fat: 19 g | Saturated fat: 6 g | Cholesterol: 55 mg | Sodium: 510 mg | Total carbohydrates: 8 g | Dietary fiber: 3 g | Sugars: 4 g | Protein: 18 g

Mongolian Flank Steak

Hands-On Time: 15 minutes
Total Time: 30 minutes
Yield: Serves 4

1 pound flank steak, cut into bite-sized slices
1 tablespoon light soy sauce
1 tablespoon Chinese rice wine or dry sherry
1½ teaspoons cornstarch
2 tablespoons vegetable oil
2 cloves garlic, peeled and minced
2 medium scallions, chopped and divided
¼ cup hoisin sauce
½ teaspoon ground black pepper

1. Place beef in a medium bowl and add soy sauce, rice wine or sherry, and cornstarch. Marinate for 15 minutes.

2. Heat a wok or medium skillet over medium-high heat until it is nearly smoking. Add oil. When oil is hot, add garlic and half the scallions. Stir-fry for 10 seconds.

3. Add beef and stir-fry for 1 minute.

4. Add hoisin sauce and bring to a boil. Stir-fry for 1 additional minute until beef is cooked. Season with black pepper. Serve hot and garnish with remaining scallions.

Per Serving: Calories: 310 | Fat: 17 g | Saturated fat: 5 g | Cholesterol: 50 mg | Sodium: 350 mg | Total carbohydrates: 8 g | Dietary fiber: 1 g | Sugars: 5 g | Protein: 30 g

Mushroom Steak

Hands-On Time: 30 minutes
Total Time: 30 minutes
Yield: Serves 6

6 (5-ounce) beef tenderloin steaks
1 teaspoon steak seasoning
¼ teaspoon ground black pepper
4 tablespoons butter, divided
1 tablespoon olive oil
1 medium onion, peeled and chopped
3 cloves garlic, peeled and minced
1 pound cremini mushrooms, cleaned and halved
½ cup dry red wine
½ cup beef broth
1 tablespoon fresh thyme leaves

1. Sprinkle steaks with steak seasoning and pepper on both sides. Let stand at room temperature while you heat 2 tablespoons butter and olive oil in a large skillet.

2. Add steaks; cook 10 minutes, turning once, for medium doneness. Remove to a warm platter and cover to keep warm. You can put the steaks in a 250°F oven while you make the sauce.

3. Add onion and garlic to pan; cook for 3 minutes. Then add mushrooms; cook and stir for 3 minutes longer. Add wine, beef broth, and thyme leaves; bring to a boil. Boil hard over high heat for 2–3 minutes until sauce reduces slightly.

4. Remove pan from heat and swirl in remaining 2 tablespoons butter. Immediately pour over the steaks and serve.

Per Serving: Calories: 361 | Fat: 20 g | Saturated fat: 9 g | Cholesterol: 125 mg | Sodium: 260 mg | Total carbohydrates: 6 g | Dietary fiber: 1 g | Sugars: 2 g | Protein: 36 g

Cheeseburger Soup (pictured)

Hands-On Time: 20 minutes
Total Time: 30 minutes
Yield: Serves 6

1 pound lean ground beef
2 tablespoons butter
1 medium onion, peeled and
 chopped
1 medium stalk celery, chopped
1 medium carrot, peeled and
 chopped
3 tablespoons all-purpose flour
2 cups chicken broth
2 cups whole milk
8 ounces cream cheese, cubed
1 (8-ounce) package shredded
 sharp Cheddar cheese
¼ teaspoon ground black pepper

1. Heat a 6- or 8-quart Dutch oven or soup pot over medium heat. Add the ground beef and cook until thoroughly browned, about 10 minutes. Remove from the pot and reserve.

2. To the pot add the butter and once melted add the onion, celery, and carrots, and cook until tender, about 8 minutes. Add the beef back to the pan, then sprinkle the flour over the vegetables and cook, stirring constantly, for 2 minutes. Slowly add the chicken broth and milk and bring just to a boil, then reduce the heat to medium-low and simmer for 10 minutes, stirring occasionally, until the soup has thickened.

3. Add the cream cheese and stir until melted, then reduce the heat to low and add the shredded cheese in three portions, waiting until the cheese has completely melted before adding the next portion. Season with pepper and serve hot.

Per Serving: Calories: 560 | Fat: 43 g | Saturated fat: 23 g | Cholesterol: 145 mg | Sodium: 740 mg | Total carbohydrates: 15 g | Dietary fiber: 1 g | Sugars: 7 g | Protein: 30 g

Burger with Greek Spices, Pine Nuts, and Feta

Hands-On Time: 25 minutes
Total Time: 25 minutes
Yield: Serves 4

1½ pounds ground beef
3 cloves garlic, peeled and minced
¼ teaspoon salt
¼ teaspoon ground black pepper
1 teaspoon dried oregano
½ teaspoon crushed red pepper
 flakes
¼ cup pine nuts (pignoles)
½ cup crumbled feta cheese
8 slices Italian bread, toasted
4 butter lettuce leaves

1. Preheat grill to medium.

2. Mix the ground beef with garlic, salt, pepper, oregano, crushed red pepper, pine nuts, and cheese, tossing carefully. Form mixture into 4 patties without too much patting and squeezing; this keeps them juicy.

3. Grill until brown and done to preference. Serve on Italian bread with lettuce.

Per Serving: Calories: 530 | Fat: 31 g | Saturated fat: 13 g | Cholesterol: 130 mg | Sodium: 650 mg | Total carbohydrates: 22 g | Dietary fiber: 0 g | Sugars: 2 g | Protein: 38 g

Beef with Bok Choy

Hands-On Time: 30 minutes
Total Time: 30 minutes
Yield: Serves 4

2 teaspoons sesame oil

3 cloves garlic, minced

1 tablespoon minced fresh ginger

1 small onion, thinly sliced

2 pounds baby bok choy, sliced

1 teaspoon sodium-free beef
    bouillon granules

½ teaspoon ground white pepper

½ cup water

½ pound grilled steak, cut into
    thin slices

2 cups cooked rice

1. Heat the oil in a large wok over medium heat. Add the garlic, ginger, and onion, and cook, stirring, for 30 seconds.

2. Add the bok choy and stir-fry for 2 minutes. Add the bouillon, pepper, and water, raise the heat to high, and cook, stirring, for 5–6 minutes.

3. Add the steak and heat until cooked through. Remove from heat and serve immediately over rice.

Per Serving: Calories: 280 | Fat: 7 g | Saturated fat: 2 g | Cholesterol: 50 mg | Sodium: 250 mg | Total carbohydrates: 31 g | Dietary fiber: 3 g | Sugars: 4 g | Protein: 23 g

Easy Cottage Pie

Hands-On Time: 10 minutes
Total Time: 25 minutes
Yield: Serves 2

1 (4-ounce) package instant
    mashed potatoes

1 large egg yolk

½ pound cooked ground beef

½ cup canned corn

3 tablespoons tomato sauce or
    ketchup

½ teaspoon minced fresh thyme

¼ teaspoon salt

⅛ teaspoon ground black pepper

1. Preheat oven to 400°F.

2. Prepare the mashed potatoes according to package instructions. Stir in the egg yolk.

3. Combine the ground beef, corn, tomato sauce, thyme, salt, and pepper in a medium-sized bowl. Divide the mixture into 2 small, individual ramekins. Spread ½ cup of the mashed potatoes on top of each ramekin in an even layer, completely covering the beef mixture. (Store the leftover potatoes in a sealed container in the refrigerator to use at another time.)

4. Bake for 15 minutes or until heated through.

Per Serving: Calories: 470 | Fat: 24 g | Saturated fat: 8 g | Cholesterol: 190 mg | Sodium: 890 mg | Total carbohydrates: 31 g | Dietary fiber: 2 g | Sugars: 10 g | Protein: 33 g

Thai Steak and Vegetable Bowl

Hands-On Time: 15 minutes
Total Time: 15 minutes
Yield: Serves 2

2 tablespoons sesame oil, divided
1 cup peeled and sliced carrots
1 cup chopped lemongrass
2 tablespoons low-sodium soy sauce
12 ounces lean beef, sliced into ¼" strips
1 cup peapods
1 tablespoon curry powder
1 teaspoon garlic powder
2 cups cooked rice noodles
½ cup peeled and shredded carrots

1. Coat a large skillet with 1 tablespoon sesame oil and heat over medium heat. Add carrots and lemongrass and cook until slightly softened, about 7 minutes.

2. Drizzle 1 tablespoon sesame oil and soy sauce in skillet and add beef and peapods. Season with curry powder and garlic powder and stir while cooking for 5–7 minutes or until beef is cooked through.

3. Add rice noodles to skillet and toss to combine ingredients thoroughly. Remove from heat.

4. Pour equal amounts of noodles into each of two serving bowls.

5. Pour equal amounts of stir-fry mixture over noodles. Garnish each with ¼ cup shredded carrots. Serve hot.

Per Serving: Calories: 650 | Fat: 24 g | Saturated fat: 6 g | Cholesterol: 105 mg | Sodium: 760 mg | Total carbohydrates: 64 g | Dietary fiber: 6 g | Sugars: 5 g | Protein: 44 g

Burritos

Hands-On Time: 20 minutes
Total Time: 20 minutes
Yield: Serves 8

1 cup refried beans
1 cup cooked rice
1 cup shredded cooked beef
½ pound Cheddar cheese
8 (10") flour tortillas
1 cup tomato salsa
½ cup red chili sauce

1. Heat the beans, rice, and beef separately in 3 small pans over low heat. Shred the cheese.

2. Lay each tortilla flat. Add ¼ cup of the beans, ¼ cup beef, ¼ cup rice, and 1 tablespoon salsa to the middle of each tortilla. Drizzle 1 teaspoon of chili sauce on top. Roll up.

Per Serving: Calories: 467 | Fat: 15 g | Saturated fat: 8 g | Cholesterol: 45 mg | Sodium: 1,274 mg | Total carbohydrates: 54 g | Dietary fiber: 4 g | Sugars: 6 g | Protein: 20 g

Southwestern Fried Cauliflower "Rice" Bowl (pictured)

Hands-On Time: 20 minutes
Total Time: 20 minutes
Yield: Serves 2

1 tablespoon olive oil

1 (12-ounce) bag frozen cauliflower "rice"

⅔ cup cooked shredded beef

2 tablespoons fresh lime juice

¼ cup chopped cilantro

⅓ cup diced strawberries

1 medium avocado, peeled, pitted, and diced

½ small jalapeño pepper, seeded and diced

¼ teaspoon kosher salt

¼ teaspoon ground black pepper

1. In a large skillet, melt olive oil over medium-high heat. Add cauliflower "rice" and sauté 10 minutes until golden brown.

2. Add shredded beef and lime juice. Sauté 5–10 minutes until heated through.

3. Remove from heat and stir in cilantro, strawberries, avocado, and jalapeño. Season with salt and pepper.

Per Serving: Calories: 471 | Fat: 29 g | Saturated fat: 6 g | Cholesterol: 78 mg | Sodium: 274 mg | Total carbohydrates: 21 g | Dietary fiber: 12 g | Sugars: 6 g | Protein: 36 g

Mexican-Style Beef "Torta"

Hands-On Time: 10 minutes
Total Time: 10 minutes
Yield: Serves 4

¾ pound trimmed skirt steak

2 tablespoons olive oil

1 teaspoon ground cumin

¼ teaspoon salt

⅛ teaspoon ground black pepper

4 large soft rolls

2 cups shredded iceberg lettuce

1 large ripe tomato, sliced

1 small red onion, peeled and sliced

1 medium ripe Hass avocado, peeled, pitted, and sliced

1 small lime, cut in half

1 teaspoon Mexican hot sauce

1. Rub the steak with the oil, cumin, salt, and pepper. Sear in a medium-sized pan on high heat for 3 minutes per side. Allow the meat to rest while you assemble the rest of the sandwich.

2. Pile the rolls with the lettuce, tomato, onion, and avocado. Squeeze the lime over the avocado.

3. Slice the meat across the grain into ¼" slices and pile on the rolls. Sprinkle with hot sauce and enjoy.

Per Serving: Calories: 500 | Fat: 28 g | Saturated fat: 7 g | Cholesterol: 85 mg | Sodium: 470 mg | Total carbohydrates: 33 g | Dietary fiber: 4 g | Sugars: 7 g | Protein: 30 g

Hambágu (Hamburger Steak)

Hands-On Time: 20 minutes
Total Time: 30 minutes
Yield: Serves 4

½ cup panko bread crumbs or soft
  white bread crumbs

2 tablespoons whole milk

2 tablespoons butter, divided

1 small onion, peeled and finely
  diced

¾ pound lean ground beef

¼ pound ground pork

1 teaspoon salt

½ teaspoon ground black pepper

¼ teaspoon ground nutmeg

1 large egg

1 tablespoon cooking oil

½ cup red wine

¼ cup ketchup

¼ cup Worcestershire sauce or
  tonkatsu sauce

1. In a small bowl combine panko and milk. Let stand for 5 minutes or until milk is completely absorbed.

2. In a large skillet over medium heat, add 1 tablespoon butter. Once it foams, add onion and cook, stirring constantly, until softened and translucent, about 3 minutes. Remove from heat and cool to room temperature.

3. In a large bowl combine beef, pork, salt, pepper, nutmeg, and egg with the softened panko and onions. Using your hands mix gently until everything is well combined.

4. Divide mixture into 4 oval-shaped patties. Toss each patty back and forth between your hands 10 times to release the air in the meat. Place the patties on a plate and press your thumb gently into the center of each patty to form a slight dent.

5. Heat the skillet over medium heat. Once the skillet is hot, add oil. When the oil shimmers, add meat patties. Cook for 5 minutes per side or until each side is dark golden brown. Cover the pan with a lid and cook for 5 minutes more or until patties reach an internal temperature of 155°F. Transfer patties to a plate and loosely cover with foil while you prepare the sauce.

6. With the skillet over medium heat, add the wine. Cook, scraping the bottom of the pan to lift any brown bits of meat, until the wine is reduced by half, about 3 minutes. Add remaining butter, ketchup, and Worcestershire or *tonkatsu* sauce and cook until sauce thickens slightly, about 3 minutes. Pour sauce over the patties and serve.

Per Serving: Calories: 440 | Fat: 28 g | Saturated fat: 11 g | Cholesterol: 140 mg | Sodium: 990 mg | Total carbohydrates: 16 g | Dietary fiber: 0 g | Sugars: 7 g | Protein: 24 g

Pan-Fried Steak with Italian Pesto

Hands-On Time: 5 minutes
Total Time: 15 minutes
Yield: Serves 4

2 teaspoons lemon-pepper
    seasoning
½ teaspoon salt
4 (1-pound) beef tenderloin
    steaks
1 tablespoon olive oil
½ cup pesto

1. Rub lemon-pepper seasoning and salt over the steaks. Heat olive oil in a large skillet over medium-high heat. Add the steaks to the pan and cook to medium (135°F–145°F), about 8–10 minutes, turning halfway through cooking.

2. Serve the steaks with a spoonful of pesto on top.

Per Serving: Calories: 366 | Fat: 31 g | Saturated fat: 8 g | Cholesterol: 83 mg | Sodium: 641 mg | Total carbohydrates: 2 g | Dietary fiber: 1 g | Sugars: 1 g | Protein: 24 g

Steak with Brown Sauce

Hands-On Time: 20 minutes
Total Time: 30 minutes
Yield: Serves 4

1½ tablespoons butter
1 tablespoon all-purpose flour
½ cup beef broth
1 tablespoon Worcestershire
    sauce
½ teaspoon honey mustard
½ teaspoon granulated sugar
⅛ teaspoon red pepper flakes
½ teaspoon seasoned salt
½ teaspoon ground black pepper
4 (5-ounce) beef tenderloin
    steaks
2 tablespoons vegetable oil
1 small shallot, peeled and
    chopped
¼ cup red wine

1. In a small saucepan, melt the butter on low heat. Add the flour and blend it into the melted butter, stirring continually until it thickens and forms a roux. Add the beef broth. Stir in the Worcestershire sauce, mustard, sugar, and red pepper flakes. Bring to a boil, stirring continually. Remove from heat and set aside.

2. Rub the salt and pepper over the steaks to season.

3. Heat the oil in a large skillet over medium-high heat. Add the steaks. Cook for 4–5 minutes until the steak is browned on the bottom. Add the shallots to the pan. Turn the steak over and cook for another 4–5 minutes. Remove the steak and shallots from the pan. Pour off any excess fat.

4. Add the red wine to the pan and bring to a boil. Deglaze the pan by using a rubber spatula to scrape up any browned bits from the meat (do not remove the browned bits: they add extra flavor to the liquid).

5. Add the brown sauce to the pan and cook at medium-low heat until it is heated through. Pour the sauce over the steak.

Per Serving: Calories: 470 | Fat: 33 g | Saturated fat: 12 g | Cholesterol: 135 mg | Sodium: 518 mg | Total carbohydrates: 4 g | Dietary fiber: 0 g | Sugars: 1 g | Protein: 34 g

Roast Beef Sandwich Au Jus (pictured)

Hands-On Time: 10 minutes
Total Time: 10 minutes
Yield: Serves 1

1 cup beef broth

2 teaspoons Worcestershire sauce

1 French roll, top and bottom
buttered and split lengthwise

¼ pound roast beef deli meat,
thinly sliced

1. In a small saucepan over medium heat, combine the beef broth with the Worcestershire sauce. Bring to a simmer; reduce heat to low and keep warm until ready to serve.

2. Preheat a panini press. Layer slices of roast beef onto the bottom half of roll. Close sandwich with top half and place on panini press. Close lid and cook for 3–5 minutes.

3. Remove sandwich from panini press and cut in half. Serve warm with a small bowl of the warm beef broth for dipping.

Per Serving: Calories: 330 | Fat: 8 g | Saturated fat: 2.5 g | Cholesterol: 65 mg | Sodium: 1,950 mg | Total carbohydrates: 35 g | Dietary fiber: 3 g | Sugars: 4 g | Protein: 28 g

Layered Mexican Taco Pizzas

Hands-On Time: 20 minutes
Total Time: 30 minutes
Yield: Serves 8

1 tablespoon olive oil

1 medium onion, peeled and
chopped

2 small jalapeño peppers, seeded
and minced

1 pound ground beef

1 (15-ounce) can refried beans

½ cup chunky salsa

2 teaspoons chili powder

8 (8") flour tortillas

2 cups shredded Cheddar cheese

2 medium tomatoes, seeded and
diced

1 cup shredded lettuce

1. Preheat oven to 400°F.

2. In large saucepan, heat olive oil over medium heat. Add onion; cook and stir for 5 minutes. Add jalapeño peppers; cook and stir for 2–3 minutes longer. Add beef and sauté until the beef is cooked through and any juices have cooked off.

3. Remove from heat and stir in refried beans, salsa, and chili powder; mix well.

4. Place 2 tortillas on two cookie sheets. Spread with ¼ of the shredded cheese, ¼ of the beef and bean mixture, and ¼ of the tomatoes. Add another tortilla on top and repeat layers until all the ingredients are used.

5. Bake for 10 minutes or until tortillas are crisp and cheeses are melted and beginning to brown. Sprinkle with lettuce and serve immediately.

Per Serving: Calories: 450 | Fat: 22 g | Saturated fat: 10 g | Cholesterol: 65 mg | Sodium: 990 mg | Total carbohydrates: 38 g | Dietary fiber: 3 g | Sugars: 4 g | Protein: 25 g

The Basic Burger

Hands-On Time: 15 minutes
Total Time: 15 minutes
Yield: Serves 4

1¼ pounds ground round beef
½ teaspoon seasoned salt
½ teaspoon ground black pepper

1. Lightly mix the ground round with salt and pepper and form into 4 evenly sized patties. Cook by your choice of the following methods.

2. To grill: Clean grill rack and lightly oil to prevent sticking. Preheat grill to medium-high. Cook for about 5 minutes per side for medium, turning once. Transfer burgers to a plate and tent with foil to keep warm. Let rest for 1–2 minutes to allow the juices to reabsorb. Serve hot. If using an indoor grill, follow manufacturer's directions.

3. To broil: Clean broiler rack and lightly oil to prevent sticking. Set broiler rack 4" from heat source. Preheat broiler to medium-high. Cook for about 5 minutes per side for medium, turning once. Transfer burgers to a plate and tent with foil to keep warm. Let rest for 1–2 minutes to allow the juices to reabsorb. Serve hot.

Per Serving: Calories: 310 | Fat: 22 g | Saturated fat: 4.5 g | Cholesterol: 90 mg | Sodium: 250 mg | Total carbohydrates: 0 g | Dietary fiber: 0 g | Sugars: 0 g | Protein: 28 g

Baked Egg Pizza Subs

Hands-On Time: 15 minutes
Total Time: 30 minutes
Yield: Serves 6

8 ounces bulk hot pork sausage
8 ounces lean ground beef
3 teaspoons salt-free seasoning
2 cloves garlic, peeled and minced
3 submarine sandwich rolls, cut in half lengthwise
3 tablespoons butter, softened
¾ cup pizza sauce
1½ cups shredded Cheddar cheese
3 slices deli ham
6 large eggs

1. Preheat oven to 400°F. Line a large baking sheet with parchment paper.

2. Sauté sausage and ground beef in large skillet over medium-high heat until cooked through, about 8–10 minutes. Add seasoning and garlic and cook 2 minutes more.

3. Lay sub roll halves on prepared baking sheet. Spread a little butter onto each roll and toast in the oven for just 3 minutes to slightly brown the bread.

4. Spoon pizza sauce onto each bread half, top with some of the meat mixture, then top with cheese.

5. Tear the ham slices into small pieces and place on top of the cheese.

6. Press a deep well into the middle of each sub with the back of a large spoon. Crack an egg into each well.

7. Bake for 15 minutes or until eggs are done to your liking.

Per Serving: Calories: 493 | Fat: 30 g | Saturated fat: 15 g | Cholesterol: 275 mg | Sodium: 1,000 mg | Total carbohydrates: 17 g | Dietary fiber: 1 g | Sugars: 3 g | Protein: 31 g

Chili Mac and Cheese

Hands-On Time: 15 minutes
Total Time: 30 minutes
Yield: Serves 6

2 tablespoons olive oil

1 medium yellow onion, peeled and chopped

1 pound lean ground beef

1 teaspoon kosher salt

1 (14.5-ounce) can diced tomatoes, drained

1 packet chili seasoning

1 (24-ounce) jar prepared pasta sauce

1 (16-ounce) box cooked elbow macaroni

1 (11-ounce) can Mexican-style corn

2 cups shredded Mexican-blend cheese, divided

½ cup chopped fresh cilantro

1. Preheat oven to 350°F.

2. Add olive oil to a large heavy-bottomed skillet over medium-high heat. Add onions and sauté for 5 minutes. Add ground beef and cook until browned, about 6–8 minutes. Add salt, tomatoes, chili seasoning, and pasta sauce. Stir to combine. Reduce heat to medium-low and simmer for 5 minutes.

3. Place pasta in a large bowl. Stir in corn and 1½ cups cheese. Once combined, stir in the chili mixture. Pour into a large, deep casserole dish and top with remaining cheese. Bake for 15 minutes. Remove from oven and serve topped with cilantro.

Per Serving: Calories: 710 | Fat: 25 g | Saturated fat: 11 g | Cholesterol: 85 mg | Sodium: 1,230 mg | Total carbohydrates: 82 g | Dietary fiber: 6 g | Sugars: 14 g | Protein: 38 g

Chapter 9

Pork, Lamb, and Venison Main Dishes

Speedy Pork Meatloaf

Hands-On Time: 5 minutes
Total Time: 25 minutes
Yield: Serves 8

1½ pounds ground pork
¾ cup plus 2 tablespoons tomato sauce, divided
¼ cup chopped onion
1 tablespoon balsamic vinegar
½ cup grated Parmesan cheese

1. In a large bowl, combine all the ingredients.
2. Shape into a loaf and place in a microwave-safe casserole dish. Cover with microwave-safe wax paper.
3. Microwave on high heat for 15 minutes, 5 minutes at a time, rotating the dish a quarter turn between each cooking period. If the meatloaf is not cooked after 15 minutes, continue to cook for 1 minute at a time until done. (Total cooking time should be about 15 minutes.) The meatloaf is cooked when the internal temperature reaches 160°F.
4. Let stand for 5 minutes. Pour any fat off the dish and serve.

Per Serving: Calories: 290 | Fat: 20 g | Saturated fat: 8 g | Cholesterol: 85 mg | Sodium: 530 mg | Total carbohydrates: 3 g | Dietary fiber: 1 g | Sugars: 2 g | Protein: 24 g

Orange Pork with Carrots

Hands-On Time: 10 minutes
Total Time: 30 minutes
Yield: Serves 6

1½ pounds pork tenderloin, cut in chunks
2 tablespoons cornstarch
1 clove fresh garlic, minced
½ teaspoon all-purpose seasoning
1 cup chicken broth
½ cup orange juice
3 tablespoons low-sodium soy sauce
1 teaspoon chili powder
2 cups sliced carrots
1 teaspoon ground ginger
1 cup sliced yellow onions
½ teaspoon black pepper

1. Coat a large skillet with nonstick spray. Add pork, cornstarch, garlic, and all-purpose seasoning. Sauté on medium-high heat for 8 minutes, stirring often.
2. Mix remaining ingredients and add to skillet. Simmer for 8–10 minutes. Add water if mixture gets too dry.

Per Serving: Calories: 180 | Fat: 3.5 g | Saturated fat: 1 g | Cholesterol: 70 mg | Sodium: 160 mg | Total carbohydrates: 12 g | Dietary fiber: 2 g | Sugars: 5 g | Protein: 24 g

Raspberry Pineapple Pork Chops

Hands-On Time: 15 minutes
Total Time: 25 minutes
Yield: Serves 4

4 (4-ounce) boneless pork chops
¼ teaspoon salt
⅛ teaspoon ground black pepper
1 tablespoon olive oil
¼ cup fat-free chicken broth
3 tablespoons raspberry vinegar
1 tablespoon low-sodium soy sauce
⅓ cup seedless raspberry jam
½ cup fresh raspberries
½ cup pineapple tidbits

1. Sprinkle chops with salt and pepper. Heat olive oil in medium skillet over medium heat. Add chops; brown well on both sides, turning once, about 6–7 minutes total.

2. Add chicken broth, vinegar, and soy sauce to pan. Bring to a boil, then cover pan, reduce heat to low, and simmer for 10 minutes or until pork is just cooked and still slightly pink in center.

3. Uncover pan and remove pork to serving platter. Add jam to sauce in pan and stir to blend. Pour sauce over chops, sprinkle with raspberries and pineapple, and serve immediately.

Per Serving: Calories: 300 | Fat: 10 g | Saturated fat: 3 g | Cholesterol: 85 mg | Sodium: 640 mg | Total carbohydrates: 18 g | Dietary fiber: 2 g | Sugars: 12 g | Protein: 36 g

DIY Italian Sausage

Hands-On Time: 15 minutes
Total Time: 15 minutes
Yield: Serves 12

2 pounds pork shoulder
1 teaspoon ground black pepper
1 teaspoon dried parsley
1 teaspoon dried rosemary
1 teaspoon dried oregano
1 teaspoon garlic powder
¾ teaspoon crushed anise seeds
⅛ teaspoon red pepper flakes
½ teaspoon paprika
½ teaspoon instant minced onion flakes
1 teaspoon kosher salt

1. Remove all fat from meat; cut the meat into cubes. Put in food processor; grind to desired consistency.

2. Add remaining ingredients to the meat in the food processor; mix until well blended. You can put sausage mixture in casings, but this recipe also works if you broil the meat well or grill as patties.

Per Serving: Calories: 70 | Fat: 3 g | Saturated fat: 1 g | Cholesterol: 30 mg | Sodium: 190 mg | Total carbohydrates: 1 g | Dietary fiber: 0 g | Sugars: 0 g | Protein: 9 g

Shredded Pork Sandwiches (pictured)

Hands-On Time: 15 minutes
Total Time: 25 minutes
Yield: Serves 4

1 (20-ounce) package cooked
    pork roast au jus
1 tablespoon olive oil
1 medium onion, chopped
3 cloves garlic, minced
1 medium green bell pepper,
    seeded and chopped
⅓ cup ketchup
¼ cup chili sauce
¼ cup mustard
½ cup beef broth
1 teaspoon dried thyme leaves
4 hoagie buns, split and toasted

1. Remove pork from package; drain off juice and reserve. Shred pork and set aside.

2. In large saucepan, heat olive oil over medium heat. Add onion and garlic; cook and stir 5 minutes. Add bell pepper, ketchup, chili sauce, and mustard; simmer 3 minutes. Add pork; simmer 3–4 minutes longer until hot.

3. Place the juice in a small saucepan and add beef broth and thyme; bring to a simmer. Make sandwiches with pork mixture and buns. Serve sandwiches with the juice for dipping.

Per Serving: Calories: 677 | Fat: 29 g | Saturated fat: 10 g | Cholesterol: 105 mg | Sodium: 2,320 mg | Total carbohydrates: 53 g | Dietary fiber: 4 g | Sugars: 16 g | Protein: 46 g

Pan-Fried Pork Chops with Apple and Sage

Hands-On Time: 15 minutes
Total Time: 15 minutes
Yield: Serves 4

4 boneless pork loin chops
½ teaspoon salt
¼ teaspoon ground black pepper
1 tablespoon olive oil
1 medium apple, cored and sliced
2 tablespoons butter
¾ cup apple cider
1 tablespoon whole-grain Dijon
    mustard
2 tablespoons chopped fresh
    sage

1. Season pork chops with salt and pepper.

2. In a large skillet over medium-high heat, heat oil until shimmering. Carefully add pork chops and cook for 2–3 minutes, flip and cook an additional 1–2 minutes. Transfer to a warm plate and tent with aluminum foil. Remove all but 1 tablespoon of fat from pan.

3. In the hot skillet, cook the apple slices in the fat until lightly browned on both sides. Add butter and melt, stirring to remove browned bits from bottom of pan. Stir or whisk in apple cider, mustard, and sage.

4. Serve pork chops with apples and sauce.

Per Serving: Calories: 470 | Fat: 31 g | Saturated fat: 12 g | Cholesterol: 115 mg | Sodium: 530 mg | Total carbohydrates: 12 g | Dietary fiber: 1 g | Sugars: 10 g | Protein: 36 g

Pork Burgers with Apples

Hands-On Time: 20 minutes
Total Time: 20 minutes
Yield: Serves 4

1 medium green apple, peeled,
    cored, and diced
1 tablespoon soy sauce
2 medium green onions, minced
1 clove garlic, minced
½ teaspoon salt
½ teaspoon ground black pepper
1 pound lean ground pork

1. Using a fork, lightly blend all ingredients together in large bowl.
2. Heat grill to high. Form meat and apple mixture into burgers. Sear quickly, turn heat to low, and cook for 5 minutes per side.

Per Serving: Calories: 160 | Fat: 4.5 g | Saturated fat: 1.5 g | Cholesterol: 65 mg | Sodium: 590 mg | Total carbohydrates: 7 g | Dietary fiber: 1 g | Sugars: 4 g | Protein: 25 g

Bangkok-Style Roasted Pork Tenderloin

Hands-On Time: 10 minutes
Total Time: 30 minutes
Yield: Serves 4

1½ teaspoons salt, divided
¼ teaspoon ground ginger
¼ teaspoon ground cardamom
1 teaspoon ground black pepper,
    divided
2 teaspoons olive oil
2 (1-pound) pork tenderloins,
    trimmed
½ cup chicken stock

1. Place rack on bottom third of the oven, then preheat the oven to 500°F.
2. Combine 1 teaspoon salt, ginger, cardamom, ¼ teaspoon pepper, and oil in a small bowl. Rub each of the tenderloins with half of the spice mixture. Place the tenderloins in a roasting pan and cook for 10 minutes. Turn the tenderloins over and roast for 10 more minutes or until done to your liking.
3. Transfer the pork to a serving platter, cover with foil, and let rest.
4. Pour off any fat that has accumulated in the roasting pan. Place the pan on the stovetop over high heat and add the stock. Bring to a boil, scraping the bottom of the pan to loosen any cooked-on bits. Season with remaining salt and pepper.
5. To serve, cut the tenderloins into thin slices. Pour a bit of the sauce over top and save the rest to pass at the table.

Per Serving: Calories: 290 | Fat: 8 g | Saturated fat: 2.5 g | Cholesterol: 135 mg | Sodium: 1,020 mg | Total carbohydrates: 2 g | Dietary fiber: 0 g | Sugars: 0 g | Protein: 48 g

Pork Skewers with Cherry Tomatoes

Hands-On Time: 20 minutes
Total Time: 20 minutes
Yield: Serves 4

¾ pound pork tenderloin, cubed
24 cherry tomatoes
1 medium onion, cut into eighths
4 metal skewers
2 tablespoons olive oil
1 tablespoon lemon juice
1 tablespoon honey
⅛ teaspoon ground black pepper
2 tablespoons chopped flat-leaf parsley
1 tablespoon fresh oregano leaves

1. Prepare and preheat grill. Thread pork, cherry tomatoes, and onion on metal skewers. In small bowl, combine olive oil, lemon juice, honey, pepper, parsley, and oregano leaves. Brush pork skewers with olive oil mixture.

2. Grill skewers 6″ from medium coals for 8–10 minutes, turning and brushing occasionally with marinade, until pork registers 155°F.

Per Serving: Calories: 190 | Fat: 9 g | Saturated fat: 2 g | Cholesterol: 45 mg | Sodium: 50 mg | Total carbohydrates: 11 g | Dietary fiber: 2 g | Sugars: 8 g | Protein: 18 g

Herbed Tenderloin Stir-Fry

Hands-On Time: 15 minutes
Total Time: 15 minutes
Yield: Serves 4

1 (1-pound) package pork tenderloin
1½ tablespoons cornstarch
2 tablespoons low-sodium soy sauce
1 cup chicken broth
2 cloves garlic, minced
½ teaspoon dried thyme leaves
½ teaspoon dried basil leaves
½ teaspoon dried marjoram leaves
⅛ teaspoon ground black pepper
2 tablespoons vegetable oil
1 (16-ounce) package frozen stir-fry vegetables
2 tablespoons water

1. Cut tenderloin into thin strips. In medium bowl, combine cornstarch, soy sauce, broth, garlic, thyme, basil, marjoram, and pepper; stir well. Add pork and stir.

2. Heat oil over medium-high heat in a large skillet or wok. Drain pork, reserving marinade. Add pork to skillet; stir-fry until brown. Remove pork and set aside.

3. Add vegetables to skillet along with 2 tablespoons water; stir-fry until hot. Stir marinade and add to skillet along with pork. Stir-fry until bubbly and hot; serve immediately.

Per Serving: Calories: 234 | Fat: 10 g | Saturated fat: 1.5 g | Cholesterol: 55 mg | Sodium: 460 mg | Total carbohydrates: 13 g | Dietary fiber: 3 g | Sugars: 4 g | Protein: 23 g

Sausage and Onion Quesadillas

Hands-On Time: 15 minutes
Total Time: 25 minutes
Yield: Serves 8

1 tablespoon olive oil
1 pound bulk pork sausage
1 medium onion, thickly sliced
½ teaspoon paprika
½ teaspoon ground cumin
2 teaspoons chili powder
8 (10") flour tortillas
2 cups shredded Cheddar cheese
2 tablespoons olive oil

1. Preheat oven to 375°F. In heavy skillet over medium heat, heat oil. Add sausage and onion, stirring with a wooden spoon to break up sausage, about 5–7 minutes. When sausage is browned and onions are softened, drain off most of the fat. Sprinkle with seasonings and remove from heat.

2. Lay four tortillas on work surface. Sprinkle each with shredded cheese and the sausage and onion mixture. Top with remaining tortillas. Place on two cookie sheets and brush tortillas with olive oil. Bake for 7–10 minutes or until cheese is melted and tortillas are lightly browned. Cut into wedges and serve.

Per Serving: Calories: 520 | Fat: 31 g | Saturated fat: 11 g | Cholesterol: 85 mg | Sodium: 1,110 mg | Total carbohydrates: 37 g | Dietary fiber: 2 g | Sugars: 2 g | Protein: 23 g

Fried Pork Chops with Mustard Ale Sauce (pictured)

Hands-On Time: 15 minutes
Total Time: 25 minutes
Yield: Serves 4

4 thin-cut bone-in pork chops (about 1 pound)
½ cup all-purpose flour
½ teaspoon salt
½ teaspoon ground black pepper
1 tablespoon butter, divided
1 medium red onion, peeled and sliced
1 cup ale-style beer
3 tablespoons Dijon mustard
3 tablespoons heavy cream

1. In a heavy-duty resealable bag, combine the pork chops, flour, salt, and pepper. Shake the bag well to combine. Set aside.

2. Place a large skillet over medium-high heat. Once the pan is hot, add half the butter, and once it melts add two of the pork chops. Cook until the chops are well browned on both sides, about 3 minutes per side. Remove from the skillet to a plate and cover loosely with foil to rest. Repeat with the remaining butter and pork chops.

3. Turn the heat down to medium and add the onions. Cook until they are tender, about 3 minutes, then add the beer. With a wooden spoon, scrape the browned bits from the bottom of the pan. Simmer 10 minutes until beer is reduced by half, then stir in the mustard and heavy cream. Add the chops back to the pan and turn to coat in the sauce.

Per Serving: Calories: 310 | Fat: 11 g | Saturated fat: 6 g | Cholesterol: 100 mg | Sodium: 630 mg | Total carbohydrates: 17 g | Dietary fiber: 1 g | Sugars: 1 g | Protein: 27 g

Sweet and Sour Pork with Rice

Hands-On Time: 25 minutes
Total Time: 25 minutes
Yield: Serves 8

¼ cup apple cider vinegar

¾ cup water

2 tablespoons reduced-sodium teriyaki sauce

½ teaspoon crushed red pepper

¼ cup brown sugar

2 pounds lean pork roast, cut into 1" cubes

1 teaspoon salt

1 teaspoon ground black pepper

1 tablespoon cornstarch

2 tablespoons olive oil

1 (15-ounce) can pineapple chunks

1 medium green bell pepper, seeded and sliced

1 medium red bell pepper, seeded and sliced

3 cups cooked rice

1. In a medium mixing bowl, combine vinegar, water, teriyaki sauce, crushed red pepper, and sugar. Mix well and set aside.

2. Season pork with salt and pepper. Toss with cornstarch.

3. In large frying pan, add olive oil and heat over medium-high heat. Add pork to the frying pan. Sauté pork until brown, but it may still be pink inside, about 10 minutes.

4. Add pineapple and peppers. Cook until the peppers begin to soften, about 5 minutes. Add the sauce and cook until bubbly and thickened, about 5 minutes.

5. Serve over rice.

Per Serving: Calories: 380 | Fat: 16 g | Saturated fat: 4.5 g | Cholesterol: 65 mg | Sodium: 410 mg | Total carbohydrates: 35 g | Dietary fiber: 1 g | Sugars: 16 g | Protein: 24 g

Italian Crispy Pork Chops

Hands-On Time: 20 minutes
Total Time: 30 minutes
Yield: Serves 8

8 (4-ounce) thin-cut boneless
   pork chops
2 large eggs, beaten
2 tablespoons water
½ cup grated Parmesan cheese
1 cup panko bread crumbs
1 teaspoon dried Italian seasoning
½ teaspoon dried basil leaves
2 tablespoons butter
3 tablespoons olive oil

1. Place pork chops between two pieces of plastic wrap and pound with a rolling pin or meat mallet until about ⅓" thick.

2. In shallow bowl, combine eggs and water and beat until blended.

3. On shallow plate, combine cheese, panko, Italian seasoning, and basil and mix well. Dip pork chops into egg mixture and then into cheese mixture, pressing the cheese mixture firmly onto the chops. Place on wire rack when coated. Let stand for 10 minutes.

4. Heat butter and olive oil in a large skillet over medium-high heat. Fry the pork chops, 2–4 minutes on each side, until brown and crisp and just slightly pink inside. Serve immediately.

Per Serving: Calories: 240 | Fat: 15 g | Saturated fat: 5 g | Cholesterol: 100 mg | Sodium: 440 mg | Total carbohydrates: 8 g | Dietary fiber: 1 g | Sugars: 1 g | Protein: 19 g

Island Grilled Pork Patties

Hands-On Time: 30 minutes
Total Time: 30 minutes
Yield: Serves 4

1 pound lean ground pork
1 tablespoon lime zest
1 teaspoon jerk seasoning
½ teaspoon ground allspice
½ teaspoon cayenne pepper
¼ teaspoon garlic salt
2 tablespoons chopped fresh
   cilantro

1. Lightly mix together all the ingredients in a large bowl and form into 4 patties, each about 4 ounces.

2. Spray a medium skillet with nonstick cooking spray and heat over medium-high heat.

3. Cook patties for 7–9 minutes per side, turning once, until cooked throughout. Transfer to a plate and tent with foil to keep warm. Let rest for 1–2 minutes to allow the juices to reabsorb. Serve hot.

Per Serving: Calories: 230 | Fat: 17 g | Saturated fat: 6 g | Cholesterol: 75 mg | Sodium: 260 mg | Total carbohydrates: 2 g | Dietary fiber: 0 g | Sugars: 0 g | Protein: 21 g

Pork and Fennel Meatballs (pictured)

Hands-On Time: 30 minutes
Total Time: 30 minutes
Yield: Serves 12

1 pound lean ground pork
¼ cup roughly chopped fresh flat-leaf parsley, divided
3 tablespoons gluten-free panko bread crumbs
1 large egg
⅛ teaspoon garlic powder
¼ teaspoon salt
½ teaspoon ground black pepper
1½ tablespoons olive oil
2 teaspoons fennel seeds

1. In a medium mixing bowl, combine pork, half of parsley, bread crumbs, egg, garlic powder, salt, and pepper. Stir to combine or mix well with hands. Shape into 1" meatballs.

2. In a medium skillet, heat oil over medium heat and toast fennel seeds until fragrant, about 4 minutes. Add meatballs to pan.

3. Brown meatballs on all sides, cooking about 4–5 minutes per side, 20 minutes total. Meatballs are cooked through when no longer pink inside. Garnish with remaining parsley.

Per Serving: Calories: 110 | Fat: 8 g | Saturated fat: 2 g | Cholesterol: 40 mg | Sodium: 80 mg | Total carbohydrates: 1 g | Dietary fiber: 0 g | Sugars: 0 g | Protein: 7 g

Grilled Pork and Onion Kebabs

Hands-On Time: 30 minutes
Total Time: 30 minutes
Yield: Serves 4

4 teaspoons finely ground whole coriander seeds
4 teaspoons finely ground anise seeds
1 tablespoon minced garlic
1 tablespoon ground paprika
¼ teaspoon cayenne pepper
1 teaspoon salt, divided
½ teaspoon ground black pepper, divided
½ cup olive oil, divided
1½ pounds boneless pork roast, cubed
1 large onion, peeled and sliced
8 metal skewers

1. Preheat grill to medium heat.

2. Place the ground coriander and anise seeds in a medium-sized bowl. Add the garlic, paprika, cayenne pepper, ½ teaspoon salt, ¼ teaspoon black pepper, and ¼ cup olive oil; stir until combined. Add the pork and stir to coat. Set aside.

3. In a medium-sized bowl, combine the onions, remaining salt, remaining pepper, and the remaining olive oil. Toss to coat.

4. Divide the pork and onions among 8 skewers. Thread the pork cubes and onions on the skewers, alternating a piece of meat with a slice of onion.

5. Grill the kebabs until well browned and the pork is cooked through, 10–15 minutes. Serve hot.

Per Serving: Calories: 460 | Fat: 31 g | Saturated fat: 5 g | Cholesterol: 105 mg | Sodium: 671 mg | Total carbohydrates: 6 g | Dietary fiber: 2 g | Sugars: 1 g | Protein: 40 g

Southwest Pork Chops

Hands-On Time: 15 minutes
Total Time: 20 minutes
Yield: Serves 6

3 tablespoons olive oil
6 (6-ounce) boneless pork chops
1 teaspoon salt
⅛ teaspoon cayenne pepper
1 tablespoon chili powder
1 medium chipotle chili, minced
2 tablespoons adobo sauce
½ cup salsa
1 (8-ounce) can tomato sauce

1. Place olive oil in large heavy skillet and heat over medium heat.

2. Sprinkle pork chops with salt, cayenne pepper, and chili powder and rub into meat. Add pork chops to skillet and cook for 4 minutes.

3. Meanwhile, combine chipotle chili, adobo sauce, salsa, and tomato sauce in a small bowl.

4. Turn pork chops and cook for 2 minutes. Then add tomato sauce mixture to skillet, bring to a simmer, and simmer for 5 minutes until chops are cooked and tender. Serve immediately.

Per Serving: Calories: 280 | Fat: 17 g | Saturated fat: 4 g | Cholesterol: 65 mg | Sodium: 1,810 mg | Total carbohydrates: 6 g | Dietary fiber: 2 g | Sugars: 3 g | Protein: 25 g

Japanese Fried Pork (Tonkatsu)

Hands-On Time: 25 minutes
Total Time: 25 minutes
Yield: Serves 4

1 cup panko bread crumbs
½ cup all-purpose flour
2 large eggs
2 tablespoons whole milk
4 pork loin pieces, pounded to ½″ thickness
¼ teaspoon kosher salt
¼ teaspoon ground black pepper
½ cup vegetable oil
4 lemon wedges

1. Place bread crumbs in a shallow dish and place flour in another dish. In a small bowl, whisk together eggs and milk.

2. Season pork with salt and pepper. Working in batches, dredge one to two pieces of pork in flour, then egg mixture, and finally bread crumbs to coat, shaking off excess between each step. Repeat with remaining pork.

3. Heat oil in a large wok over medium-high heat. In batches, slide in two pieces of pork and fry until golden brown, approximately 2–3 minutes on each side. Remove meat from pan and drain on plates lined with paper towels. Repeat with remaining pork. Serve with lemon wedges.

Per Serving: Calories: 470 | Fat: 27 g | Saturated fat: 5 g | Cholesterol: 160 mg | Sodium: 220 mg | Total carbohydrates: 25 g | Dietary fiber: 1 g | Sugars: 2 g | Protein: 29 g

Broiled Pork Chops with Dill

Hands-On Time: 10 minutes
Total Time: 20 minutes
Yield: Serves 2

2 (10-ounce, ½"-thick) boneless pork loin chops
⅛ teaspoon seasoned salt
⅛ teaspoon ground black pepper
1 tablespoon olive oil
1 teaspoon chopped dill
⅛ teaspoon garlic powder
1 teaspoon Worcestershire sauce

1. Oil a broiler rack and position about 4" from the heat source. Preheat oven broiler to medium-high.

2. Trim excess fat from the chops and pierce in several places with a fork. Season with salt and pepper. Combine the olive oil, dill weed, garlic powder, and Worcestershire in a medium-sized bowl and mix to combine. Add the chops and turn to coat evenly.

3. Broil the chops for about 4 minutes on each side until cooked through. Transfer to a plate, tent with foil, and let rest for 3–4 minutes. Serve hot with any accumulated juices. Store remaining chop with juices tightly sealed in the refrigerator. Reheat, covered, in a preheated 375°F oven for about 10–14 minutes until warmed throughout.

Per Serving: Calories: 240 | Fat: 16 g | Saturated fat: 3 g | Cholesterol: 70 mg | Sodium: 180 mg | Total carbohydrates: 1 g | Dietary fiber: 0 g | Sugars: 0 g | Protein: 23 g

Indian Pork Fried Rice (Pork Wale Chawal)

Hands-On Time: 20 minutes
Total Time: 20 minutes
Yield: Serves 5

2 tablespoons soy sauce
1 tablespoon white vinegar
1 teaspoon cornstarch
3 tablespoons vegetable oil
1" piece fresh gingerroot, peeled and julienned
2 garlic cloves, minced
¼ pound boneless pork cut into 1" cubes
3 cups cold cooked basmati rice

1. Combine the soy sauce, vinegar, and cornstarch in a small bowl; set aside.

2. In a large nonstick skillet, heat the vegetable oil on high. Add the ginger and garlic and sauté for 1 minute.

3. Add the pork; sauté for 7–8 minutes or until the pork is cooked through.

4. Give the soy sauce mixture a quick stir to recombine it and add it to the pan. Add the cold rice and mix well. Sauté for about 2–3 minutes or until the rice has completely heated through. Serve hot.

Per Serving: Calories: 245 | Fat: 11 g | Saturated fat: 2 g | Cholesterol: 14 mg | Sodium: 412 mg | Total carbohydrates: 29 g | Dietary fiber: 1 g | Sugars: 0 g | Protein: 7 g

Pork Chops with Balsamic Glaze

Hands-On Time: 15 minutes
Total Time: 15 minutes
Yield: Serves 4

4 (5-ounce) center-cut pork
   chops
1 teaspoon salt, divided
¼ teaspoon ground black pepper
2 tablespoons olive oil
½ cup balsamic vinegar
2 teaspoons agave nectar

1. Season pork chops with ½ teaspoon salt and pepper.

2. Heat oil in a large pan over medium-high heat. Cook pork in pan. Turn pork over once to cook, about 3 minutes on each side. Transfer pork to a plate, cover, and set aside.

3. Add vinegar, agave nectar, and remaining salt to the pan. Cook until liquid begins to thicken, about 1–2 minutes.

4. Turn heat down to medium-low; return pork to the pan and coat well with sauce. Cook for 3–4 minutes; a thermometer inserted into pork should read 150°F.

5. Remove pork from the pan, turn heat up to medium, and allow remaining sauce to thicken. Pour sauce over pork chops before serving.

Per Serving: Calories: 270 | Fat: 11 g | Saturated fat: 2.5 g | Cholesterol: 90 mg | Sodium: 680 mg | Total carbohydrates: 9 g | Dietary fiber: 0 g | Sugars: 7 g | Protein: 33 g

Miso-Glazed Pork Belly (pictured)

Hands-On Time: 5 minutes
Total Time: 20 minutes
Yield: Serves 2

2 tablespoons low-sodium soy
   sauce
1 tablespoon miso paste
1 tablespoon honey
1 tablespoon mirin
1 tablespoon water
1 teaspoon sesame oil
2 garlic cloves, minced
1 tablespoon vegetable oil
½ pound pork belly, sliced into ½"
   pieces
1 medium scallion, green part
   only, thinly sliced

1. In a small bowl, whisk together the soy sauce, miso paste, honey, mirin, water, sesame oil, and garlic. Set aside.

2. Heat a large wok over medium heat and add the vegetable oil. Swirl the pan and add the pork belly. Cook for 1–2 minutes on each side until both sides of the pork belly have turned golden brown and some of the fat has rendered out. You may need to use paper towels to blot out excess fat.

3. Pour the soy sauce glaze into the wok and lower the heat to medium-low. Cover and simmer the pork for 6–8 minutes, flipping the pork halfway through.

4. Sprinkle scallions over the pork belly and serve immediately.

Per Serving: Calories: 240 | Fat: 19 g | Saturated fat: 1 g | Cholesterol: 30 mg | Sodium: 420 mg | Total carbohydrates: 8 g | Dietary fiber: 0 g | Sugars: 5 g | Protein: 10 g

Chops with Mint and Garlic

Hands-On Time: 15 minutes
Total Time: 20 minutes
Yield: Serves 4

3 tablespoons minced fresh mint
1 tablespoon minced garlic
2 tablespoons olive oil
1 tablespoon lemon juice
4 (4-ounce) pork chops
⅛ teaspoon salt
⅛ teaspoon white pepper

1. Prepare and preheat grill. In small bowl, combine mint, garlic, olive oil, and lemon juice and mix well.

2. Sprinkle pork chops with salt and pepper. Brush with sauce and place on grill. Grill 6" from medium coals for 5–6 minutes per side until internal temperatures reach 155°F, brushing with mint sauce. Discard any remaining mint sauce. Let chops stand for 5 minutes, then serve.

Per Serving: Calories: 200 | Fat: 11 g | Saturated fat: 2 g | Cholesterol: 55 mg | Sodium: 280 mg | Total carbohydrates: 2 g | Dietary fiber: 0 g | Sugars: 1 g | Protein: 23 g

Venison Medallions with Cranberry Chutney

Hands-On Time: 25 minutes
Total Time: 25 minutes
Yield: Serves 4

1 cup fresh cranberries
1 teaspoon honey
1 teaspoon fresh chopped
    rosemary
2 teaspoons butter, divided
½ teaspoon salt, divided
½ teaspoon ground black pepper,
    divided
8 (2.5-ounce) venison medallions
2 small shallots, minced
1 cup dry red wine
¼ cup cider vinegar
½ cup chicken stock
1 tablespoon red currant jelly

1. In a small nonstick sauté pan, combine the cranberries, honey, rosemary, and 1 teaspoon of the butter. Season with half of salt and pepper. Cook over low heat for about 3–5 minutes until the cranberries just start to pop. Remove from the heat and set aside.

2. Season the venison with remaining salt and pepper. Melt the remaining butter in a large nonstick sauté pan over high heat until very hot. Add the venison and sear for about 2 minutes or until golden brown. Turn over and sear for another 2 minutes. The meat should be medium-rare at this point. Transfer to a warm platter and keep warm.

3. Return the sauté pan to medium heat. Add the shallots and cook for about 2 minutes or until tender. Add the wine, the vinegar, and the stock. Raise the heat to high and cook for about 10 minutes or until the liquid is reduced to about ½ cup. Stir in the jelly.

4. Spoon a small amount of the cranberry sauce on top of each venison medallion. Ladle the sauce on top and around the venison.

Per Serving: Calories: 250 | Fat: 5 g | Saturated fat: 2.5 g | Cholesterol: 125 mg | Sodium: 370 mg | Total carbohydrates: 10 g | Dietary fiber: 1 g | Sugars: 6 g | Protein: 33 g

Seared Venison Steaks with Saffron Butter

Hands-On Time: 15 minutes
Total Time: 25 minutes
Yield: Serves 4

4 (6-ounce) venison steaks
1 teaspoon salt
¼ cup butter
2 tablespoons water
2 tablespoons lemon juice
½ teaspoon crumbled saffron
2 tablespoons olive oil
1 teaspoon fresh thyme leaves

1. Preheat oven to 350°F. Grease a broiler pan with non-stick cooking spray. Season steaks with salt.

2. Put butter, water, lemon juice, and saffron in a microwave-safe liquid measuring cup. Heat on 50 percent in 15-second increments, stirring each time, until butter is melted. Whisk mixture until smooth and creamy.

3. In a large heavy skillet over medium-high heat, heat oil until shimmering. Sear steaks in skillet for about 2 minutes on each side or until well browned. Transfer to prepared broiler pan and put in the center of oven to finish cooking. Internal temperature of venison should be at least 145°F, about 10 minutes.

4. Serve steak with a scoop of saffron butter on top. Sprinkle with thyme leaves.

Per Serving: Calories: 370 | Fat: 22 g | Saturated fat: 10 g | Cholesterol: 175 mg | Sodium: 650 mg | Total carbohydrates: 1 g | Dietary fiber: 0 g | Sugars: 0 g | Protein: 39 g

Stuffed Greek-Style Lamb Patties

Hands-On Time: 15 minutes
Total Time: 15 minutes
Yield: Serves 6

1 pound ground lamb
½ cup dry bread crumbs
2 tablespoons finely chopped onion
2 tablespoons chopped fresh parsley
1 clove garlic, peeled and crushed
1 teaspoon dried mint
¾ cup diced feta cheese

1. Preheat the broiler, lightly grease the rack or spray with cooking oil, and adjust the rack to 5½"–6" from the heating element.

2. Combine all ingredients, except the feta, mixing well. Divide the mixture into 6 portions and shape into 4" balls. Push one-sixth of the feta into the center of each ball and flatten into 4" patties.

3. Place on the rack of broiler pan and broil 4–5 minutes per side, turning once, or to desired doneness.

Per Serving: Calories: 230 | Fat: 14 g | Saturated fat: 7 g | Cholesterol: 65 mg | Sodium: 280 mg | Total carbohydrates: 8 g | Dietary fiber: 1 g | Sugars: 1 g | Protein: 16 g

Souvlaki with Raita (pictured)

Hands-On Time: 15 minutes
Total Time: 15 minutes
Yield: Serves 6

1 teaspoon olive oil
1 pound diced boneless lamb (fat removed)
2 teaspoons ground black pepper
6 skewers
¼ cup chopped fresh oregano
1 cup raita

1. Preheat broiler.

2. Brush the lamb with oil, season with pepper, and thread on 6 skewers. Broil skewers 5–8 minutes, turning often. Transfer skewers to a platter and sprinkle with oregano.

3. Serve skewers with raita on the side.

Per Serving: Calories: 200 | Fat: 14 g | Saturated fat: 3 g | Cholesterol: 90 mg | Sodium: 530 mg | Total carbohydrates: 2 g | Dietary fiber: 0 g | Sugars: 2 g | Protein: 17 g

Mexican-Style Lamb Chops

Hands-On Time: 10 minutes
Total Time: 20 minutes
Yield: Serves 4

2 tablespoons olive oil
1 teaspoon ground cumin
1 teaspoon chili powder
8 (3-ounce) lamb chops
1 cup jarred chimichurri steak sauce

1. Preheat the broiler on high heat. Spray the broiling rack with nonstick cooking spray. In a small bowl, combine the olive oil, ground cumin, and chili powder.

2. Place the lamb chops on the broiling rack and brush with half the olive oil mixture. Place the rack 3″ from the heat source.

3. Broil the lamb chops for 8–10 minutes until they are cooked to the desired level of doneness, turning halfway through and brushing with the remainder of the olive oil mixture.

4. To serve, spoon the chimichurri on the lamb chops.

Per Serving: Calories: 650 | Fat: 51 g | Saturated fat: 20 g | Cholesterol: 117 mg | Sodium: 567 mg | Total carbohydrates: 17 g | Dietary fiber: 0 g | Sugars: 12 g | Protein: 26 g

Grilled Rosemary Lamb Chops

Hands-On Time: 15 minutes
Total Time: 25 minutes
Yield: Serves 4

2 tablespoons olive oil

2 tablespoons minced fresh rosemary

2 cloves garlic, chopped

1½ tablespoons lemon juice

2 teaspoons grated lemon zest

4 (⅓-pound) bone-in lamb chops

½ teaspoon salt

½ teaspoon ground black pepper

1. Preheat grill to 450°F. In a small bowl, make a paste of the first five ingredients. Trim the lamb chops of all fat. Sprinkle the chops with salt and pepper. Brush the paste on both sides of the chops.

2. Grill the chops for 5 minutes per side or to desired doneness. Let the chops rest for 5 minutes before serving.

Per Serving: Calories: 300 | Fat: 19 g | Saturated fat: 8 g | Cholesterol: 75 mg | Sodium: 360 mg | Total carbohydrates: 2 g | Dietary fiber: 0 g | Sugars: 0 g | Protein: 22 g

Spicy Moroccan Lamb Stew

Hands-On Time: 20 minutes
Total Time: 30 minutes
Yield: Serves 4

2 tablespoons extra-virgin olive oil

½ medium onion, peeled and chopped

1 medium carrot, peeled and chopped

½ large parsnip, peeled and chopped

¼ cup chopped fresh parsley

1 teaspoon salt

½ teaspoon ground black pepper

4 medium-sized lamb chops

1 (14.5-ounce) can diced tomatoes with juice

1 (19-ounce) can chickpeas, drained and rinsed

3 tablespoons spicy harissa

1 tablespoon Moroccan spice

1. Heat the olive oil in a large Dutch oven over medium-high heat. Add the onion, carrot, parsnip, parsley, salt, and pepper. Cook 4–6 minutes or until softened. Add the lamb chops and cook until browned on both sides, about 5 minutes. Add the tomatoes, chickpeas, harissa, and Moroccan spice.

2. Reduce to low and simmer until most of the liquid has evaporated, about 10 minutes. Serve hot.

Per Serving: Calories: 500 | Fat: 28 g | Saturated fat: 9 g | Cholesterol: 90 mg | Sodium: 1,320 mg | Total carbohydrates: 30 g | Dietary fiber: 9 g | Sugars: 5 g | Protein: 31 g

Curried Lamb with Wild Rice

Hands-On Time: 25 minutes
Total Time: 25 minutes
Yield: Serves 4

2 tablespoons vegetable oil

1 pound lean boneless lamb, cut into ½" cubes

2 garlic cloves, crushed

½ medium onion, peeled and chopped

¼ teaspoon red pepper flakes

2 teaspoons curry powder

1 medium tomato, thinly sliced

¼ cup beef broth

1 tablespoon chopped cilantro leaves

1 tablespoon tomato paste

¼ teaspoon salt

¼ teaspoon ground black pepper

2 cups cooked wild rice

1. Heat the oil in a large skillet over medium-high heat. Add the lamb. Let the meat brown for 5–7 minutes, then turn down the heat to medium and cook, stirring, for 4–5 minutes, until the meat loses its pinkness. Remove the lamb from the pan.

2. Add the garlic, onion, red pepper flakes, and curry powder. Sauté for 2–3 minutes until the onion begins to soften. Add the tomato slices. Cook for 3 minutes, pressing down on the tomato so that it releases its juices. Add the beef broth and cilantro. Stir in the tomato paste. Return the lamb to the pan.

3. Cook, stirring, for another 5 minutes to mix everything together. Season with salt and pepper. Serve hot over the cooked rice.

Per Serving: Calories: 329 | Fat: 15 g | Saturated fat: 3 g | Cholesterol: 66 mg | Sodium: 291 mg | Total carbohydrates: 22 g | Dietary fiber: 3 g | Sugars: 3 g | Protein: 27 g

Grilled Rack of Lamb

Hands-On Time: 10 minutes
Total Time: 30 minutes
Yield: Serves 10

1 (5-pound) rack of lamb

½ bulb garlic, minced

2 tablespoons olive oil

½ teaspoon ground black pepper

1 teaspoon coarse salt

1. "French" the ends of the lamb rack by cutting away suet, fat, etc., from the bone ends just past the "center" chop area. Scrape the bones clean and cover the bare bones with foil. Preheat the grill.

2. In a small bowl, mix together the garlic, oil, pepper, and salt.

3. Thoroughly rub the lamb with the prepared garlic oil.

4. Grill the lamb on all sides to desired doneness (anywhere from 10–20 minutes) and serve.

Per Serving: Calories: 520 | Fat: 25 g | Saturated fat: 10 g | Cholesterol: 265 mg | Sodium: 370 mg | Total carbohydrates: 0 g | Dietary fiber: 0 g | Sugars: 0 g | Protein: 73 g

Chapter 10

Fish and Seafood Main Dishes

Beer-Battered Fish

Hands-On Time: 20 minutes
Total Time: 20 minutes
Yield: Serves 4

2 cups vegetable oil
1 cup McCormick Golden Dipt
    Beer Batter Seafood Batter
    mix
⅔ cup beer
1½ pounds cod fillets

1. Pour oil into a deep fryer or large heavy skillet. Heat oil to 375°F.

2. In a medium bowl, stir batter mix and beer until smooth. Cut fish into serving-sized pieces. Dip fish into batter and set on a wire rack.

3. Carefully add the fish three pieces at a time into the hot oil. Cook 3–5 minutes, turning once to brown evenly. Drain on paper towels and serve hot.

Per Serving: Calories: 280 | Fat: 7 g | Saturated fat: 0.5 g | Cholesterol: 75 mg | Sodium: 770 mg | Total carbohydrates: 18 g | Dietary fiber: 0 g | Sugars: 0 g | Protein: 32 g

Baked Sole

Hands-On Time: 10 minutes
Total Time: 30 minutes
Yield: Serves 4

¾ cup bread crumbs
1 tablespoon fresh dill
1 large egg, beaten
¼ cup skim milk
½ teaspoon salt
4 (4-ounce) sole fillets

1. Preheat oven to 400°F.

2. Mix bread crumbs with dill in a shallow bowl. Combine eggs, milk, and salt in second shallow bowl.

3. Dip each sole fillet in the egg mixture and then roll in bread crumbs. Place breaded sole on a baking sheet and bake for 20 minutes or until fish flakes.

Per Serving: Calories: 130 | Fat: 3.5 g | Saturated fat: 1 g | Cholesterol: 100 mg | Sodium: 690 mg | Total carbohydrates: 5 g | Dietary fiber: 0 g | Sugars: 1 g | Protein: 17 g

Shrimp Scampi

Hands-On Time: 10 minutes
Total Time: 10 minutes
Yield: Serves 10

1 pound medium fresh, uncooked
     shrimp
2 tablespoons olive oil
1 teaspoon ground black pepper
3 cloves garlic, peeled and
     minced
3 tablespoons lemon juice
½ cup dry white wine
½ cup fish stock
¼ cup cold unsalted butter
½ cup chopped parsley

1. Peel and devein the shrimp (leave the tails intact).

2. Heat the oil over medium heat in a large sauté pan. Season the shrimp with pepper and add to the hot oil. Sauté for 1 minute, stirring constantly.

3. Add the garlic, then lemon juice and wine, stirring constantly. Sauté for 1 minute, then add the stock. Cook for 3 minutes.

4. Add the cold butter, stir until melted, and remove from heat. Sprinkle with the parsley and serve.

Per Serving: Calories: 210 | Fat: 19 g | Saturated fat: 8 g | Cholesterol: 40 mg | Sodium: 95 mg | Total carbohydrates: 3 g | Dietary fiber: 0 g | Sugars: 1 g | Protein: 2 g

Stovetop-Poached Fresh Cod

Hands-On Time: 10 minutes
Total Time: 25 minutes
Yield: Serves 6

3 medium celery stalks
½ medium bunch fresh parsley
     stems
1½ pounds fresh cod, cut into
     4-ounce portions
1 bay leaf
2 cups fish stock
1 tablespoon lemon juice
¼ teaspoon ground black pepper
½ teaspoon kosher salt

1. Roughly chop the celery and parsley. Place the celery and parsley in the bottom of a large sauté pan and arrange the cod pieces on top. Add the bay leaf, stock, and lemon juice, and place over medium-high heat. Cover with parchment paper or a loose-fitting lid.

2. Bring to a simmer and cook covered until the fish flakes, approximately 15–20 minutes, depending on the thickness of the fish. Remove from heat and season with pepper and salt. Serve with poaching liquid.

Per Serving: Calories: 100 | Fat: 1 g | Saturated fat: 0 g | Cholesterol: 50 mg | Sodium: 550 mg | Total carbohydrates: 1 g | Dietary fiber: 0 g | Sugars: 0 g | Protein: 20 g

Oven-Fried Fish (pictured)

Hands-On Time: 10 minutes
Total Time: 25 minutes
Yield: Serves 4

1 large egg
½ teaspoon salt
½ teaspoon ground black pepper
2 tablespoons all-purpose flour
1 cup corn bread crumbs
½ teaspoon dried thyme
4 (4-ounce) cod fillets
1 tablespoon olive oil

1. Preheat oven to 425°F.
2. Beat the egg, salt, and pepper in a shallow bowl. Place flour in another shallow bowl. In a third small bowl, combine corn bread crumbs with thyme.
3. Dredge both sides of the fish in flour. Dip fillets in beaten egg mixture and then corn bread mixture.
4. Place coated fish on baking pan and drizzle olive oil over each piece.
5. Bake for 15 minutes or until fillets are crisp and golden.

Per Serving: Calories: 230 | Fat: 7 g | Saturated fat: 1.5 g | Cholesterol: 110 mg | Sodium: 650 mg | Total carbohydrates: 18 g | Dietary fiber: 0 g | Sugars: 0 g | Protein: 24 g

Crispy Potato Chip and Cheese Baked Shrimp

Hands-On Time: 10 minutes
Total Time: 30 minutes
Yield: Serves 4

Nonstick cooking spray
3 cloves garlic, minced
2 tablespoons extra-virgin olive oil
⅔ cup crushed gluten-free kettle-style potato chips
¼ cup gluten-free chicken broth
½ teaspoon crushed red pepper
½ teaspoon chili powder
½ teaspoon salt
½ teaspoon ground black pepper
1 pound large uncooked shrimp, peeled and deveined
⅓ cup shredded part-skim mozzarella cheese
2 cups baby arugula

1. Preheat oven to 375°F. Grease a large oven-safe skillet with gluten-free nonstick cooking spray.
2. In a medium bowl, mix the garlic, olive oil, kettle chips, broth, crushed red pepper, chili powder, salt, and pepper.
3. Lay shrimp in the bottom of the prepared skillet. Press the potato chip mixture over the top of the shrimp with a spatula. Sprinkle with cheese.
4. Bake for at least 20 minutes or until cheese is melted and the shrimp is pink. Remove from oven and serve over arugula.

Per Serving: Calories: 230 | Fat: 13 g | Saturated fat: 2.5 g | Cholesterol: 150 mg | Sodium: 1,050 mg | Total carbohydrates: 9 g | Dietary fiber: 0 g | Sugars: 1 g | Protein: 20 g

Breaded Fish

Hands-On Time: 15 minutes
Total Time: 30 minutes
Yield: Serves 6

4 (1-ounce) slices French bread
2 teaspoons herbes de Provence
¼ teaspoon ground black pepper
2 large lemons
1½ pounds halibut fillets
Spectrum Naturals Canola Spray
   Oil with Butter Flavor

1. Preheat the oven to 375°F. Treat a large baking dish with nonstick spray.

2. Add the bread, herbes de Provence, and pepper to the bowl of a food processor or a blender; process to mix and create bread crumbs. Set aside.

3. Cut 1 lemon into thin slices. Arrange the slices in the bottom of the prepared dish. Grate the zest from the second lemon, then cut it in half and squeeze the juice into a shallow dish. Combine the grated zest with the prepared bread crumbs; set aside.

4. Dip the fish pieces in the lemon juice and set them on the lemon slices in the baking dish. Sprinkle the bread crumb mixture evenly over the fish pieces. Lightly mist the bread crumbs with the spray oil. Bake until the crumbs are lightly browned and the fish is opaque, about 10–15 minutes. Serve immediately.

Per Serving: Calories: 160 | Fat: 2 g | Saturated fat: 0 g | Cholesterol: 55 mg | Sodium: 190 mg | Total carbohydrates: 11 g | Dietary fiber: 0 g | Sugars: 1 g | Protein: 23 g

Grilled Shrimp with Asian Seasonings

Hands-On Time: 15 minutes
Total Time: 15 minutes
Yield: Serves 4

2 tablespoons soy sauce
1 tablespoon grated ginger
1 tablespoon toasted sesame oil
1 teaspoon Splenda
Juice of 1 lime
1 tablespoon dry English mustard
16 jumbo raw, fresh shrimp,
   peeled
Extra lime wedges for serving

1. In a medium bowl, mix the first six ingredients together and coat the shrimp. Set grill on high.

2. Grill the shrimp for 2 minutes per side. Serve with extra lime wedges.

Per Serving: Calories: 60 | Fat: 1 g | Saturated fat: 0.5 g | Cholesterol: 95 mg | Sodium: 470 mg | Total carbohydrates: 1 g | Dietary fiber: 0 g | Sugars: 0 g | Protein: 10 g

Cilantro Citrus Caribbean Mahi-Mahi

Hands-On Time: 10 minutes
Total Time: 20 minutes
Yield: Serves 6

1 tablespoon olive oil
1 clove garlic, peeled and minced
½ teaspoon all-purpose seasoning
½ cup sliced yellow onions
½ cup chopped cilantro
2 teaspoons chopped parsley
¼ cup freshly squeezed orange juice
¼ cup freshly squeezed lemon juice
½ teaspoon ground cumin
6 (5-ounce) mahi-mahi fillets
1 medium lemon, cut in wedges

1. Combine oil, garlic, seasoning, onions, cilantro, parsley, orange juice, lemon juice, and cumin in a shallow dish. Add fish fillets and turn to coat.

2. Spray a large skillet with nonstick spray and heat over medium heat. Add fish mixture and lemon wedges to skillet.

3. Cover and cook for 10–12 minutes or until fish flakes easily.

Per Serving: Calories: 150 | Fat: 3 g | Saturated fat: 0.5 g | Cholesterol: 105 mg | Sodium: 125 mg | Total carbohydrates: 3 g | Dietary fiber: 0 g | Sugars: 2 g | Protein: 27 g

Fish Cakes

Hands-On Time: 20 minutes
Total Time: 20 minutes
Yield: Serves 6

1 pound boneless cod fillets
2 tablespoons chopped parsley
1 teaspoon chopped dill
1 large leek, trimmed and chopped
1 teaspoon ground white pepper
1 large egg
1 tablespoon avocado oil

1. Place cod in a food processor and pulse until finely chopped. Add parsley, dill, leeks and pepper and pulse 2 or 3 times. Transfer mixture to a medium bowl.

2. Beat egg in a small bowl, then stir into fish mixture. Form the mixture into 6 patties.

3. Heat the oil in a large skillet over medium-high heat. Fry the fish cakes for 4–6 minutes on each side. Drain on paper towels.

Per Serving: Calories: 100 | Fat: 3.5 g | Saturated fat: 0.5 g | Cholesterol: 65 mg | Sodium: 60 mg | Total carbohydrates: 3 g | Dietary fiber: 0 g | Sugars: 1 g | Protein: 15 g

Orange-Glazed Fish Fillets (pictured)

Hands-On Time: 5 minutes
Total Time: 15 minutes
Yield: Serves 4

2 tablespoons olive oil
2 tablespoons orange juice
1 tablespoon Worcestershire sauce
2 teaspoons chopped fresh cilantro
½ teaspoon paprika
1½ pounds red snapper fillets

1. Spray a rack with nonstick cooking spray.
2. In a small bowl, whisk together the olive oil, orange juice, Worcestershire sauce, cilantro, and paprika. Brush the olive oil mixture over the fish fillets.
3. Broil the fish for 4 minutes. Turn over, brush the other side with the olive oil mixture and broil for another 4–5 minutes, until the fish is cooked through. (Be sure not to overcook the fish.)

Per Serving: Calories: 216 | Fat: 6 g | Saturated fat: 1 g | Cholesterol: 67 mg | Sodium: 126 mg | Total carbohydrates: 1 g | Dietary fiber: 0 g | Sugars: 1 g | Protein: 37 g

Mahi-Mahi Tacos with Avocado and Fresh Cabbage

Hands-On Time: 15 minutes
Total Time: 30 minutes
Yield: Serves 4

1 pound mahi-mah fillets
½ teaspoon salt
½ teaspoon ground black pepper
1 teaspoon paprika
1 teaspoon olive oil
1 medium avocado
4 (6") corn tortillas
2 cups shredded cabbage
2 limes, quartered

1. Season the fish with salt, pepper, and paprika. Heat the oil in a large frying pan on medium. Once the oil is hot, sauté the fish for about 3–4 minutes on each side.
2. Slice the avocado in half. Remove the pit and, using a spoon, remove the flesh from the skin. Slice the avocado halves into ½"-thick slices.
3. In a small pan, warm the corn tortillas and cook for about 1 minute on each side.
4. Place one-fourth of the mahi-mahi on each tortilla; top with the avocado and cabbage. Serve with lime wedges.

Per Serving: Calories: 230 | Fat: 8 g | Saturated fat: 1 g | Cholesterol: 85 mg | Sodium: 410 mg | Total carbohydrates: 17 g | Dietary fiber: 5 g | Sugars: 2 g | Protein: 24 g

Shrimp Creole

Hands-On Time: 10 minutes
Total Time: 25 minutes
Yield: Serves 6

2 teaspoons canola oil

1 medium onion, peeled and finely diced

1 medium bell pepper, seeded finely diced

2 medium stalks celery, finely diced

3 cloves garlic, minced

2 (15-ounce) cans no-salt-added diced tomatoes

1 (8-ounce) can no-salt-added tomato sauce

⅓ cup white wine

½ teaspoon apple cider vinegar

2 bay leaves

2 teaspoons salt-free chili seasoning

1 teaspoon ground sweet paprika

½ teaspoon ground black pepper

⅛ teaspoon ground cayenne pepper

1 pound frozen, raw shrimp, peeled and tails removed

1. Heat oil in a large sauté pan over medium heat. Add the onion, bell pepper, celery, and garlic and cook, stirring, for 5 minutes.

2. Add the remaining ingredients except shrimp and stir well to combine. Simmer for 10 minutes, stirring frequently. Cover and reduce heat to medium-low if sauce begins to splatter.

3. Stir in the shrimp and simmer for 5 minutes.

4. Remove from heat and remove bay leaves from pan. Serve immediately.

Per Serving: Calories: 131 | Fat: 2 g | Saturated fat: 0 g | Cholesterol: 122 mg | Sodium: 176 mg | Total carbohydrates: 9 g | Dietary fiber: 3 g | Sugars: 5 g | Protein: 17 g

Seared Ahi Tuna Steaks

Hands-On Time: 5 minutes
Total Time: 10 minutes
Yield: Serves 2

2 (6-ounce) tuna steaks
2 teaspoons kosher salt
2 teaspoons ground black pepper
3 tablespoons olive oil
1 medium lemon, cut into 4
    wedges

1. Season the tuna steaks evenly with the salt and pepper. In a medium pan, heat the oil over medium heat.

2. Place the tuna steaks in the hot oil and sear for 1½ minutes on each side.

3. Make sure that every corner has been seared. This will give you a rare temperature. Cook for another minute on each side for medium-rare.

4. Serve immediately and squeeze lemon juice (from wedges) on steaks.

Per Serving: Calories: 210 | Fat: 4 g | Saturated fat: 0 g | Cholesterol: 75 mg | Sodium: 2,390 mg | Total carbohydrates: 2 g | Dietary fiber: 1 g | Sugars: 1 g | Protein: 39 g

Red Snapper with Peppers

Hands-On Time: 20 minutes
Total Time: 30 minutes
Yield: Serves 10

5 small red snapper fillets
2 sprigs fresh thyme
¼ cup barley flour
2 tablespoons olive oil
1 medium red bell pepper, seeded
    and finely sliced
1 medium green bell pepper,
    seeded and finely sliced
2 medium carrots, peeled and cut
    into matchsticks
1 medium onion, peeled and finely
    sliced
3 cloves garlic, finely sliced
½ teaspoon ground black pepper
¼ cup wine vinegar

1. Gently clean the fish in ice-cold water and pat dry with paper towels. Remove the leaves from the sprigs of thyme and discard the stems.

2. Lightly flour the fillets. Heat the oil over medium heat in a large sauté pan. Add the fish, sauté for 2 minutes, and turn. Add the peppers, carrots, onion, garlic, thyme leaves, black pepper, and vinegar.

3. Cover and cook for 5–10 minutes until the fish is flaky and the peppers are lightly cooked. Serve immediately.

Per Serving: Calories: 170 | Fat: 4.5 g | Saturated fat: 0.5 g | Cholesterol: 40 mg | Sodium: 80 mg | Total carbohydrates: 7 g | Dietary fiber: 1 g | Sugars: 2 g | Protein: 23 g

Oven-Fried Shrimp (pictured)

Hands-On Time: 15 minutes
Total Time: 25 minutes
Yield: Serves 4

1 cup unsweetened coconut flakes
2 large eggs
2 cups ice-cold water
2 cups rice flour
1 pound (about 24) large frozen, raw shrimp, peeled, deveined, tail on

1. Preheat the oven to 450°F. Spray a baking sheet with nonstick cooking spray. Place the coconut flakes in a small bowl.

2. In a medium bowl, beat the eggs and then stir in the ice water.

3. Add the flour to the eggs and stir until the batter has a runny consistency similar to pancake batter. Add more flour or ice water if needed.

4. Use your fingers to coat each shrimp in the batter. Dip each shrimp into the coconut, holding it by the tail, and then lay it on the baking sheet. Continue with the remainder of the shrimp.

5. Bake the shrimp until it is golden brown on the bottom (4–5 minutes). Turn over and cook the other side for about 5 minutes until done. Serve immediately.

Per Serving: Calories: 400 | Fat: 10 g | Saturated fat: 7 g | Cholesterol: 90 mg | Sodium: 40 mg | Total carbohydrates: 67 g | Dietary fiber: 4 g | Sugars: 1 g | Protein: 9 g

Jumbo Sweet and Spicy Shrimp Skewers

Hands-On Time: 10 minutes
Total Time: 45 minutes
Yield: Serves 2

2 tablespoons honey
1 tablespoon hot sauce
1 tablespoon lemon juice
1 teaspoon fresh thyme leaves
12 jumbo fresh, raw shrimp, peeled, deveined, tail on
1 shallot, quartered
2 medium white asparagus spears, trimmed and cut in 3" pieces
2 wooden skewers
3 tablespoons peanut oil
⅛ teaspoon salt
⅛ teaspoon ground black pepper

1. In a large pot or bowl, combine honey, hot sauce, lemon juice, and thyme leaves. Add shrimp and cover. Refrigerate for 30 minutes. Remove shrimp from marinade and pat dry.

2. Preheat grill or broiler on high. Thread wooden skewers with six shrimp each, alternating with half of the shallot and asparagus pieces. Rub with the oil and season with salt and pepper.

3. Grill or broil skewers for about 2 minutes per side.

4. Brush the honey marinade over the shrimp. Cook for 1 minute on each side. Serve hot.

Per Serving: Calories: 200 | Fat: 7 g | Saturated fat: 1 g | Cholesterol: 90 mg | Sodium: 360 mg | Total carbohydrates: 24 g | Dietary fiber: 2 g | Sugars: 17 g | Protein: 16 g

Mediterranean-Style Shrimp

Hands-On Time: 10 minutes
Total Time: 25 minutes
Yield: Serves 6

1 clove fresh garlic, minced
½ teaspoon all-purpose seasoning
¼ cup freshly squeezed lemon
    juice
1 teaspoon thyme
2 tablespoons capers
½ teaspoon olive oil
½ cup chopped white onions
1½ pounds frozen, raw shrimp,
    peeled and deveined
2 cups marinara sauce
4 cups cooked spaghetti squash

1. Coat a large skillet with nonstick spray. Add all ingredients except marinara and spaghetti squash to skillet. Sauté on medium heat for 7 minutes, stirring often.

2. Add marinara sauce to skillet and simmer for 8 minutes, stirring often. Serve over spaghetti squash.

Per Serving: Calories: 170 | Fat: 4 g | Saturated fat: 0.5 g | Cholesterol: 140 mg | Sodium: 590 mg | Total carbohydrates: 13 g | Dietary fiber: 3 g | Sugars: 6 g | Protein: 20 g

Crisp Mustard Broiled Fish

Hands-On Time: 15 minutes
Total Time: 25 minutes
Yield: Serves 6

1½ pounds mild white fish fillets
½ teaspoon salt
⅛ teaspoon ground black pepper
½ cup minced onion
2 cloves minced garlic
1 tablespoon olive oil
¼ cup Dijon mustard
2 cups soft fresh bread crumbs
2 teaspoons dried parsley flakes
½ teaspoon dried oregano

1. Preheat broiler. Place fish on sprayed broiler pan and sprinkle with salt and pepper; set aside. In small pan, cook onion and garlic in olive oil over medium-high heat until tender.

2. Remove from heat and stir in mustard. On plate, combine bread crumbs, parsley, and oregano.

3. Broil fish for 3 minutes on one side, then carefully turn with spatula. Spread with mustard mixture and sprinkle with bread crumb mixture to heavily coat.

4. Return to broiler and broil other side for 5–6 minutes, watching carefully, until bread crumb topping is crisp and browned. Serve immediately.

Per Serving: Calories: 198 | Fat: 5 g | Saturated fat: 1.5 g | Cholesterol: 55 mg | Sodium: 590 mg | Total carbohydrates: 9 g | Dietary fiber: 1 g | Sugars: 1 g | Protein: 26 g

Orange Teriyaki Salmon

Hands-On Time: 10 minutes
Total Time: 25 minutes
Yield: Serves 6

2 tablespoons soy sauce

1 clove garlic, peeled and minced

½ teaspoon all-purpose sodium-free seasoning

1 tablespoon agave syrup

1 tablespoon rice vinegar

3 tablespoons fresh orange juice

½ cup sliced green onions

6 (4-ounce) salmon fillets

1 small orange, cut into very thin slices

1. Preheat oven to 350°F.

2. Mix all ingredients except salmon fillets and orange slices in a medium bowl.

3. Spray a 9″ x 13″ baking dish with nonstick spray. Place salmon in the dish. Pour mixture over the fish and top with orange slices.

4. Cover with foil; bake 15 minutes or until fish flakes easily.

Per Serving: Calories: 200 | Fat: 6 g | Saturated fat: 1 g | Cholesterol: 60 mg | Sodium: 446 mg | Total carbohydrates: 8 g | Dietary fiber: 1 g | Sugars: 6 g | Protein: 28 g

Jambalaya Stir-Fry

Hands-On Time: 20 minutes
Total Time: 20 minutes
Yield: Serves 4

2 tablespoons olive oil, divided

1 garlic clove, finely chopped

½ medium onion, finely chopped

1 medium red bell pepper, seeded and thinly sliced

2 cups fresh, cooked shrimp

1½ cups cooked rice

⅛ teaspoon salt

⅛ teaspoon ground black pepper

¼ teaspoon Tabasco sauce

1 cup canned chopped tomatoes with juice

1 teaspoon chopped fresh thyme leaves

1. Heat 2 tablespoon oil in a large, heavy skillet or wok over medium-high heat. Add the garlic and onion. Stir-fry for about 2 minutes, until the onion begins to soften. Add the red bell pepper. Stir-fry for 1 minute, until tender. Add the cooked shrimp. Cook for 1 minute. Stir in the cooked rice, stirring until it begins to turn light brown. Stir the salt, pepper, and Tabasco sauce into the rice. Add the tomatoes with juice and thyme leaves to the rice. Bring to a boil.

2. Add the shrimp and vegetables. Cook for another minute, stirring to mix everything together. Serve hot.

Per Serving: Calories: 278 | Fat: 7 g | Saturated fat: 1 g | Cholesterol: 214 mg | Sodium: 333 mg | Total carbohydrates: 23 g | Dietary fiber: 2 g | Sugars: 4 g | Protein: 30 g

Risotto with Mixed Seafood

Hands-On Time: 25 minutes
Total Time: 25 minutes
Yield: Serves 6

2 cups water
2½ cups low-sodium chicken broth
2 tablespoons olive oil
1 medium onion, peeled and minced
3 cloves garlic, minced
1½ cups Arborio rice
1 cup chopped celery
1 tablespoon fresh dill weed
¼ cup dry white wine
½ pound sole fillets, chopped
¼ pound small frozen, raw shrimp
½ pound frozen bay scallops
¼ cup grated Parmesan cheese
1 tablespoon butter
¼ cup minced fresh chives

1. In medium saucepan, combine water and broth and heat over low heat. Keep mixture on heat.

2. In large saucepan, heat olive oil over medium heat. Add onion and garlic; cook and stir until crisp-tender, about 3 minutes. Add rice; cook and stir for 3 minutes.

3. Start adding broth mixture a cup at a time to the rice mixture, stirring frequently, adding liquid when previous addition is absorbed. When only 1 cup of broth remains to be added, stir in celery, dill, wine, fish fillets, shrimp, and scallops to rice mixture. Add last cup of broth.

4. Cook, stirring constantly, for 5–7 minutes or until fish is cooked and rice is tender and creamy. Stir in Parmesan, butter, and chives; stir and serve.

Per Serving: Calories: 340 | Fat: 9 g | Saturated fat: 3 g | Cholesterol: 60 mg | Sodium: 380 mg | Total carbohydrates: 41 g | Dietary fiber: 1 g | Sugars: 2 g | Protein: 24 g

Grilled Swordfish with Pineapple Salsa

Hands-On Time: 15 minutes
Total Time: 15 minutes
Yield: Serves 4

½ whole pineapple, cut into small chunks

2 tablespoons finely chopped cilantro

2 medium limes, juiced and zested

1 medium orange, juiced and zested

1 shallot, finely chopped

1 red chili pepper, finely chopped

¼ teaspoon kosher salt

½ teaspoon ground black pepper

4 (3.5-ounce, 1"-thick) swordfish steaks

2 tablespoons olive oil

1. In a medium bowl, combine pineapple, cilantro, lime and orange juice and zest, shallot, and chili pepper; set aside.

2. Set a gas grill to medium-high or heat a cast-iron grill pan over medium-high heat. Mix salt and pepper together in a small bowl.

3. Brush swordfish with oil and sprinkle with salt and pepper. Grill fish 5 minutes on one side and 3 minutes on other side. Transfer swordfish to plates; top with pineapple salsa.

Per Serving: Calories: 260 | Fat: 13 g | Saturated fat: 2.5 g | Cholesterol: 55 mg | Sodium: 220 mg | Total carbohydrates: 19 g | Dietary fiber: 2 g | Sugars: 13 g | Protein: 18 g

Shrimp Spring Roll Bowl (pictured)

Hands-On Time: 10 minutes
Total Time: 10 minutes
Yield: Serves 2

3 tablespoons natural peanut
  butter

2 tablespoons warm water

1½ tablespoons coconut aminos

1 tablespoon lime juice

½ tablespoon grated fresh ginger

1½ cups shredded red cabbage

1 large carrot, julienned

1 medium cucumber, julienned

½ pound extra-large fresh, cooked
  shrimp

2 tablespoons chopped peanuts

¼ cup chopped cilantro leaves

2 tablespoons chopped mint
  leaves

1. In a small bowl, whisk together the peanut butter, warm water, aminos, lime juice, and ginger. Add more water, 1 teaspoon at a time, if you prefer a thinner sauce. Set sauce aside.

2. Divide the cabbage between two bowls and top with carrots and cucumbers. Arrange the shrimp on top of the vegetables. Sprinkle with peanuts, cilantro, and mint.

3. Drizzle the peanut sauce over the top and serve.

Per Serving: Calories: 410 | Fat: 19 g | Saturated fat: 2.5 g | Cholesterol: 230 mg | Sodium: 650 mg | Total carbohydrates: 20 g | Dietary fiber: 6 g | Sugars: 10 g | Protein: 38 g

Grilled Tuna

Hands-On Time: 10 minutes
Total Time: 10 minutes
Yield: Serves 4

4 ahi tuna steaks

2 tablespoons olive oil

¼ teaspoon salt

¼ teaspoon ground black pepper

1 cup black bean and tomato
  salsa

1. Brush tuna steaks with oil. Season with salt and pepper.

2. Grill on both sides over medium heat for about 7 minutes total.

3. Serve with salsa on top.

Per Serving: Calories: 207 | Fat: 7 g | Saturated fat: 1 g | Cholesterol: 55 mg | Sodium: 210 mg | Total carbohydrates: 0 g | Dietary fiber: 0 g | Sugars: 0 g | Protein: 33 g

Seared Snapper with Vegetables and Cream Sauce

Hands-On Time: 20 minutes
Total Time: 20 minutes
Yield: Serves 4

4 (6-ounce) grouper fillets, cleaned and dried
½ teaspoon salt
¼ teaspoon ground black pepper
1 teaspoon dried lemon zest
1 tablespoon olive oil
1 tablespoon butter
2 large carrots, peeled and cut into long strips
2 medium parsnips, peeled and cut into long strips
1 medium green bell pepper, seeded and sliced
1 pound baby spinach
½ teaspoon chopped red chili pepper
½ cup white wine
½ teaspoon chopped fresh thyme
¼ cup cream

1. Season fish fillets with salt, pepper, and lemon zest.
2. Heat oil in a large skillet over medium-high heat until shimmering. Add fillets and cook for about 2 minutes until browned. Turn fish. Add butter, carrots, parsnips, green bell pepper, spinach, chili pepper, wine, and thyme to the skillet. Reduce to medium-low, cover, and cook for 3 minutes or until fish flakes easily with a fork and vegetables are tender.
3. Remove fish and vegetables to a warm platter. Stir cream into skillet and cook until sauce is smooth and creamy. Serve vegetables and fish with sauce.

Per Serving: Calories: 385 | Fat: 14 g | Saturated fat: 6 g | Cholesterol: 90 mg | Sodium: 510 mg | Total carbohydrates: 24 g | Dietary fiber: 7 g | Sugars: 7 g | Protein: 38 g

Pan-Fried Tilapia

Hands-On Time: 15 minutes
Total Time: 15 minutes
Yield: Serves 4

3 tablespoons olive oil
1 cup all-purpose flour
⅛ teaspoon garlic powder
⅛ teaspoon salt
⅛ teaspoon ground black pepper
2 large eggs, beaten
4 tilapia fillets

1. Heat oil in large skillet over low heat.
2. In a small bowl, mix flour with garlic powder, salt, and pepper. Add beaten eggs to another small dish. Dip each fish fillet in egg, and then flour mixture.
3. Pan-fry until golden brown, 5–6 minutes on each side, turning once. Serve hot.

Per Serving: Calories: 340 | Fat: 15 g | Saturated fat: 3 g | Cholesterol: 140 mg | Sodium: 160 mg | Total carbohydrates: 24 g | Dietary fiber: 1 g | Sugars: 0 g | Protein: 28 g

Fish in Red Sauce

Hands-On Time: 20 minutes
Total Time: 20 minutes
Yield: Serves 6

8 ounces pimientos, cut into ¼"
   pieces

3 large tomatoes, cut into ¼"
   pieces

½ teaspoon salt

½ teaspoon ground black pepper

1 (28-ounce) can tomato purée

2 medium stalks celery, minced

2 garlic cloves, peeled and
   minced

¼ cup water

3 tablespoons fresh lemon juice

6 (3-ounce) cod fillets

1 teaspoon white granulated
   sugar

2 teaspoons fresh thyme leaves

1. In a large saucepan, combine the pimientos, tomatoes, salt, pepper, and tomato purée. Bring to a boil. Add the celery and garlic. Cook for 3 minutes.

2. Stir in the water and lemon juice. Place the fish into the pan without stirring. Baste the fish with the liquid. Sprinkle the sugar on top of the fish but do not stir. Continue basting periodically.

3. When the fish is opaque and cooked through, remove from heat. Top with sauce and sprinkle with thyme to serve.

Per Serving: Calories: 146 | Fat: 1 g | Saturated fat: 0 g | Cholesterol: 39 mg | Sodium: 346 mg | Total carbohydrates: 20 g | Dietary fiber: 5 g | Sugars: 11 g | Protein: 19 g

Sheet Pan Herb-Crusted Cod

Hands-On Time: 10 minutes
Total Time: 25 minutes
Yield: Serves 4

2 tablespoons olive oil, divided
½ medium red onion, peeled and
   minced
1 clove garlic, peeled and minced
1 teaspoon salt, divided
1 teaspoon ground black pepper,
   divided
1 tablespoon red wine vinegar
½ cup crushed melba toasts
2 teaspoons chopped fresh basil
16 ounces cod fillets
½ cup white wine
1 pound fresh asparagus

1. Preheat oven to 400°F. Line a large baking sheet with aluminum foil and spray lightly with nonstick cooking spray.

2. Heat 1 tablespoon oil in a small skillet over medium-high heat. Sauté onion and garlic until softened, about 5 minutes. Add ½ teaspoon salt, ½ teaspoon pepper, and vinegar. Mix to combine and transfer to one side of the prepared baking sheet.

3. Combine toast crumbs, basil, 1 tablespoon oil, ½ teaspoon salt, and ½ teaspoon pepper. Mix thoroughly. Coat the fish on both sides with the toast mixture. Place fish on top of the onion mixture and add wine without pouring over the coating.

4. Place asparagus on the other end of the baking sheet.

5. Bake for 15–20 minutes or until the fish flakes easily and asparagus is tender.

Per Serving: Calories: 211 | Fat: 7 g | Saturated fat: 1 g | Cholesterol: 48 mg | Sodium: 664 mg | Total carbohydrates: 7 g | Dietary fiber: 2 g | Sugars: 2 g | Protein: 23 g

Fettuccine with Shrimp, Red Pepper, and Mushrooms

Hands-On Time: 15 minutes
Total Time: 15 minutes
Yield: Serves 6

1 pound medium fresh, raw shrimp, peeled

½ teaspoon salt

¼ teaspoon lemon pepper

3 tablespoons olive oil

1 small onion, peeled and chopped

1 medium red bell pepper, seeded and sliced

8 ounces button mushrooms, sliced

1½ cups heavy cream

1 (16-ounce) package fettuccine, cooked and drained

1 cup grated Parmesan cheese

1 tablespoon chopped parsley

1. Dry shrimp with a paper towel and season with salt and lemon pepper.

2. In a large saucepan over medium-high, heat olive oil. Add onion and cook, stirring often, for 4–5 minutes or until tender. Add bell pepper and mushrooms; cook over medium heat for 4–5 minutes or until mushrooms are tender and cooked through and peppers are crisp-tender.

3. Add shrimp and cook until they curl and turn pink, about 2 minutes. Stir in cream and heat for 2 minutes. Add cooked pasta, tossing gently to combine. Cook over medium heat for 3–4 minutes until sauce is slightly thickened and pasta is hot. Add cheese and stir gently to coat. Sprinkle with parsley and serve immediately.

Per Serving: Calories: 520 | Fat: 24 g | Saturated fat: 18 g | Cholesterol: 205 mg | Sodium: 610 mg | Total carbohydrates: 29 g | Dietary fiber: 2 g | Sugars: 4 g | Protein: 26 g

Grilled Haddock with Mango Salsa (pictured)

Hands-On Time: 15 minutes
Total Time: 25 minutes
Yield: Serves 4

2 tablespoons olive oil
2 tablespoons lime juice
¼ teaspoon salt
⅛ teaspoon ground black pepper
2 (8-ounce) haddock fillets
1 cup mango salsa

1. Mix olive oil, lime juice, salt, and pepper in a shallow dish; add haddock. Turn and coat fish with marinade. Set aside 10 minutes.
2. Heat gas or charcoal grill. Spray large piece of aluminum foil with nonstick cooking spray.
3. Place fillets on foil; cook 7–8 minutes on each side or until fish is tender when pierced with a fork.
4. Top each piece of fish with ½ cup salsa.

Per Serving: Calories: 181 | Fat: 7 g | Saturated fat: 1 g | Cholesterol: 58 mg | Sodium: 677 mg | Total carbohydrates: 11 g | Dietary fiber: 0 g | Sugars: 4 g | Protein: 18 g

Sweet and Sour Fish

Hands-On Time: 30 minutes
Total Time: 30 minutes
Yield: Serves 6

1½ cups long grain rice
3 cups water
6 frozen crunchy fish nuggets
2 tablespoons olive oil
1 medium onion, peeled and chopped
2 cloves garlic, peeled and minced
1 medium green bell pepper, seeded and chopped
1 medium red bell pepper, seeded and chopped
1 (8-ounce) can pineapple tidbits
⅓ cup ketchup
2 tablespoons sugar
2 tablespoons apple cider vinegar
2 tablespoons cornstarch
2 tablespoons soy sauce
½ teaspoon ground ginger
⅛ teaspoon cayenne pepper

1. In large saucepan, combine rice and water and bring to a boil. Reduce heat, cover, and simmer for 20–25 minutes or until rice is tender and liquid is absorbed. Preheat oven to 350°F. Prepare fish as directed on package.
2. Meanwhile, in large saucepan heat olive oil over medium heat. Add onion and garlic; stir-fry for 3 minutes. Add bell pepper and stir-fry for 3–5 minutes longer.
3. Drain pineapple, reserving juice. Add pineapple to saucepan with vegetables and stir. In small bowl, combine reserved pineapple juice, ketchup, sugar, vinegar, cornstarch, soy sauce, ginger, and pepper and mix well. Add to saucepan, bring to a simmer, and cook until thickened, about 3–5 minutes. Add fish pieces and stir to combine.
4. When rice is done, place on serving plate and top with sweet and sour fish.

Per Serving: Calories: 451 | Fat: 14 g | Saturated fat: 3 g | Cholesterol: 16 mg | Sodium: 526 mg | Total carbohydrates: 69 g | Dietary fiber: 3 g | Sugars: 15 g | Protein: 11 g

Poached Salmon Italian-Style

Hands-On Time: 20 minutes
Total Time: 25 minutes
Yield: Serves 4

1 cup chicken stock

1 cup halved cherry tomatoes

¼ cup diced green peppers

½ cup thinly sliced yellow onion

1 cup thinly sliced mushrooms

½ cup thinly sliced zucchini

1 teaspoon minced garlic

2 teaspoons dried Italian
seasoning

¼ teaspoon salt

⅛ teaspoon ground black pepper

4 (6-ounce) skinless salmon
fillets, about 1" thick each

2 tablespoons grated Parmesan
cheese

1. Combine the stock, tomatoes, peppers, onion, mushrooms, zucchini, garlic, seasoning, salt, and pepper in a large skillet over medium-high heat. Cover and bring to a boil.

2. Use a spatula to move the vegetables aside and carefully add the salmon fillets. Reduce the heat to medium, cover, and gently simmer until the fish is opaque and firm throughout when tested with a fork.

3. Use a slotted spatula to transfer the salmon to serving plates. Spoon the vegetable mixture over the fish and sprinkle with Parmesan. Serve hot.

Per Serving: Calories: 260 | Fat: 9 g | Saturated fat: 2 g | Cholesterol: 85 mg | Sodium: 590 mg | Total carbohydrates: 5 g | Dietary fiber: 1 g | Sugars: 3 g | Protein: 39 g

Shrimp Pesto

Hands-On Time: 20 minutes
Total Time: 25 minutes
Yield: Serves 4

1 pound gemelli pasta or spiral-
shaped pasta, uncooked

2 tablespoons olive oil

3 cloves garlic, diced

½ pound fresh, raw shrimp, shells
removed

2 cups cherry tomatoes, halved

¼ cup prepared pesto

¼ cup grated Parmesan cheese

1. Bring a large pot of water to a boil and cook pasta according to directions on package. Drain.

2. Heat the oil in a large skillet and sauté the garlic 1 minute. Add shrimp and sauté 3 minutes or until shrimp turns pink. Add tomatoes and pasta. Add enough pesto to lightly cover the pasta. Add Parmesan cheese and toss. Serve hot.

Per Serving: Calories: 693 | Fat: 24 g | Saturated fat: 6 g | Cholesterol: 105 mg | Sodium: 836 mg | Total carbohydrates: 91 g | Dietary fiber: 5 g | Sugars: 7 g | Protein: 40 g

Pan-Roasted Sea Scallops

Hands-On Time: 10 minutes
Total Time: 10 minutes
Yield: Serves 4

2 tablespoons butter
1 tablespoon extra-virgin olive oil
¾ pound sea scallops
¼ teaspoon salt
⅛ teaspoon ground black pepper
½ pound sliced cremini
    mushrooms
¼ cup minced red bell pepper
¼ cup minced green bell pepper
¼ cup minced white onion
2 teaspoons minced thyme
¼ cup dry white wine

1. Heat the butter and oil in a large skillet over medium-high heat until the butter stops bubbling. Season the scallops with salt and pepper. Lay them in the pan in a single layer with some room between each scallop. Increase heat to high and don't move the scallops for about 2 minutes. Allow them to brown well on one side.

2. Turn the scallops over and add the mushrooms, bell peppers, onion, and thyme to the pan. Stir to coat the vegetables with the butter. Cook over high heat until the water that releases from the mushrooms evaporates.

3. Add the wine and cook for about 1 minute. Serve immediately.

Per Serving: Calories: 170 | Fat: 10 g | Saturated fat: 4 g | Cholesterol: 35 mg | Sodium: 480 mg | Total carbohydrates: 7 g | Dietary fiber: 1 g | Sugars: 2 g | Protein: 12 g

Fish in Lemon Basil Sauce

Hands-On Time: 30 minutes
Total Time: 30 minutes
Yield: Serves 4

4 (6-ounce) cod fillets
½ teaspoon salt
½ teaspoon ground black pepper
3 tablespoons olive oil, divided
2 small zucchini, sliced
1 cup lemon basil leaves
1 tablespoon grated lemon zest
3 tablespoons lemon juice

1. Rinse the fish fillets and pat dry with paper towels. Sprinkle with salt and pepper. Set aside.

2. Place a large skillet over medium heat and add 2 tablespoons oil. Slide two fillets into the skillet and cook on each side for 4–5 minutes or until the center is almost opaque and the fish begins to flake on the tips. Place on a clean plate to keep warm. Cook the remaining fish and add to the plate. Keep warm.

3. Add remaining tablespoon olive oil to the pan before adding the zucchini slices.

4. Sprinkle the basil, lemon zest, and a pinch of salt and pepper over the zucchini. Cover the pan and steam for 1 minute before tossing. Place the fish on top of the zucchini and sprinkle with lemon juice. Cover the skillet for 2–3 minutes to warm the fish and finish cooking the zucchini. Serve immediately.

Per Serving: Calories: 240 | Fat: 11 g | Saturated fat: 2 g | Cholesterol: 70 mg | Sodium: 400 mg | Total carbohydrates: 3 g | Dietary fiber: 1 g | Sugars: 2 g | Protein: 30 g

Cauliflower with Dilled Shrimp Sauce

Hands-On Time: 25 minutes
Total Time: 25 minutes
Yield: Serves 4

1 tablespoon olive oil

3 tablespoons butter, divided

3 cloves garlic, finely chopped

1 small onion, finely chopped

1 pound small cooked shrimp, peeled

2 tablespoons flour

½ cup vegetable broth

⅔ cup whole milk

1 medium head cauliflower, separated into florets and steamed

¼ teaspoon salt

¼ teaspoon black pepper

¼ cup fresh dill

1. Melt the olive oil and 1 tablespoon of butter in a large skillet over medium heat. Add garlic and onion and sauté gently until the onion is translucent, stirring occasionally. Stir in the shrimp and cook 5 minutes.

2. Melt the remaining 2 tablespoons of butter in a large pot over medium heat, then stir in the flour to make a roux. Whisking constantly, pour the vegetable broth and milk into the roux in a steady stream until the sauce thickens and begins to bubble.

3. Divide cooked cauliflower and shrimp onto 4 serving plates. Top with sauce, black pepper, and fresh dill.

Per Serving: Calories: 308 | Fat: 14 g | Saturated fat: 7 g | Cholesterol: 240 mg | Sodium: 350 mg | Total carbohydrates: 15 g | Dietary fiber: 4 g | Sugars: 6 g | Protein: 33 g

Poached Salmon with Béarnaise Sauce

Hands-On Time: 10 minutes
Total Time: 20 minutes
Yield: Serves 4

½ cup water
¼ cup white wine
2 (6-ounce) salmon steaks
¼ cup mayonnaise
2 tablespoons lemon juice
1 tablespoon Dijon mustard
1 teaspoon sugar
1 teaspoon tarragon
¼ teaspoon salt
¼ teaspoon ground black pepper
4 medium sprigs fresh dill

1. In large skillet, bring water and wine to a gentle simmer. Add salmon and cook without boiling for 8–10 minutes or until fish flakes easily when tested with a fork. Divide steaks in half and arrange on warmed plates.

2. In small saucepan, whisk together mayonnaise, lemon juice, mustard, sugar, and tarragon. Cook over medium-low heat, whisking, for about 3 minutes or until warmed through but not boiling. Season with salt and pepper. Spoon over salmon. Garnish with dill.

Per Serving: Calories: 320 | Fat: 23 g | Saturated fat: 4 g | Cholesterol: 70 mg | Sodium: 310 mg | Total carbohydrates: 3 g | Dietary fiber: 0 g | Sugars: 2 g | Protein: 22 g

White Beans with Shrimp

Hands-On Time: 20 minutes
Total Time: 20 minutes
Yield: Serves 8

1 tablespoon olive oil
1 medium red bell pepper, seeded and sliced
1 small onion, peeled and chopped
2 garlic cloves, peeled and minced
1 medium celery stalk, sliced
2 tablespoons chopped parsley
2 tablespoons chopped thyme
⅛ teaspoon crushed red pepper
4 tablespoons unsalted butter
1 pound large fresh, raw shrimp, peeled and deveined
2 (15-ounce) cans Great Northern beans, drained and rinsed
3 tablespoons lemon juice

1. Place a large skillet over medium heat and once it is heated, add the oil, bell pepper, and onion. Cook for 5–7 minutes or until the vegetables are softened but not browned. Add the garlic and celery. Stir to combine before adding in the herbs, crushed red pepper, and butter.

2. Stir continually until the butter is melted and starts to turn brown. Swirl the skillet occasionally.

3. Place the shrimp in the skillet and cook on each side for 1–2 minutes. Stir in the beans and lemon juice and cook until warmed through. Serve immediately.

Per Serving: Calories: 473 | Fat: 9 g | Saturated fat: 4.5 g | Cholesterol: 86 mg | Sodium: 338 mg | Total carbohydrates: 68 g | Dietary fiber: 17 g | Sugars: 2 g | Protein: 33 g

Chapter 11

Vegetarian Main Dishes

Vegetarian Stroganoff

Hands-On Time: 20 minutes
Total Time: 20 minutes
Yield: Serves 4

1 tablespoon extra-virgin olive oil
2 (14-ounce) packages extra-firm tofu, crumbled
1 medium yellow onion, minced
1 cup sliced mushrooms
1 teaspoon garlic powder
2 tablespoons low-sodium soy sauce
1 (12-ounce) container nonfat cottage cheese
2 tablespoons plain low-fat Greek-style yogurt
16 ounces 100 percent whole-wheat noodles, cooked
2 teaspoons ground black pepper

1. Prepare a large skillet with olive oil and place over medium heat.

2. Sauté tofu crumbles and onion in the olive oil for 7 minutes or until cooked through. Add the mushrooms, garlic powder, and soy sauce and combine well. Stir in the cottage cheese and Greek-style yogurt until the ingredients form a thick sauce. Remove from the heat.

3. In a large bowl, combine the cooked noodles, tofu mixture, and pepper. Blend well. Serve immediately.

Per Serving: Calories: 360 | Fat: 11 g | Saturated fat: 1.5 g | Cholesterol: 45 mg | Sodium: 80 mg | Total carbohydrates: 40 g | Dietary fiber: 7 g | Sugars: 6 g | Protein: 29 g

Easiest-Ever Vegetarian Lasagna

Hands-On Time: 7 minutes
Total Time: 25 minutes
Yield: Serves 2

½ cup diced tomatoes
⅓ cup ricotta cheese
½ cup grated mozzarella cheese, divided
1 tablespoon grated Parmesan cheese
⅛ teaspoon dried oregano
⅛ teaspoon dried basil
6 "oven-ready" lasagna noodles

1. Place the diced tomatoes in a medium bowl. Stir in the ricotta, then 1/3 cup mozzarella, and then the Parmesan. Make sure each cheese is thoroughly mixed in before adding the next. Stir in the oregano and basil.

2. Lay out 2 lasagna noodles in a large bowl or small (½-quart) microwave-safe casserole dish. Break the noodles in half or as needed to fit the shape of the dish. Spoon approximately ⅓ of the tomato and cheese mixture evenly over the top. Repeat the layering 2 more times. Sprinkle the remaining mozzarella cheese over the top.

3. Cover the dish with wax paper. Microwave on high heat for 3 minutes. Turn the bowl and microwave on high heat for another 5 minutes until the cheese is cooked. Let stand for 10 minutes before serving.

Per Serving: Calories: 370 | Fat: 14 g | Saturated fat: 8 g | Cholesterol: 60 mg | Sodium: 270 mg | Total carbohydrates: 42 g | Dietary fiber: 3 g | Sugars: 3 g | Protein: 20 g

Classic Margherita Pizza

Hands-On Time: 10 minutes
Total Time: 20 minutes
Yield: Serves 6

1 pound pizza dough
½ cup crushed, peeled tomatoes
¼ teaspoon dried basil
¼ teaspoon dried oregano
¼ teaspoon garlic powder
1 teaspoon lemon juice
¼ teaspoon salt
⅛ teaspoon ground black pepper
¼ pound fresh mozzarella, thinly sliced
3 tablespoons finely grated Grana Padano cheese
1 cup small basil leaves

1. Preheat oven to 500°F. Preheat baking stone in oven.

2. Mix crushed tomatoes, dry basil, dry oregano, garlic powder, lemon juice, salt, and black pepper together, then spread on rolled, prepared pizza dough.

3. Arrange sliced mozzarella on top and sprinkle with grated Grana Padano.

4. Bake on stone for 8–10 minutes until the crust is brown and tomato sauce is bubbly. Remove from oven and top with basil leaves.

Per Serving: Calories: 220 | Fat: 9 g | Saturated fat: 3.5 g | Cholesterol: 15 mg | Sodium: 500 mg | Total carbohydrates: 27 g | Dietary fiber: 1 g | Sugars: 3 g | Protein: 12 g

Bean Tacos

Hands-On Time: 20 minutes
Total Time: 30 minutes
Yield: Serves 8

1 tablespoon olive oil
1 large onion, peeled and chopped
5 cloves garlic, peeled and minced
2 small jalapeño peppers, seeded and minced
2 (14-ounce) cans black beans, drained and rinsed
1 cup frozen corn kernels, thawed
1 cup sour cream
2 medium tomatoes, chopped
½ teaspoon salt
⅛ teaspoon ground black pepper
8 (6") flour tortillas
2 cups shredded Pepper Jack cheese

1. Preheat oven to 400°F. Heat a large skillet over medium heat. Add olive oil, onion, garlic, and jalapeño pepper and sauté until the vegetables are tender. Add the beans and corn and continue to cook until the beans are hot. Remove from heat.

2. Add sour cream, tomatoes, salt, and pepper; mix well.

3. Fold tortillas over and fill with bean mixture and shredded cheese and move to a baking sheet. Bake for 10 minutes or until the edges of the tortillas are brown and crunchy. Serve immediately.

Per Serving: Calories: 552 | Fat: 9 g | Saturated fat: 3 g | Cholesterol: 60 mg | Sodium: 1,358 mg | Total carbohydrates: 50 g | Dietary fiber: 9 g | Sugars: 3 g | Protein: 28 g

Spinach and Potato Curry (Saag Aloo) (pictured)

Hands-On Time: 5 minutes
Total Time: 20 minutes
Yield: Serves 4

1 tablespoon minced ginger
½ tablespoon minced garlic
1 medium jalapeño pepper,
  seeded and diced
1 teaspoon garam masala, divided
¼ cup vegetable stock
½ cup vegetable oil
1 large russet potato, peeled and
  cubed
½ cup diced white onions
1 (16-ounce) bag frozen spinach,
  thawed, drained, and chopped
1 tablespoon water
¼ teaspoon cayenne
½ teaspoon kosher salt
2 tablespoons plain low-fat yogurt

1. In a blender, purée the ginger, garlic, jalapeño, ½ teaspoon garam masala, and vegetable stock. Set aside.

2. Heat the oil in a large wok over medium-high heat. Fry the potato cubes for 2 minutes or until golden brown. Remove to a paper towel–lined plate.

3. Lower the heat to medium and carefully discard all but 1 tablespoon oil from the wok. Add the onions and cook for 2 minutes until browned. Stir in the remaining ½ teaspoon garam masala and allow the spice to toast for 30 seconds.

4. Add the spinach with water and allow 1–2 minutes for the leaves to wilt.

5. Stir in the puréed ginger and garlic mixture and reduce heat to medium low. Cook, stirring often, for about 5–6 minutes until the spinach has broken down and melded into the liquids.

6. Stir in the cayenne, salt, and yogurt. Add fried potatoes to the spinach mixture and cover. Simmer for 2–3 minutes to allow the flavors to marry. Serve warm.

Per Serving: Calories: 170 | Fat: 4 g | Saturated fat: 1 g | Cholesterol: 0 mg | Sodium: 450 mg | Total carbohydrates: 26 g | Dietary fiber: 7 g | Sugars: 3 g | Protein: 7 g

Asparagus, Swiss, and Ricotta Frittata

Hands-On Time: 10 minutes
Total Time: 25 minutes
Yield: Serves 4

8 medium stalks fresh asparagus
1 shallot, finely diced
1¼ cups liquid egg replacement
¼ cup shredded Swiss cheese
1 cup nonfat ricotta cheese
¼ teaspoon ground black pepper

1. Move rack to top of the oven and preheat to 450°F.

2. Trim the asparagus and cut into thirds. Steam the asparagus over high heat for 5 minutes.

3. Spray a large ovenproof skillet with cooking oil. Place over medium heat, add shallot, and sauté for 2 minutes. Add liquid egg replacement to pan and remove from heat. Top with asparagus and Swiss. Dollop ricotta over top and season with ground black pepper.

4. Place skillet on top rack in oven and bake for 10 minutes.

5. Remove from oven. Slide a heatproof spatula around and under frittata to loosen. Remove and cut into wedges. Serve immediately.

Per Serving: Calories: 130 | Fat: 2 g | Saturated fat: 1 g | Cholesterol: 15 mg | Sodium: 200 mg | Total carbohydrates: 10 g | Dietary fiber: 1 g | Sugars: 3 g | Protein: 16 g

Zucchini Bake

Hands-On Time: 15 minutes
Total Time: 30 minutes
Yield: Serves 6

1 teaspoon olive oil
1 clove garlic, peeled and minced
4 large zucchini, sliced
1 cup sliced white mushrooms
1 (15-ounce) can Italian-style
   stewed tomatoes
½ cup Italian-style bread crumbs
¼ cup grated low-fat Parmesan
   cheese
¼ cup shredded low-fat
   mozzarella cheese

1. Preheat oven to 350°F.

2. Coat a 9" x 13" baking dish with nonstick spray.

3. Heat oil in a large skillet over medium heat. Add garlic and sauté 1 minute. Add zucchini to skillet and sauté for 5 minutes. Add mushrooms to skillet and sauté for 5 minutes. Remove from heat and stir in tomatoes.

4. Pour zucchini mixture into the prepared baking dish. Cover with bread crumbs. Sprinkle both cheeses over bread crumbs.

5. Bake for 15 minutes or until cheese melts and sauce is bubbly around the edges.

Per Serving: Calories: 120 | Fat: 3 g | Saturated fat: 1 g | Cholesterol: 5 mg | Sodium: 490 mg | Total carbohydrates: 17 g | Dietary fiber: 3 g | Sugars: 8 g | Protein: 6 g

Provençal Ratatouille

Hands-On Time: 10 minutes
Total Time: 10 minutes
Yield: Serves 8

2 tablespoons olive oil

2 cloves garlic, peeled and minced

1½ cups sliced Japanese eggplant

1½ cups sliced zucchini

1½ cups sliced yellow squash

1 cup diced red bell pepper

2 cups diced plum tomatoes

½ teaspoon dried thyme leaves

¼ cup minced parsley

1 teaspoon salt

½ teaspoon ground black pepper

1. In a large saucepan, heat olive oil over medium-high heat. Add garlic and sauté over medium-high heat for 1 minute.

2. Add eggplant, zucchini, squash, bell pepper, and tomatoes. Sauté, stirring often, until vegetables are crisp and tender and tomatoes are soft, about 6–8 minutes.

3. Add thyme, parsley, salt, and pepper and serve.

Per Serving: Calories: 55 | Fat: 4 g | Saturated fat: 1 g | Cholesterol: 0 mg | Sodium: 296 mg | Total carbohydrates: 5 g | Dietary fiber: 2 g | Sugars: 3 g | Protein: 1 g

Spinach and Ricotta Pizza

Hands-On Time: 10 minutes
Total Time: 20 minutes
Yield: Serves 6

1 (11-ounce) can refrigerated pizza crust
1 tablespoon olive oil
1 tablespoon grated Parmesan cheese
¼ teaspoon garlic powder
½ teaspoon salt
½ teaspoon ground black pepper
½ small red onion, peeled and thinly sliced
1 cup fresh spinach
1 cup grated mozzarella cheese
½ cup part-skim ricotta
¼ teaspoon crushed red pepper

1. Preheat oven to 450°F.
2. Unroll dough and spread on a pizza pan or baking sheet. Brush the dough with olive oil and sprinkle evenly with Parmesan and garlic powder. Season with salt and pepper.
3. Scatter onions, spinach, and mozzarella over the pizza. Top with spoonfuls of ricotta. Sprinkle with crushed red pepper.
4. Bake for 8–10 minutes until golden and bubbly.

Per Serving: Calories: 227 | Fat: 8 g | Saturated fat: 4 g | Cholesterol: 16 mg | Sodium: 618 mg | Total carbohydrates: 28 g | Dietary fiber: 1 g | Sugars: 4 g | Protein: 10 g

Quinoa Black Bean Burgers (pictured)

Hands-On Time: 5 minutes
Total Time: 15 minutes
Yield: Serves 4

1 (15-ounce) can black beans, drained and rinsed
1 teaspoon chili powder
½ teaspoon salt
¾ cup cooked quinoa
¾ cup shredded carrots
1 tablespoon olive oil
2 cups lettuce
1 large tomato, sliced
½ small red onion, peeled and sliced
1 medium avocado, peeled, pitted, and sliced

1. Place the black beans, chili powder, salt, quinoa, and carrots in a food processor and process for 3–4 minutes or until everything is combined and holds together.
2. Heat the olive oil in a large pan over medium-high heat. Form four patties out of the bean mixture and place in the pan. Cook for 5 minutes on each side.
3. Serve the bean burgers on lettuce with tomato, onion, and avocado on top.

Per Serving: Calories: 240 | Fat: 10 g | Saturated fat: 1 g | Cholesterol: 0 mg | Sodium: 650 mg | Total carbohydrates: 30 g | Dietary fiber: 8 g | Sugars: 3 g | Protein: 9 g

Coconut Cauliflower Curry

Hands-On Time: 10 minutes
Total Time: 30 minutes
Yield: Serves 6

1 tablespoon canola oil

1 medium onion, diced

6 cloves garlic, minced

1 tablespoon minced fresh ginger

1 tablespoon salt-free garam masala

1 teaspoon ground turmeric

2 tablespoons salt-free tomato paste

2 cups low-sodium vegetable broth

1 cup light coconut milk

1 medium head cauliflower, cut into florets

3 medium potatoes or sweet potatoes, diced

2 medium carrots, sliced

1 (15-ounce) can no-salt-added diced tomatoes

1½ cups fresh or frozen peas

½ teaspoon ground black pepper

¼ cup chopped fresh cilantro

1. Heat oil in a large stockpot over medium heat. Add onion, garlic, and ginger and cook, stirring, for 5 minutes. Add the garam masala and turmeric and sauté until fragrant, roughly 30 seconds to 1 minute.

2. Stir in the tomato paste, broth, coconut milk, cauliflower, potatoes, carrots, and tomatoes with juice and stir well to combine. Raise heat slightly and bring to a boil. Once boiling, lower heat to medium-low, cover, and simmer for 20 minutes. Stir in the peas and black pepper and cook 2-3 minutes more.

3. Remove from heat and stir in the cilantro. Serve immediately.

Per Serving: Calories: 200 | Fat: 4.5 g | Saturated fat: 1.5 g | Cholesterol: 0 mg | Sodium: 150 mg | Total carbohydrates: 35 g | Dietary fiber: 7 g | Sugars: 10 g | Protein: 7 g

Zucchini Noodle Lasagna

Hands-On Time: 10 minutes
Total Time: 25 minutes
Yield: Serves 4

2 cups crushed tomatoes
1¼ cups cottage cheese
¼ cup shredded mozzarella cheese
¼ teaspoon dried basil
¼ teaspoon dried oregano
⅛ teaspoon black pepper
2 medium zucchini, sliced in long, thin strips
1 cup frozen spinach, thawed and drained
3 tablespoons grated Parmesan cheese

1. In a medium bowl, stir together the crushed tomatoes and the cottage cheese. Stir in the mozzarella cheese, basil, oregano, and pepper.

2. Lay out one of the zucchini strips in a deep-sided casserole dish that is microwave-safe. Add half of the spinach.

3. Spoon about half of the cheese and tomato mixture over the spinach. Repeat with the remainder of the zucchini, spinach, and cheese and tomato mixture.

4. Cover the dish with microwave-safe wax paper. Microwave on high heat for 3 minutes. Give the dish a quarter turn and microwave on high for 2 minutes at a time until the cheese is cooked (total cooking time should be 7–9 minutes).

5. Sprinkle the Parmesan cheese over the top. Let stand for at least 5 minutes before serving.

Per Serving: Calories: 154 | Fat: 5 g | Saturated fat: 3 g | Cholesterol: 13 mg | Sodium: 615 mg | Total carbohydrates: 14 g | Dietary fiber: 3.5 g | Sugars: 7 g | Protein: 14 g

Vegetarian Black Bean Burrito

Hands-On Time: 10 minutes
Total Time: 30 minutes
Yield: Serves 6

3 cups black beans
1 cup frozen corn
½ teaspoon all-purpose seasoning
1 clove fresh garlic, minced
1 teaspoon chipotle sauce
½ cup fat-free sour cream
½ cup chopped white onion
1 tablespoon chopped cilantro
6 (8") flour tortillas
½ cup shredded low-fat Cheddar cheese

1. Preheat oven to 375°F.

2. Coat a 9" x 13" baking dish with nonstick spray.

3. In a medium bowl, mix all ingredients except tortillas and cheese.

4. Divide mixture equally among 6 tortillas and fold each tortilla into a burrito. Place each burrito in dish and top with Cheddar cheese.

5. Cover with foil and bake for 20 minutes or until cheese melts.

Per Serving: Calories: 280 | Fat: 5 g | Saturated fat: 2.5 g | Cholesterol: 10 mg | Sodium: 320 mg | Total carbohydrates: 46 g | Dietary fiber: 9 g | Sugars: 3 g | Protein: 14 g

Asian Cashew Wraps (pictured)

Hands-On Time: 15 minutes
Total Time: 15 minutes
Yield: Serves 2

1 tablespoon coconut oil
1 clove garlic, finely chopped
1 cup raw cashews
¼ cup fresh lime juice
2 tablespoons coconut aminos
2 tablespoons honey
6 medium butter lettuce leaves
½ cup chopped pineapple
2 tablespoons chopped cilantro
2 tablespoons chopped scallions
1 tablespoon sesame seeds

1. In a large skillet over medium-high heat, melt coconut oil and add garlic, then immediately reduce heat to medium-low.

2. Add cashews and lime juice to the skillet. Cook until the lime juice is reduced. Add coconut aminos and honey, then cook until glazed and golden brown.

3. Serve in lettuce leaves topped with pineapple, cilantro, scallions, and sesame seeds.

Per Serving: Calories: 520 | Fat: 33 g | Saturated fat: 10 g | Cholesterol: 0 mg | Sodium: 290 mg | Total carbohydrates: 47 g | Dietary fiber: 4 g | Sugars: 28 g | Protein: 12 g

Broccoli, Red Pepper, and Fontina Pizza

Hands-On Time: 10 minutes
Total Time: 30 minutes
Yield: Serves 16

1 pound pizza dough
1 tablespoon olive oil
1½ cups pizza sauce
4 cups small broccoli florets, blanched
1 large red bell pepper, seeded and sliced
2 cups shredded fontina cheese

1. Roll or press pizza dough into two 12" circles, slightly thicker at the edges than in the center. Grease 2 pizza pans with olive oil and place one dough circle in pan. Preheat oven to 400°F.

2. Spread ¾ cup sauce in the center of each pizza, leaving 1" around the edges bare.

3. Distribute 2 cups broccoli florets evenly over each pizza, leaving edges bare. Arrange bell pepper slices over broccoli. Top with 1 cup fontina sprinkled over each pizza.

4. If using a hot stone or tiles, use a well-floured pizza peel to carefully lift one pizza from preparation surface and place on stone. If using pizza pans, place first pizza in the center of the oven. Bake for 15–20 minutes or until the crust is lightly browned and cheese is melted.

5. Remove pizza from oven carefully. Set aside to rest briefly before slicing. Repeat baking process with second pie.

Per Serving: Calories: 150 | Fat: 6 g | Saturated fat: 3 g | Cholesterol: 15 mg | Sodium: 360 mg | Total carbohydrates: 17 g | Dietary fiber: 1 g | Sugars: 3 g | Protein: 7 g

Lentil Taco Bowl

Hands-On Time: 10 minutes
Total Time: 10 minutes
Yield: Serves 2

3 cups coarsely chopped romaine lettuce leaves
1 cup cooked lentils
1 cup diced red, orange, and yellow bell peppers
¼ cup prepared fresh salsa
¼ cup prepared guacamole
2 tablespoons lime juice
¼ cup chopped cilantro
½ teaspoon salt
½ teaspoon ground black pepper

1. Divide the lettuce between two medium bowls.

2. Top each bowl of lettuce with ½ cup cooked lentils, ½ cup diced peppers, 2 tablespoons salsa, and 2 tablespoons guacamole. Drizzle the lime juice over the bowls.

3. Sprinkle with cilantro, salt, and pepper, then serve.

Per Serving: Calories: 220 | Fat: 6 g | Saturated fat: 1 g | Cholesterol: 0 mg | Sodium: 970 mg | Total carbohydrates: 33 g | Dietary fiber: 13 g | Sugars: 8 g | Protein: 12 g

Vegetarian Tacos

Hands-On Time: 10 minutes
Total Time: 30 minutes
Yield: Serves 8

1 tablespoon olive oil

1 small onion, peeled and
   chopped

½ small yellow bell pepper,
   seeded and chopped

1 medium jalapeño pepper,
   seeded and minced

1 (15-ounce) can black beans,
   drained

2 cups frozen corn

½ teaspoon oregano leaves

⅛ teaspoon cayenne pepper

2 teaspoons chili powder

8 crisp corn taco shells

2 cups shredded romaine lettuce

1 medium tomato, chopped

1 cup shredded low-fat Cheddar
   cheese

1. In large skillet, heat olive oil over medium heat. Add onion, bell pepper, and jalapeño pepper; cook and stir for 6 minutes. Add black beans, corn, oregano, pepper, and chili powder; cook and stir until hot. Remove from heat.

2. Heat taco shells as directed on package. Fill shells with lettuce, black bean mixture, tomatoes, and cheese.

Per Serving: Calories: 200 | Fat: 8 g | Saturated fat: 2.5 g | Cholesterol: 5 mg | Sodium: 330 mg | Total carbohydrates: 26 g | Dietary fiber: 6 g | Sugars: 3 g | Protein: 10 g

Tomato and Vegetable Frittata

Hands-On Time: 20 minutes
Total Time: 20 minutes
Yield: Serves 4

2 teaspoons olive oil

2 teaspoons unsalted butter, melted and cooled

¼ cup minced onion

2 cups halved cherry tomatoes

2 cups chopped fresh spinach

4 large eggs

½ teaspoon dried basil

¼ teaspoon dried parsley

⅛ teaspoon ground black pepper

⅛ teaspoon chili powder

⅛ teaspoon mustard powder

⅛ teaspoon crushed red pepper

¼ cup grated Parmesan cheese

1. Spray a large, nonstick, ovenproof sauté pan with a thin coating of nonstick baking spray. Bring to temperature over medium heat. Add the olive oil and butter. When the butter sizzles, add the onion; sauté for 3 minutes or until almost tender. Add tomatoes and sauté for 5 minutes or until most of the moisture from the tomatoes has evaporated from the pan. Remove from heat and stir in spinach.

2. In a small bowl, whisk together the eggs, basil, parsley, pepper, chili powder, mustard powder, and crushed red pepper. Pour the mixture over the sautéed vegetables in the pan. Use a spoon or spatula to gently stir the eggs into the vegetables so that some of the eggs run to the bottom of the pan. Cook about 3 minutes until eggs just begin to set in the center.

3. Remove the pan from the burner and sprinkle the Parmesan cheese evenly over the top of the frittata. Place the pan under the broiler for 1–2 minutes until the cheese is melted and lightly browned. Gently lift the edges of the frittata away from the pan with a spatula, then slide it onto a serving platter.

Per Serving: Calories: 150 | Fat: 10 g | Saturated fat: 4 g | Cholesterol: 195 mg | Sodium: 180 mg | Total carbohydrates: 6 g | Dietary fiber: 2 g | Sugars: 2 g | Protein: 9 g

Easy Eggplant Parmigiana

Hands-On Time: 5 minutes
Total Time: 30 minutes
Yield: Serves 4

½ teaspoon dried basil

½ teaspoon dried oregano

⅛ teaspoon garlic salt

1 cup spaghetti sauce

1 medium eggplant, cut into ¼" slices

6 slices mozzarella cheese

1. Preheat oven to 350°F. Spray an 8" x 8" baking pan with nonstick cooking spray.

2. Stir the dried basil, dried oregano, and garlic salt into the spaghetti sauce.

3. Layer the eggplant slices flat in the prepared baking pan. Spoon the spaghetti sauce over the top and around the eggplant.

4. Cover the eggplant with foil and bake for 20 minutes or until tender. Remove from the oven. Uncover and lay the mozzarella slices on top.

5. Bake for another 5 minutes until the cheese melts.

Per Serving: Calories: 200 | Fat: 11 g | Saturated fat: 6 g | Cholesterol: 35 mg | Sodium: 600 mg | Total carbohydrates: 14 g | Dietary fiber: 6 g | Sugars: 9 g | Protein: 12 g

Individual Zucchini Gratins

Hands-On Time: 10 minutes
Total Time: 30 minutes
Yield: Serves 4

1 tablespoon olive oil
½ teaspoon salt
½ teaspoon ground black pepper
1 tablespoon chopped fresh
  rosemary
1 cup whole milk
¼ teaspoon ground nutmeg
4 medium zucchini, cut into ¼"
  slices
1 large onion, peeled and thinly
  sliced
¾ cup shredded Swiss cheese

1. Preheat oven to 350°F. Grease 4 individual shallow ovenproof bowls with olive oil.

2. In a small bowl, whisk together salt, black pepper, and rosemary.

3. In a microwave-safe measuring cup, stir together milk and nutmeg and heat in microwave on high for 60 seconds.

4. Into each prepared bowl, arrange zucchini slices in a single layer, alternating with a sprinkle of the salt mixture, onion slices, and cheese. Top the layers with the remaining cheese.

5. Bake 20 minutes or until milk is bubbling and cheese is browned.

Per Serving: Calories: 205 | Fat: 12 g | Saturated fat: 6 g | Cholesterol: 29 mg | Sodium: 338 mg | Total carbohydrates: 14 g | Dietary fiber: 3 g | Sugars: 9 g | Protein: 10 g

Mushroom Risotto

Hands-On Time: 30 minutes
Total Time: 30 minutes
Yield: Serves 6

4 cups vegetable stock
1 cup Arborio rice
1 tablespoon olive oil
3 tablespoons butter, divided
1½ cups fresh button mushrooms,
  trimmed and sliced
1 cup grated Parmesan cheese
2 teaspoons chopped parsley
  leaves

1. In a medium saucepan over medium heat, heat vegetable stock. Reduce to low and continue to heat while you prepare the vegetables and rice.

2. Meanwhile, in a large sauté pan over medium-high heat, heat oil and 1 tablespoon of butter. Add the mushrooms; cook, stirring often, until edges are browned and mushrooms give up their liquid and the liquid evaporates, about 6–8 minutes. Stir in rice; cook and stir for 3–4 minutes, until rice is opaque. Add the stock to the rice mixture about 1 cup at a time, stirring until the liquid is absorbed each time.

3. When all the stock is added and rice is tender, remove from the heat, stir in cheese and remaining 2 tablespoons of butter, cover, and let stand for 5 minutes. Stir, sprinkle with chopped parsley, and serve immediately.

Per Serving: Calories: 270 | Fat: 13 g | Saturated fat: 7 g | Cholesterol: 30 mg | Sodium: 740 mg | Total carbohydrates: 31 g | Dietary fiber: 0 g | Sugars: 1 g | Protein: 8 g

Buddha Bowl with Sesame Brittle (pictured)

Hands-On Time: 15 minutes
Total Time: 25 minutes
Yield: Serves 2

Sesame Seed Brittle
⅓ cup black sesame seeds
1 teaspoon sesame oil
1 tablespoon honey

Buddha Bowl
3 tablespoons olive oil, divided
2 cloves garlic, minced
1 (15-ounce) can chickpeas, drained and dried
1 large baked sweet potato, peeled and cut into chunks
2 tablespoons honey
2 tablespoons coconut aminos
4 cups baby kale
1 lemon, freshly juiced
1½ cups cooked brown rice

1. In a small skillet, heat sesame seeds, sesame oil, and honey together over high heat. Stirring constantly, cook until honey begins to sizzle. Transfer immediately to a piece of parchment paper. Place in refrigerator or freeze until cool. Crack or crumble into bite-sized pieces.

2. In a large skillet, heat 2 tablespoons olive oil over medium-high heat. Add garlic and chickpeas, frying chickpeas for 2 minutes. Add sweet potatoes to skillet and continue to sauté until sweet potato and chickpeas are golden brown, about 10 minutes. Add honey and coconut aminos, then stir and cook until caramelized, about 5 minutes. Set aside.

3. In a large serving bowl, combine kale with lemon juice and 1 tablespoon olive oil. Toss to coat.

4. To assemble bowl, place kale and sweet potato mixture over brown rice. Top with sesame brittle. Enjoy hot or cold.

Per Serving: Calories: 860 | Fat: 38 g | Saturated fat: 6 g | Cholesterol: 0 mg | Sodium: 820 mg | Total carbohydrates: 117 g | Dietary fiber: 16 g | Sugars: 34 g | Protein: 20 g

Quinoa Caprese Bowl

Hands-On Time: 10 minutes
Total Time: 10 minutes
Yield: Serves 1

1 cup cooked quinoa
½ cup mozzarella balls
½ cup cherry tomatoes
¼ cup chopped fresh basil
3 tablespoons Italian dressing

Place quinoa in a medium bowl. Top with mozzarella, tomatoes, and basil. Drizzle with Italian dressing and serve.

Per Serving: Calories: 620 | Fat: 40 g | Saturated fat: 13 g | Cholesterol: 15 mg | Sodium: 530 mg | Total carbohydrates: 44 g | Dietary fiber: 6 g | Sugars: 4 g | Protein: 22 g

Spinach-Stuffed Portobello Mushrooms

Hands-On Time: 15 minutes
Total Time: 30 minutes
Yield: Serves 6

2 tablespoons olive oil, divided
1 medium onion, peeled and
  chopped
10 ounces washed spinach leaves
1 teaspoon salt
½ teaspoon ground black pepper
1 cup quartered artichoke hearts
1½ cups shredded Gruyère or
  Emmentaler cheese, divided
6 large portobello mushrooms

1. Heat 1 tablespoon olive oil over medium heat in a large skillet and cook the onion until translucent, 5 minutes. Add the spinach. Season with salt and pepper and cook until spinach is wilted. Transfer to a plate to cool and then squeeze any excess water from the spinach. Chop the spinach and mix in the artichokes and ⅔ of the cheese.

2. Remove the mushroom stems; scoop out some of the dark ribs in the center of the caps. Divide the spinach mixture into the mushroom caps. Mushrooms can be cooked immediately or refrigerated for cooking later.

3. Heat the broiler. Heat remaining 1 tablespoon olive oil in a large skillet. Transfer the stuffed mushrooms to the pan, cover, and cook over medium heat for 10–15 minutes or until cooked through. Uncover, sprinkle with remaining cheese, and broil until cheese is molten and bubbly.

Per Serving: Calories: 210 | Fat: 14 g | Saturated fat: 6 g | Cholesterol: 30 mg | Sodium: 620 mg | Total carbohydrates: 12 g | Dietary fiber: 3 g | Sugars: 6 g | Protein: 12 g

Skillet Frittata

Hands-On Time: 15 minutes
Total Time: 25 minutes
Yield: Serves 6

1 tablespoon butter
1 tablespoon olive oil
½ cup diced onion
1 pound asparagus, chopped
1 cup chopped zucchini
¼ cup fresh or frozen peas
1 cup crumbled feta cheese
1 teaspoon dried oregano
1 teaspoon dried dill
1 teaspoon dried parsley
½ teaspoon dried basil
½ teaspoon salt
½ teaspoon ground black pepper
7 large eggs

1. Preheat oven to 325°F. Heat the butter and oil in a 12″ cast-iron skillet over medium heat. Sauté the onion, asparagus, zucchini, and peas until the onions are soft, about 8–10 minutes.

2. Meanwhile, in a medium bowl, whisk together the feta, oregano, dill, parsley, basil, salt, pepper, and eggs.

3. Pour the egg mixture over the vegetables in the skillet. Tilt the skillet slightly to coat all of the ingredients with the egg mixture. Cook over medium heat until the eggs are just beginning to set, about 4 minutes.

4. Place skillet in the oven and bake for 10 minutes or until the mixture is cooked through and just beginning to brown.

5. Remove frittata from the pan and slice. Serve immediately.

Per Serving: Calories: 220 | Fat: 15 g | Saturated fat: 7 g | Cholesterol: 245 mg | Sodium: 520 mg | Total carbohydrates: 7 g | Dietary fiber: 2 g | Sugars: 4 g | Protein: 13 g

Vegetarian Chop Suey

Hands-On Time: 20 minutes
Total Time: 20 minutes
Yield: Serves 4

½ cup vegetable broth

2 tablespoons soy sauce

1 teaspoon cornstarch

2 tablespoons vegetable or peanut oil

4 thin slices ginger, minced

1 medium onion, peeled and chopped

1 (14-ounce) package frozen stir-fry vegetable mix

1 cup mung bean sprouts

¼ teaspoon salt

½ cup cashews

1 teaspoon sugar

¼ teaspoon ground black pepper

1. In a small bowl, combine vegetable broth and soy sauce. Whisk in cornstarch.

2. Heat a wok or medium skillet over medium-high heat until it is nearly smoking. Add oil. When oil is hot, add sliced ginger and stir-fry for about 10 seconds.

3. Add onion. Stir-fry onion until it begins to soften (about 2 minutes). Add stir-fry vegetable mix. Stir-fry according to package directions or until vegetables are tender but still crisp.

4. Add mung bean sprouts and salt. Stir-fry for about 30 seconds. Add vegetable broth mixture to wok. Bring to a boil, stirring continually. Stir in cashews and sugar. Add black pepper. Serve hot.

Per Serving: Calories: 230 | Fat: 15 g | Saturated fat: 2 g | Cholesterol: 0 mg | Sodium: 780 mg | Total carbohydrates: 19 g | Dietary fiber: 4 g | Sugars: 8 g | Protein: 6 g

Raw "Pasta" Primavera

Hands-On Time: 10 minutes
Total Time: 10 minutes
Yield: Serves 4

3 medium zucchini

1 cup halved cherry tomatoes

¼ cup thinly sliced red onion

¼ cup extra-virgin olive oil

¼ cup grated aged Parmesan cheese

1. Process the zucchini into noodles using a spiral slicer. Alternatively, grate the zucchini or slice into strips.

2. Toss the zucchini noodles with the chopped vegetables.

3. Pour the oil over the noodles and vegetables and serve in four pasta bowls, topped with grated Parmesan.

Per Serving: Calories: 180 | Fat: 16 g | Saturated fat: 3 g | Cholesterol: 5 mg | Sodium: 125 mg | Total carbohydrates: 8 g | Dietary fiber: 2 g | Sugars: 5 g | Protein: 4 g

One-Pot Tomato-Basil Pasta (pictured)

Hands-On Time: 20 minutes
Total Time: 20 minutes
Yield: Serves 4

½ cup olive oil

3 cloves garlic

¾ cup Brazil nuts

⅓ cup nutritional yeast

1 teaspoon sea salt

¾ teaspoon Italian seasoning

½ teaspoon cayenne pepper

2 large zucchini, spiralized

2 cups sliced baby bella
    mushrooms

1 pound cherry tomatoes, halved

½ cup chopped fresh basil

1 teaspoon salt

½ teaspoon ground black pepper

1. In a small food processor or high-speed blender, combine olive oil, garlic, Brazil nuts, nutritional yeast, sea salt, Italian seasoning, and cayenne pepper. Pulse until the consistency of pesto sauce.

2. Transfer sauce to a large pot. Add spiralized zucchini, mushrooms, and tomatoes. Cook on stovetop over high heat, tossing every 3–5 minutes with tongs until the noodles begin to wilt and pot starts steaming (about 15 minutes of cooking time).

3. Garnish with fresh basil, salt, and pepper before serving.

Per Serving: Calories: 500 | Fat: 45 g | Saturated fat: 8 g | Cholesterol: 0 mg | Sodium: 1,540 mg | Total carbohydrates: 19 g | Dietary fiber: 7 g | Sugars: 8 g | Protein: 10 g

Quinoa Mango Salad

Hands-On Time: 10 minutes
Total Time: 10 minutes
Yield: Serves 4

2 tablespoons lime juice

1 tablespoon orange juice

4 tablespoons extra-virgin olive oil

¼ cup minced fresh cilantro leaves

1 teaspoon salt

½ teaspoon ground black pepper

1 (15-ounce) can black beans, drained and rinsed

2 cups cooked quinoa

1 cup diced mango

½ cup finely diced red bell pepper

1. In a small bowl whisk together the lime juice, orange juice, olive oil, and cilantro. Add salt and pepper.

2. Place the black beans, quinoa, mango, and bell pepper in a large bowl. Pour in the dressing and toss gently until coated. Serve immediately or store in the refrigerator for up to 8 hours before serving.

Per Serving: Calories: 350 | Fat: 16 g | Saturated fat: 2 g | Cholesterol: 0 mg | Sodium: 920 mg | Total carbohydrates: 42 g | Dietary fiber: 8 g | Sugars: 8 g | Protein: 10 g

Mediterranean Chickpea Bake

Hands-On Time: 10 minutes
Total Time: 20 minutes
Yield: Serves 4

5 tablespoons olive oil

1 large onion, peeled and finely chopped

4 cloves garlic, peeled and minced

1 large tomato, seeded and chopped

2 teaspoons ground cumin

1 teaspoon ground paprika

2 cups baby spinach

1 (15-ounce) can chickpeas, drained and rinsed

½ teaspoon salt

¼ teaspoon ground black pepper

2 teaspoons grated lemon zest

1. Heat olive oil in a large pan over medium heat. Sauté onion and garlic for 2–3 minutes until the onion starts to become translucent, then add tomato, cumin, and paprika. Continue cooking for 5 minutes.

2. Add spinach and chickpeas to the pan. Reduce the heat to medium-low and cover with a lid. Cook, stirring frequently, until the spinach is wilted and the chickpeas are heated through. Add salt, pepper, and lemon zest. Serve hot.

Per Serving: Calories: 280 | Fat: 20 g | Saturated fat: 2.5 g | Cholesterol: 0 mg | Sodium: 440 mg | Total carbohydrates: 22 g | Dietary fiber: 6 g | Sugars: 6 g | Protein: 6 g

Quinoa, Black Bean, and Vegetable Burritos

Hands-On Time: 10 minutes
Total Time: 25 minutes
Yield: Serves 4

1 cup cooked quinoa

1 cup frozen corn kernels, thawed

1 (15-ounce) can black beans, drained and rinsed

1 small red bell pepper, seeded and diced

1 medium green bell pepper, seeded and diced

2 tablespoons chopped cilantro

4 (10") large flour tortillas

1 cup shredded Monterrey Jack cheese

½ cup sour cream

1. Preheat oven to 375°F. Line a baking sheet with parchment paper.

2. In a large bowl, combine quinoa, corn, beans, bell peppers, and cilantro.

3. Lay tortillas out on a work surface. Scatter cheese over tortillas. Scoop about 1 cup of quinoa mixture onto center of each tortilla and roll up. Place filled tortillas on prepared baking sheet.

4. Bake for 15 minutes or until cheese is melted and filling is warm. Serve with sour cream.

Per Serving: Calories: 550 | Fat: 20 g | Saturated fat: 10 g | Cholesterol: 40 mg | Sodium: 976 mg | Total carbohydrates: 73 g | Dietary fiber: 7 g | Sugars: 6 g | Protein: 22 g

Three-Cheese Calzones

Hands-On Time: 20 minutes
Total Time: 30 minutes
Yield: Serves 4

Cornmeal to sprinkle under the crusts

1½ pounds pizza dough

8 ounces pizza sauce

1 cup mozzarella cheese, shredded

½ cup grated Parmesan cheese

1 cup ricotta cheese

1 cup loosely packed fresh shredded basil leaves

2 tablespoons fresh oregano leaves or 2 teaspoons dried

¼ teaspoon red pepper flakes

½ teaspoon salt

½ teaspoon ground black pepper

1 large egg yolk, beaten

1. Heat oven to 425°F. Spread cornmeal on a board. Roll out the pizza dough into 4 rounds, each 6" in diameter.

2. Mix the sauce, cheeses, herbs, and red pepper flakes. Season with salt and pepper. Spread ¼ of the filling on each calzone, covering only half of the dough. Fold the halves that are not sauced over the filling and crimp the edges with a fork.

3. Place calzones on a heavy baking sheet or pizza stone. Brush with egg and use a fork to prick the top of the dough in two places. Bake for about 10 minutes or until browned and bubbly.

Per Serving: Calories: 390 | Fat: 31 g | Saturated fat: 9 g | Cholesterol: 50 mg | Sodium: 650 mg | Total carbohydrates: 11 g | Dietary fiber: 2 g | Sugars: 5 g | Protein: 18 g

Creamy Polenta

Hands-On Time: 30 minutes
Total Time: 30 minutes
Yield: Serves 10

3 cups vegetable stock
2 cups whole milk
¼ cup unsalted butter
1½ cups cornmeal
½ cup grated Parmesan cheese
½ teaspoon ground black pepper
½ teaspoon kosher salt

1. Bring the stock, milk, and butter to a simmer over medium to medium-high heat in a large saucepan.

2. Slowly whisk in the cornmeal, stirring constantly to avoid lumps.

3. Reduce heat to low. Cook for 20–25 minutes uncovered, stirring frequently until thick and creamy.

4. Sprinkle with the cheese and season with pepper and salt.

Per Serving: Calories: 180 | Fat: 8 g | Saturated fat: 4.5 g | Cholesterol: 20 mg | Sodium: 270 mg | Total carbohydrates: 23 g | Dietary fiber: 1 g | Sugars: 4 g | Protein: 4 g

Pesto Quinoa Bowl (pictured)

Hands-On Time: 5 minutes
Total Time: 10 minutes
Yield: Serves 1

1½ cups cooked quinoa
¼ cup prepared pesto
1 large egg, hard-boiled and cut in half
2 tablespoons pine nuts, toasted

1. Heat quinoa in microwave, if needed. Stir in pesto until well mixed.

2. Top with egg, sprinkle with pine nuts, and serve.

Per Serving: Calories: 770 | Fat: 47 g | Saturated fat: 8 g | Cholesterol: 185 mg | Sodium: 690 mg | Total carbohydrates: 65 g | Dietary fiber: 9 g | Sugars: 5 g | Protein: 24 g

Colorful Grilled Corn Salad

Hands-On Time: 25 minutes
Total Time: 25 minutes
Yield: Serves 8

- **6 medium ears corn, shucked and cleaned**
- **1 (19-ounce) can black beans, drained and rinsed**
- **1 medium red bell pepper, seeded and chopped**
- **2 medium tomatoes, chopped**
- **½ cup diced red onion**
- **½ cup chopped fresh cilantro**
- **1 medium jalapeño pepper, seeded and finely diced**
- **½ cup olive oil**
- **½ cup red wine vinegar**
- **2 tablespoons lime juice**
- **1 tablespoon agave nectar or sugar**
- **1 teaspoon salt**
- **1 clove garlic, minced**
- **½ teaspoon ground cumin**
- **½ teaspoon ground black pepper**
- **1 teaspoon chili powder**
- **⅛ teaspoon hot pepper sauce**
- **1 medium avocado, peeled, pitted, and chopped**

1. Grill corn over medium heat for 15 minutes, turning occasionally, until slightly blackened in areas. Allow to cool and cut off corn kernels into a medium bowl. Add black beans, red pepper, tomato, red onion, cilantro, and jalapeño pepper.

2. In a small bowl, whisk to combine the olive oil, red wine vinegar, lime juice, agave nectar, salt, garlic, cumin, black pepper, chili powder, and hot sauce.

3. Pour over corn mixture and stir to coat. Top with chopped avocado right before serving.

Per Serving: Calories: 310 | Fat: 20 g | Saturated fat: 2.5 g | Cholesterol: 0 mg | Sodium: 490 mg | Total carbohydrates: 27 g | Dietary fiber: 7 g | Sugars: 5 g | Protein: 6 g

Zucchini Pasta with Veggie Meatballs

Hands-On Time: 15 minutes
Total Time: 15 minutes
Yield: Serves 4

4 large zucchini
1 tablespoon grapeseed oil
3 cloves garlic, minced
1 teaspoon salt
½ teaspoon ground black pepper
1 (8.5-ounce) package vegetarian meatballs defrosted according to package directions
1 (24-ounce) jar marinara sauce
3 tablespoons grated Parmesan cheese

1. Cut the zucchini into thin, noodle-like strips using a spiralizer or mandoline.

2. Heat the oil in a large skillet over medium-high heat. Add zucchini and garlic; cook and stir until just tender, about 5 minutes. Season with salt and pepper.

3. In a large saucepan over medium heat, combine veggie meatballs and sauce. Cook, stirring occasionally, until heated through, about 10 minutes.

4. Top zucchini noodles with sauce and meatballs. Sprinkle with Parmesan cheese.

Per Serving: Calories: 270 | Fat: 11 g | Saturated fat: 2 g | Cholesterol: 5 mg | Sodium: 1,710 mg | Total carbohydrates: 27 g | Dietary fiber: 2 g | Sugars: 14 g | Protein: 17 g

Spanish Artichoke and Zucchini Paella

Hands-On Time: 25 minutes
Total Time: 25 minutes
Yield: Serves 4

3 cloves garlic, peeled and minced
1 medium yellow onion, peeled and diced
2 tablespoons olive oil
1 cup uncooked white rice
½ cup chopped sun-dried tomatoes
1 medium red or yellow bell pepper, seeded and chopped
½ cup chopped artichoke hearts
2 medium zucchini, sliced
2 cups vegetable broth
1 tablespoon paprika
½ teaspoon turmeric
½ teaspoon salt

1. In a large skillet, heat garlic and onion in olive oil over medium-high heat 3–4 minutes until onion is almost soft. Add rice, stirring well to coat, and heat another minute, stirring to prevent burning.

2. Add tomatoes, peppers, artichokes, and zucchini, stirring to combine. Add vegetable broth and remaining ingredients, cover, and simmer 15–20 minutes until rice is done.

Per Serving: Calories: 330 | Fat: 10 g | Saturated fat: 2 g | Cholesterol: 0 mg | Sodium: 760 mg | Total carbohydrates: 54 g | Dietary fiber: 6 g | Sugars: 8 g | Protein: 8 g

Black Bean Cakes with Avocado and Cilantro Cream

Hands-On Time: 20 minutes
Total Time: 25 minutes
Yield: Serves 8

4 tablespoons extra-virgin olive oil, divided

2 small yellow onions, peeled and diced

3 cloves garlic, minced

4 (15-ounce) cans black beans, drained and rinsed

3 cups gluten-free panko bread crumbs

4 large eggs, divided

1 teaspoon cayenne pepper

⅓ cup almond meal

⅓ cup gluten-free all-purpose flour

1 tablespoon Mexican oregano

1 tablespoon crushed red pepper

1 large ripe avocado, peeled, pitted, and halved

2 tablespoons heavy cream

6 tablespoons sour cream

2 tablespoons lemon juice

¼ cup chopped cilantro

1 teaspoon salt

1 teaspoon ground black pepper

1. Heat 1 tablespoon oil in a large skillet over medium-high heat. Add onions and garlic and cook until softened and translucent, about 5 minutes. Remove from heat and put into a food processor.

2. Add beans, bread crumbs, 2 eggs, cayenne pepper, almond meal, and 1 tablespoon oil to onion mixture. Pulse until the mixture is smooth.

3. Whisk the remaining eggs in a shallow bowl. Combine flour, oregano, and crushed red pepper into another shallow bowl.

4. Form the bean mixture into 8 patties. Dip each into the eggs and then dredge in the flour mixture.

5. Heat the remaining 2 tablespoons of olive oil in a large skillet over medium-high heat. Add the patties and cook until browned on each side, about 6 minutes total.

6. In a medium bowl, mash avocado, heavy cream, sour cream, lemon juice, and cilantro. Add salt and pepper.

7. Garnish each black bean cake with avocado cream and serve.

Per Serving: Calories: 550 | Fat: 20 g | Saturated fat: 4 g | Cholesterol: 105 mg | Sodium: 1,310 mg | Total carbohydrates: 71 g | Dietary fiber: 11 g | Sugars: 1 g | Protein: 19 g

Portobello Burgers

Hands-On Time: 10 minutes
Total Time: 10 minutes
Yield: Serves 4

4 large portobello mushroom caps
1 tablespoon olive oil
4 hamburger rolls

1. Preheat grill.

2. Brush mushroom caps with oil. Place flat side on grill and cook for 8 minutes. Flip mushrooms over and grill another 5 minutes.

3. Remove mushrooms from grill and sandwich between rolls. Garnish with condiments of choice. Serve immediately.

Per Serving: Calories: 180 | Fat: 6 g | Saturated fat: 1.5 g | Cholesterol: 0 mg | Sodium: 230 mg | Total carbohydrates: 25 g | Dietary fiber: 2 g | Sugars: 5 g | Protein: 7 g

Chapter 12
Vegetables and Side Dishes

Orange-Glazed Carrots

Hands-On Time: 10 minutes
Total Time: 15 minutes
Yield: Serves 6

1 tablespoon butter
4 cloves garlic, minced
1 (16-ounce) bag baby carrots
½ cup frozen orange juice concentrate, thawed
2 tablespoons honey
½ teaspoon salt
⅛ teaspoon ground white pepper

1. In large saucepan, melt butter over medium heat. Add garlic; cook and stir until fragrant, about 30 seconds. Add carrots to pan; cook and stir for 4 minutes until carrots are glazed.

2. Add orange juice concentrate, honey, salt, and pepper to saucepan. Bring to a simmer, then cover, reduce heat to low, and simmer for 5 minutes until carrots are tender and glazed. Serve immediately.

Per Serving: Calories: 80 | Fat: 2 g | Saturated fat: 1 g | Cholesterol: 5 mg | Sodium: 250 mg | Total carbohydrates: 15 g | Dietary fiber: 2 g | Sugars: 10 g | Protein: 1 g

Fluffy Buttermilk Mashed Potatoes

Hands-On Time: 10 minutes
Total Time: 10 minutes
Yield: Serves 4

¾ pound potatoes, peeled and boiled
¼ cup warm buttermilk
2 teaspoons unsalted butter
1 teaspoon salt
¼ teaspoon ground white pepper

1. Place potatoes in large bowl and partially mash.

2. Add warm buttermilk and mix well, mashing potatoes completely.

3. Stir in butter, salt, and pepper. If you like your mashed potatoes creamy, add some of the potato water.

Per Serving: Calories: 90 | Fat: 2.5 g | Saturated fat: 1.5 g | Cholesterol: 5 mg | Sodium: 600 mg | Total carbohydrates: 15 g | Dietary fiber: 1 g | Sugars: 1 g | Protein: 2 g

Homemade Creamed Corn

Hands-On Time: 10 minutes
Total Time: 10 minutes
Yield: Serves 2

1 tablespoon low-fat margarine
1 cup frozen corn kernels
¼ cup skim milk
1 teaspoon granulated sugar
¼ teaspoon salt
⅛ teaspoon ground black pepper
1 teaspoon cornstarch

1. Melt the margarine over low heat in a medium-sized saucepan.

2. Add the corn, milk, sugar, salt, and pepper. Increase heat to medium and bring to a boil, stirring constantly. Reduce heat to low and simmer for 5 more minutes, stirring throughout.

3. Push the corn off to the sides of the pan. Increase heat to medium-high and add the cornstarch to the liquid in the middle of the pan, stirring constantly until thickened. Make sure there are no lumps. Stir the corn and milk 2–3 times. Serve hot.

Per Serving: Calories: 120 | Fat: 4 g | Saturated fat: 1.5 g | Cholesterol: 5 mg | Sodium: 350 mg | Total carbohydrates: 19 g | Dietary fiber: 2 g | Sugars: 5 g | Protein: 3 g

Sweet Potato Chips

Hands-On Time: 20 minutes
Total Time: 20 minutes
Yield: Serves 6

2 large sweet potatoes, peeled
3 cups canola oil
1 teaspoon salt
½ teaspoon ground black pepper

1. Slice the potatoes thinly with a mandoline.

2. Heat the oil in a deep-fat fryer to 375°F.

3. Fry for about 3–4 minutes, depending on the thickness of the chips. When the chips are very crisp, remove from the oil and drain.

4. Sprinkle chips with salt and pepper.

Per Serving: Calories: 83 | Fat: 5 g | Saturated fat: 0 g | Cholesterol: 0 mg | Sodium: 401 mg | Total carbohydrates: 9 g | Dietary fiber: 1 g | Sugars: 3 g | Protein: 1 g

Roasted Red Peppers (pictured)

Hands-On Time: 10 minutes
Total Time: 25 minutes
Yield: Serves 8

4 large red peppers
¼ cup olive oil

1. Preheat the oven to 400°F (or preheat the grill on high). Toss the whole peppers (stem and all) in the olive oil. Roast on a baking sheet pan until the skin starts to blister, about 10 minutes.

2. Immediately place the peppers in a plastic bag and seal (this makes it easy to peel them).

3. After 5 minutes, peel off and discard the skins. Cut peppers in half and remove ribs and seeds.

Per Serving: Calories: 30 | Fat: 0 g | Saturated fat: 0 g | Cholesterol: 0 mg | Sodium: 0 mg | Total carbohydrates: 5 g | Dietary fiber: 2 g | Sugars: 3 g | Protein: 1 g

Baked Plantains

Hands-On Time: 10 minutes
Total Time: 30 minutes
Yield: Serves 8

4 medium ripe plantains
Nonstick cooking spray
½ cup orange juice
1 teaspoon cinnamon
3 tablespoons brown sugar

1. Preheat oven to 350°F. Spray baking pan with nonstick cooking spray.

2. Slice each plantain in half. Place plantains flat in a shallow baking dish.

3. Pour orange juice over plantains. Sprinkle with cinnamon and sugar.

4. Spray the top of the plantains again with cooking spray. Bake for 20 minutes or until tender.

Per Serving: Calories: 140 | Fat: 0 g | Saturated fat: 0 g | Cholesterol: 0 mg | Sodium: 5 mg | Total carbohydrates: 36 g | Dietary fiber: 2 g | Sugars: 20 g | Protein: 1 g

Steamed Broccoli

Hands-On Time: 5 minutes
Total Time: 15 minutes
Yield: Serves 2

Water, as needed
4 ounces chopped broccoli

1. Fill a medium-sized saucepan with 1" of water. Place a metal steamer inside the pan. Make sure the water is not touching the bottom of the steamer. Heat the water to boiling.

2. When the water is boiling, add the broccoli pieces to the steamer. Cover and steam until the broccoli is tender, about 10 minutes. Drain and serve.

Per Serving: Calories: 20 | Fat: 0 g | Saturated fat: 0 g | Cholesterol: 0 mg | Sodium: 20 mg | Total carbohydrates: 4 g | Dietary fiber: 2 g | Sugars: 1 g | Protein: 2 g

Roasted Zucchini and Squash

Hands-On Time: 5 minutes
Total Time: 20 minutes
Yield: Serves 6

3 medium zucchini
3 medium yellow squash
½ teaspoon all-purpose seasoning

1. Slice vegetables into thin rounds. Coat a cookie sheet with nonstick spray. Lay veggie rounds on cookie sheet, being careful not to crowd them.

2. Sprinkle with all-purpose seasoning. Bake in 375°F oven for 16 minutes, flipping once.

Per Serving: Calories: 40 | Fat: 0 g | Saturated fat: 0 g | Cholesterol: 0 mg | Sodium: 70 mg | Total carbohydrates: 6 g | Dietary fiber: 2 g | Sugars: 2 g | Protein: 2 g

Sugar Snap Peas with Mint

Hands-On Time: 5 minutes
Total Time: 10 minutes
Yield: Serves 4

3 teaspoons olive oil
2 cloves garlic, minced
1 pound sugar snap peas
¼ teaspoon salt
¼ teaspoon ground black pepper
3 teaspoons chopped fresh mint

1. Heat olive oil in a medium skillet over medium heat and add garlic. Sauté 3–4 minutes or until fragrant.

2. Add sugar snap peas and continue to sauté until softened, about 4 more minutes.

3. Remove from heat and stir in salt, pepper, and mint. Serve immediately.

Per Serving: Calories: 60 | Fat: 0 g | Saturated fat: 0 g | Cholesterol: 0 mg | Sodium: 140 mg | Total carbohydrates: 10 g | Dietary fiber: 3 g | Sugars: 3 g | Protein: 3 g

Boiled Salad with Carrots, Broccoli, and Cauliflower

Hands-On Time: 15 minutes
Total Time: 15 minutes
Yield: Serves 3

1 cup cauliflower florets
1 cup broccoli florets
2 large carrots, cut into matchsticks
1 teaspoon umeboshi vinegar

1. Fill a large saucepan with 3" of water. Bring to a boil.

2. Add cauliflower and boil 3 minutes. Remove cauliflower with a strainer and place in a serving bowl. Reserve cooking water in saucepan.

3. Add broccoli and boil 2 minutes. Remove broccoli with a strainer and place broccoli in medium bowl with cauliflower.

4. Add carrots and boil 1 minute. Remove carrots with a strainer and place carrots in bowl.

5. Season with umeboshi vinegar.

Per Serving: Calories: 35 | Fat: 0 g | Saturated fat: 0 g | Cholesterol: 0 mg | Sodium: 250 mg | Total carbohydrates: 8 g | Dietary fiber: 3 g | Sugars: 3 g | Protein: 2 g

Kohlrabi with Lemon (pictured)

Hands-On Time: 5 minutes
Total Time: 20 minutes
Yield: Serves 4

1 pound kohlrabi, stems removed, peeled, and shredded
½ cup chicken broth
1 tablespoon lemon juice
½ teaspoon salt
½ teaspoon ground black pepper
½ cup chopped fresh parsley

Place the kohlrabi in a large saucepan. Add the broth, lemon juice, salt, and pepper. Simmer over low heat for 15 minutes. Sprinkle with parsley. Serve hot.

Per Serving: Calories: 40 | Fat: 0 g | Saturated fat: 0 g | Cholesterol: 0 mg | Sodium: 430 mg | Total carbohydrates: 8 g | Dietary fiber: 4 g | Sugars: 3 g | Protein: 2 g

Spiced Pineapple Kebabs

Hands-On Time: 15 minutes
Total Time: 15 minutes
Yield: Serves 4

4 teaspoons sugar
1 teaspoon ground cloves
1 teaspoon lemon juice
1 medium pineapple, peeled, cored, and cut in 1" x 3" pieces
4 skewers

1. Mix sugar, cloves, and lemon juice in a medium bowl. Thread the pineapple pieces onto the skewers and sprinkle with sugar mixture.
2. Set grill to high heat.
3. Grill skewers over hot fire until slightly brown and very hot. Serve immediately.

Per Serving: Calories: 131 | Fat: 0.3 g | Saturated fat: 0 g | Cholesterol: 0 mg | Sodium: 4 mg | Total carbohydrates: 34 g | Dietary fiber: 3 g | Sugars: 27 g | Protein: 1 g

Cheesy Potato Boats

Hands-On Time: 10 minutes
Total Time: 25 minutes
Yield: Serves 6

6 medium baking potatoes
½ teaspoon salt
⅛ teaspoon black pepper
½ cup fat-free shredded Cheddar cheese
¼ cup sliced scallions

1. Preheat oven to 475°F.
2. Cut potatoes in half and scoop out 80 percent of the pulp. Coat a large baking sheet with nonstick spray.
3. Place potato halves on sheet and sprinkle with salt and pepper. Bake potatoes for 10–15 minutes or until crispy.
4. Sprinkle potatoes with cheese and return to oven for 2 minutes. Sprinkle potatoes with scallions.

Per Serving: Calories: 50 | Fat: 0 g | Saturated fat: 0 g | Cholesterol: 0 mg | Sodium: 290 mg | Total carbohydrates: 8 g | Dietary fiber: 1 g | Sugars: 1 g | Protein: 4 g

Healthy "Creamed" Spinach

Hands-On Time: 10 minutes
Total Time: 15 minutes
Yield: Serves 6

2 pounds fresh spinach
½ cup chicken broth, divided
2 garlic cloves, minced
1 small yellow onion, peeled and diced
½ teaspoon salt
Juice from 1 large lemon

1. Steam spinach in a double boiler until completely wilted, about 3 minutes. Allow to cool and then squeeze out excess moisture.
2. Add 1 tablespoon broth to a medium skillet over medium heat; cook the garlic and onion until soft, about 5 minutes.
3. Put cooked spinach, garlic, and onion in a food processor with remaining broth, salt, and lemon juice. Process until smooth.

Per Serving: Calories: 50 | Fat: 0 g | Saturated fat: 0 g | Cholesterol: 0 mg | Sodium: 380 mg | Total carbohydrates: 7 g | Dietary fiber: 4 g | Sugars: 0 g | Protein: 4 g

Baked Zucchini Stacks

Hands-On Time: 10 minutes
Total Time: 25 minutes
Yield: Serves 4

1 large egg white, beaten
1 cup panko bread crumbs
1 teaspoon salt
1 teaspoon ground black pepper
½ teaspoon granulated garlic
2 large zucchini, sliced into ¼"
   rounds

1. Preheat oven to 450°F. Line a baking sheet with parchment paper.
2. Place egg white in a small, shallow dish. Place panko, salt, pepper, and garlic in another shallow dish.
3. Dip zucchini rounds first into the egg white then press into the bread crumbs until well coated.
4. Transfer coated zucchini to prepared baking sheet. Bake for 10–12 minutes or until exterior is crispy. Stack 3 or 4 zucchini rounds on individual plates for serving.

Per Serving: Calories: 90 | Fat: 0 g | Saturated fat: 0 g | Cholesterol: 0 mg | Sodium: 647 mg | Total carbohydrates: 10 g | Dietary fiber: 2 g | Sugars: 4 g | Protein: 4 g

Couscous with Peas

Hands-On Time: 10 minutes
Total Time: 15 minutes
Yield: Serves 6

1¾ cups water
1 teaspoon chicken-flavored
   bouillon granules
⅛ teaspoon salt
1 cup couscous, uncooked
¾ cup frozen peas, thawed

1. Combine water, bouillon granules, and salt in a medium saucepan. Bring to a boil.
2. Remove from heat. Add couscous and peas. Cover and let stand until liquid is absorbed and couscous is tender, about 5 minutes. Fluff couscous with a fork.

Per Serving: Calories: 120 | Fat: 0.5 g | Saturated fat: 0 g | Cholesterol: 0 mg | Sodium: 130 mg | Total carbohydrates: 25 g | Dietary fiber: 2 g | Sugars: 1 g | Protein: 5 g

Sweet Potato Crisps (pictured)

Hands-On Time: 5 minutes
Total Time: 30 minutes
Yield: Serves 2

1 small sweet potato
1 teaspoon olive oil
½ teaspoon seasoned salt

1. Preheat oven to 400°F.

2. Scrub sweet potato and pierce flesh several times with fork. Place on microwave-safe plate; microwave 5 minutes on high. Remove from microwave; wrap in aluminum foil. Set aside 5 minutes.

3. Remove foil; peel and cut potato into strips. Spread on baking sheet treated with nonstick cooking spray; drizzle strips with olive oil and sprinkle with seasoned salt. Bake for 10–15 minutes or until crisp. There's a risk that sweet potato strips will caramelize and burn; check often while cooking to ensure this doesn't occur. Lower oven temperature, if necessary. Serve immediately.

Per Serving: Calories: 40 | Fat: 2.5 g | Saturated fat: 0.5 g | Cholesterol: 0 mg | Sodium: 390 mg | Total carbohydrates: 5 g | Dietary fiber: 1 g | Sugars: 2 g | Protein: 1 g

Skewered Vegetables

Hands-On Time: 20 minutes
Total Time: 20 minutes
Yield: Serves 6

12 wooden skewers
1 medium par-baked sweet potato or yam
1 medium yellow bell pepper
1 medium red bell pepper
1 medium green bell pepper
1 medium zucchini
1 large shallot
1 tablespoon olive oil
½ teaspoon sea salt
½ teaspoon ground black pepper
1 Serrano pepper, finely minced

1. Soak wooden skewers in water for at least 4 hours.

2. Peel the potato and cut into 2″ cubes. Stem and seed the peppers and cut into 2″ squares. Cut the zucchini into 2″ chunks. Cut the shallot into wedges.

3. Preheat grill. Skewer the vegetables, alternating types. Brush them with the oil, sprinkle with salt and pepper, and grill until al dente. Sprinkle with Serrano pepper before serving.

Per Serving: Calories: 70 | Fat: 3 g | Saturated fat: 0.5 g | Cholesterol: 0 mg | Sodium: 140 mg | Total carbohydrates: 11 g | Dietary fiber: 2 g | Sugars: 5 g | Protein: 2 g

Grilled Asparagus

Hands-On Time: 10 minutes
Total Time: 15 minutes
Yield: Serves 6

**2 medium bunches asparagus,
    trimmed**
1 tablespoon extra-virgin olive oil
1 teaspoon lemon juice
⅛ teaspoon ground black pepper

Preheat grill to medium. Toss the asparagus in the oil, then drain on a rack and season with lemon juice and pepper. Grill the asparagus for 1–2 minutes on each side. Serve immediately.

Per Serving: Calories: 20 | Fat: 1 g | Saturated fat: 0 g | Cholesterol: 0 mg | Sodium: 0 mg | Total carbohydrates: 2 g | Dietary fiber: 1 g | Sugars: 1 g | Protein: 1 g

Spaghetti Squash

Hands-On Time: 5 minutes
Total Time: 25 minutes
Yield: Serves 4

1 (2-pound) spaghetti squash
¼ teaspoon salt
¼ teaspoon ground black pepper

1. Slice squash in half and scoop out the seeds. Wrap each half loosely in plastic wrap. Cook wrapped squash in microwave for 20 minutes on high power. Remove plastic wrap.

2. Using a fork, scoop squash pulp into a medium bowl. The squash should be stringy like spaghetti. Season with salt and pepper.

Per Serving: Calories: 50 | Fat: 1 g | Saturated fat: 0 g | Cholesterol: 0 mg | Sodium: 170 mg | Total carbohydrates: 11 g | Dietary fiber: 2 g | Sugars: 4 g | Protein: 1 g

Duchess Potatoes

Hands-On Time: 5 minutes
Total Time: 25 minutes
Yield: Serves 8

1 (12-ounce) package refrigerated mashed potatoes

1 large egg, beaten

¼ cup grated Parmesan cheese

2 tablespoons sour cream

½ teaspoon dried basil leaves

2 tablespoons whole milk

4 tablespoons grated Parmesan cheese, divided

1. Preheat oven to 375°F.

2. In a large bowl, combine all ingredients except milk and 2 tablespoons Parmesan cheese. Beat well until combined. Spoon or pipe mixture into 16 mounds onto greased baking sheets. Brush with milk and sprinkle with 2 tablespoons Parmesan cheese.

3. Bake potatoes for 15–20 minutes or until tops are beginning to brown and potatoes are hot. Serve immediately.

Per Serving: Calories: 70 | Fat: 2 g | Saturated fat: 1 g | Cholesterol: 25 mg | Sodium: 170 mg | Total carbohydrates: 9 g | Dietary fiber: 1 g | Sugars: 1 g | Protein: 3 g

Fresh Roasted Green Beans

Hands-On Time: 5 minutes
Total Time: 20 minutes
Yield: Serves 6

1 pound fresh green beans, ends trimmed

3 teaspoons olive oil

1 teaspoon sea salt

½ teaspoon garlic powder

½ teaspoon onion powder

1. Preheat oven to 400°F.

2. Arrange green beans in a single layer on a baking sheet. Dress with olive oil, salt, garlic powder, and onion powder.

3. Bake 15 minutes, stirring halfway through cooking time.

Per Serving: Calories: 40 | Fat: 2 g | Saturated fat: 0 g | Cholesterol: 0 mg | Sodium: 390 mg | Total carbohydrates: 4 g | Dietary fiber: 2 g | Sugars: 1 g | Protein: 1 g

Crispy Corn Fritters (pictured)

Hands-On Time: 20 minutes
Total Time: 20 minutes
Yield: Serves 12

1 large egg
⅓ cup whole milk
⅔ cup cornstarch
1½ teaspoons baking powder
½ teaspoon salt
1 teaspoon ground black pepper
⅛ teaspoon ground nutmeg
1 cup fresh corn kernels
2 cups canola oil

1. Place egg, milk, cornstarch, baking powder, salt, pepper, and nutmeg in a food processor and blend until smooth. Scrape into a medium bowl; fold in the corn.

2. Heat oil to 350°F in a large frying pan. Drop the fritters by the tablespoonful into the hot oil and cook for 3–5 minutes. Drain on paper towels and serve hot.

Per Serving: Calories: 80 | Fat: 4 g | Saturated fat: 0.5 g | Cholesterol: 15 mg | Sodium: 180 mg | Total carbohydrates: 10 g | Dietary fiber: 0 g | Sugars: 1 g | Protein: 1 g

Broiled Eggplant

Hands-On Time: 5 minutes
Total Time: 15 minutes
Yield: Serves 6

4 small eggplants, sliced
   lengthwise into ⅛″ pieces
4 cloves garlic, minced
1 tablespoon olive oil
2 teaspoons salt, divided
½ teaspoon ground black pepper

1. Preheat broiler.

2. Toss all ingredients, except 1 teaspoon salt, together in a large bowl. Place eggplant slices on a broiler pan or baking sheet.

3. Broil 5 minutes per side until golden brown outside and soft inside. Season with remaining salt.

Per Serving: Calories: 120 | Fat: 3 g | Saturated fat: 0 g | Cholesterol: 0 mg | Sodium: 780 mg | Total carbohydrates: 22 g | Dietary fiber: 12 g | Sugars: 12 g | Protein: 4 g

Simple Quinoa

Hands-On Time: 5 minutes
Total Time: 25 minutes
Yield: Serves 4

1 cup quinoa, rinsed and drained
2 cups vegetable broth
½ teaspoon garlic salt
1 teaspoon fresh lemon juice

1. Combine quinoa and broth in a medium saucepan over high heat. Bring to a boil and then reduce heat to low and cover. Allow to simmer 20 minutes or until quinoa is tender and fluffy.

2. Fluff quinoa with a fork and stir in garlic salt and lemon juice. Serve warm.

Per Serving: Calories: 160 | Fat: 2 g | Saturated fat: 0 g | Cholesterol: 0 mg | Sodium: 500 mg | Total carbohydrates: 30 g | Dietary fiber: 3 g | Sugars: 1 g | Protein: 6 g

Leek Potato Cakes

Hands-On Time: 10 minutes
Total Time: 30 minutes
Yield: Serves 4

2 cups finely chopped leeks, white part only
2 cups finely grated peeled potatoes
2 large eggs, beaten
2 tablespoons all-purpose flour
1 teaspoon salt
¼ teaspoon ground black pepper
¼ cup olive oil

1. Combine leeks, potatoes, eggs, flour, salt, and pepper in a medium mixing bowl; mix well. Form into 8 pancakes (3″).

2. Heat olive oil in a heavy skillet over medium heat until a piece of leek sizzles when added. Transfer 4 of the pancakes into the pan and cook gently, without moving them, until a crisp brown crust develops, about 5 minutes. Turn and brown the other side; drain on paper towels and repeat with remaining cakes.

Per Serving: Calories: 120 | Fat: 2 g | Saturated fat: 0 g | Cholesterol: 0 mg | Sodium: 610 mg | Total carbohydrates: 25 g | Dietary fiber: 3 g | Sugars: 2 g | Protein: 3 g

Herbed Wax Beans

Hands-On Time: 10 minutes
Total Time: 10 minutes
Yield: Serves 6

1 cup water
1 pound wax beans, stems trimmed
1 tablespoon olive oil
1 tablespoon minced chives
½ teaspoon salt

1. Place water and a steamer basket in a medium saucepan set over high heat. Place beans in basket and steam for 3–8 minutes or until tender.

2. Transfer beans to a serving dish, drizzle with oil, and sprinkle with chives and salt.

3. Serve hot or at room temperature.

Per Serving: Calories: 46 | Fat: 2 g | Saturated fat: 0 g | Cholesterol: 0 mg | Sodium: 195 mg | Total carbohydrates: 6 g | Dietary fiber: 2 g | Sugars: 3 g | Protein: 1 g

Blanched String Beans

Hands-On Time: 15 minutes
Total Time: 15 minutes
Yield: Serves 6

1 pound string beans
1 tablespoon olive oil
1 teaspoon lemon juice

1. Cook the beans in a large pot of boiling water for 5 minutes and then shock them in medium bowl of ice water for 5 minutes.

2. Toss with the olive oil and lemon juice.

Per Serving: Calories: 40 | Fat: 2.5 g | Saturated fat: 0.5 g | Cholesterol: 0 mg | Sodium: 5 mg | Total carbohydrates: 5 g | Dietary fiber: 2 g | Sugars: 2 g | Protein: 1 g

Kidney Bean Succotash

Hands-On Time: 10 minutes
Total Time: 10 minutes
Yield: Serves 8

16 ounces thawed corn
2 (16-ounce) cans red kidney beans, drained and rinsed
½ cup diced red onion
¼ cup red wine vinegar
¼ cup extra-virgin olive oil
¼ cup chopped parsley
1 teaspoon salt
½ teaspoon ground black pepper

Toss corn with beans, onion, vinegar, oil, and parsley; season with salt and pepper.

Per Serving: Calories: 200 | Fat: 8 g | Saturated fat: 1.5 g | Cholesterol: 0 mg | Sodium: 460 mg | Total carbohydrates: 27 g | Dietary fiber: 6 g | Sugars: 0 g | Protein: 8 g

Mashed Parsnips (pictured)

Hands-On Time: 10 minutes
Total Time: 30 minutes
Yield: Serves 6

4 pounds parsnips, peeled and
    quartered
1 cup chicken broth
1 teaspoon salt
½ teaspoon ground black pepper
2 tablespoons chopped chives

1. Put parsnips in a large stockpot with just enough water to cover. Bring to a boil over high heat and then reduce heat to low and simmer until parsnips are soft, about 20 minutes. Drain.

2. Put parsnips in a food processor with broth, salt, and pepper and process until smooth.

3. Top with chives. Serve immediately.

Per Serving: Calories: 240 | Fat: 3 g | Saturated fat: 1 g | Cholesterol: 0 mg | Sodium: 520 mg | Total carbohydrates: 38 g | Dietary fiber: 15 g | Sugars: 17 g | Protein: 6 g

Grilled Corn with Red Peppers

Hands-On Time: 15 minutes
Total Time: 25 minutes
Yield: Serves 4

4 medium ears fresh corn
1 tablespoon olive oil
1 large red onion, peeled and
    chopped
3 cloves garlic, minced
1 medium red bell pepper, seeded
    and chopped
1 tablespoon chopped fresh
    oregano
⅛ teaspoon salt
⅛ teaspoon ground black pepper
½ teaspoon ground cumin

1. Prepare and preheat grill. Remove husk and silk from corn. Grill corn about 6" from medium coals for 3–5 minutes, turning frequently, until corn is light brown. Cool for 10 minutes, then cut kernels from the cobs.

2. Place a heavy-duty medium saucepan on the grill. Add olive oil and heat. Add onion and garlic; cook and stir until tender, about 5 minutes. Add bell pepper and corn; cook and stir for 2 minutes longer. Toss with oregano, salt, black pepper, and cumin and serve.

Per Serving: Calories: 130 | Fat: 4 g | Saturated fat: 0 g | Cholesterol: 0 mg | Sodium: 80 mg | Total carbohydrates: 23 g | Dietary fiber: 4 g | Sugars: 7 g | Protein: 4 g

Buttery Mashed Cauliflower

Hands-On Time: 10 minutes
Total Time: 20 minutes
Yield: Serves 6

3 quarts water
1 tablespoon salt
1 large head cauliflower, cored and chopped
2 tablespoons butter, divided
1 tablespoon chopped fresh chives

1. Boil water in a large stockpot. Add salt and cauliflower and cook for 10 minutes. Drain well, reserving ¼ cup cooking liquid.

2. Place cauliflower in blender or food processor with 1 tablespoon butter. Process until smooth, adding reserved cooking liquid as needed to make smooth.

3. Transfer to a serving dish and top with chives and remaining butter.

Per Serving: Calories: 70 | Fat: 4 g | Saturated fat: 2.5 g | Cholesterol: 10 mg | Sodium: 117 mg | Total carbohydrates: 7 g | Dietary fiber: 3 g | Sugars: 3 g | Protein: 3 g

Lima Bean Succotash

Hands-On Time: 10 minutes
Total Time: 20 minutes
Yield: Serves 4

1 cup frozen baby lima beans
1½ cups frozen corn kernels
1 tablespoon butter
1 teaspoon fresh chopped oregano
¼ teaspoon salt
⅛ teaspoon ground black pepper
1 tomato, chopped

1. Heat a medium saucepan over medium heat. Add the lima beans and corn, bring to a simmer, and turn the heat to low. Cover and cook for 10 minutes.

2. Stir in butter, oregano, salt, and pepper. Remove from heat; toss with the tomato. Serve hot.

Per Serving: Calories: 142 | Fat: 4 g | Saturated fat: 2 g | Cholesterol: 10 mg | Sodium: 140 mg | Total carbohydrates: 23 g | Dietary fiber: 3 g | Sugars: 5 g | Protein: 5 g

Mashed Sweet Potatoes with Brown Sugar

Hands-On Time: 10 minutes
Total Time: 30 minutes
Yield: Serves 6

4 medium sweet potatoes, peeled and quartered
¼ cup whole milk
2 tablespoons butter
1 tablespoon brown sugar

1. In a large pot, cook the sweet potatoes in boiling, salted water until tender, about 20 minutes. Drain and return to the pan.

2. In a medium pan, heat the milk and butter. Add to the potatoes along with the brown sugar. Mash by hand or whip with an electric mixer.

Per Serving: Calories: 120 | Fat: 4 g | Saturated fat: 3 g | Cholesterol: 11 mg | Sodium: 53 mg | Total carbohydrates: 19.4 g | Dietary fiber: 3 g | Sugars: 6 g | Protein: 2 g

Steamed Brussels Sprouts with Butter

Hands-On Time: 10 minutes
Total Time: 10 minutes
Yield: Serves 3

8 Brussels sprouts, cut into halves
1 tablespoon butter
¼ teaspoon salt
¼ teaspoon ground black pepper

1. Place Brussels sprouts on a plate that fits into a steamer insert or basket. Set aside.

2. Fill a rice cooker pot with water to about the 4-cup mark. Cover the rice cooker and set to "Cook." When the water in the rice cooker boils, place the steamer insert or basket with the plate of Brussels sprouts into the rice cooker and steam, covered, for 4 minutes until sprouts slightly soften. Drain excess water from the Brussels sprouts and set aside.

3. Clean out the rice cooker and wipe dry. Add the butter to the rice cooker, cover, and set to "Cook." When the base of the cooker pot gets warm, add Brussels sprouts, cut-side down, and fry for about 3 minutes until tender. Before serving, add salt and black pepper. Toss well and transfer to serving dish.

Per Serving: Calories: 57 | Fat: 4 g | Saturated fat: 4 g | Cholesterol: 13 mg | Sodium: 239 mg | Total carbohydrates: 5 g | Dietary fiber: 2 g | Sugars: 1 g | Protein: 2 g

Stir-Fried Spinach

Hands-On Time: 20 minutes
Total Time: 20 minutes
Yield: Serves 4

1 tablespoon vegetable oil
18 medium spinach leaves
¼ teaspoon salt

Add the oil to a preheated wok or large skillet. When the oil is hot, add the spinach and remove from heat. Add the salt and stir-fry briefly off the heat for less than 1 minute. Serve immediately.

Per Serving: Calories: 40 | Fat: 4 g | Saturated fat: 0 g | Cholesterol: 0 mg | Sodium: 180 mg | Total carbohydrates: 2 g | Dietary fiber: 1 g | Sugars: 0 g | Protein: 1 g

Hearty Mushroom and Herb Stuffing

Hands-On Time: 20 minutes
Total Time: 20 minutes
Yield: Serves 8

2 tablespoons extra-virgin olive oil, divided
1 (16-ounce) package sliced button mushrooms
1 cup chopped celery
1 cup chopped yellow or white onions
1 cup vegetable stock, divided
1 (16-ounce) package whole button mushrooms
2 teaspoons ground sage, divided
2 teaspoons dried rosemary, divided
2 teaspoons dried basil, divided
2 teaspoons sea salt, divided
2 teaspoons ground black pepper, divided
8 slices stale 100 percent whole-wheat bread, torn into small pieces

1. In a large skillet over medium heat, combine ½ tablespoon olive oil with sliced mushrooms, celery, and onions. Sauté for about 3–5 minutes or until slightly softened. Add ½ cup stock and simmer until completely absorbed, about 5 minutes. Add the whole mushrooms to the skillet and season with 1 teaspoon each sage, rosemary, basil, sea salt, and pepper. Add ¼ cup stock and sauté until vegetables are cooked through, about 5–7 minutes.

2. In a large serving dish, toss the vegetable sauté (and all the juices that remain) with the torn bread pieces. Add the remaining stock, olive oil, and spices to the stuffing and toss. Serve hot.

Per Serving: Calories: 140 | Fat: 4.5 g | Saturated fat: 1 g | Cholesterol: 0 mg | Sodium: 790 mg | Total carbohydrates: 20 g | Dietary fiber: 3 g | Sugars: 3 g | Protein: 7 g

Cornmeal Grits

Hands-On Time: 20 minutes
Total Time: 30 minutes
Yield: Serves 4

4 cups water
1 teaspoon salt
1 cup polenta meal
2 tablespoons butter

1. Put water and salt in a medium saucepan and bring to a boil.

2. Reduce heat to medium-low and gradually add polenta, stirring constantly until it has thickened, about 15 minutes. Stir in butter.

3. Serve immediately for soft grits or pour into a greased loaf pan and let cool. When cool, grits can be sliced and fried or grilled.

Per Serving: Calories: 180 | Fat: 6 g | Saturated fat: 4 g | Cholesterol: 15 mg | Sodium: 590 mg | Total carbohydrates: 27 g | Dietary fiber: 2 g | Sugars: 0 g | Protein: 3 g

Cauliflower "Rice"

Hands-On Time: 15 minutes
Total Time: 15 minutes
Yield: Serves 4

1 medium head cauliflower
1 tablespoon lemon juice
2 tablespoons coconut oil
3 small shallots, peeled and minced
2 cloves garlic, minced
1 teaspoon kosher salt
⅛ teaspoon ground white pepper

1. Rinse cauliflower and pat dry. Break into florets. Using a box grater or a food processer, grate or process the florets until they are in tiny pieces. Toss with lemon juice in a medium bowl and set aside.

2. In a large skillet, melt coconut oil over medium-high heat. Add shallots and garlic; cook and stir until tender, about 5 minutes.

3. Add the cauliflower and sprinkle with salt and pepper. Cook for 5 minutes, stirring frequently, until cauliflower is tender but with some firmness in the center. Serve immediately.

Per Serving: Calories: 100 | Fat: 7 g | Saturated fat: 6 g | Cholesterol: 0 mg | Sodium: 420 mg | Total carbohydrates: 9 g | Dietary fiber: 3 g | Sugars: 4 g | Protein: 3 g

Chapter 13

Desserts and Beverages

Chocolate Cookies with M&M's and Jelly Beans

Hands-On Time: 10 minutes
Total Time: 25 minutes
Yield: Makes 36 cookies

4 tablespoons butter, softened
2 large eggs, beaten
1 (18-ounce) package chocolate cake mix
½ cup plain M&M's
½ cup M&M's with peanuts
½ cup jelly beans

1. Preheat oven to 350°F. Line a baking sheet with parchment paper.

2. In a large bowl, combine the butter and eggs until creamy. Stir in the cake mix until combined. Stir in candies until well combined.

3. Drop by tablespoons onto prepared baking sheets. Bake for 12–15 minutes or until cookies are set. Let cool for 5 minutes on cookie sheets, then remove to wire racks.

Per Cookie: Calories: 90 | Fat: 4 g | Saturated fat: 2 g | Cholesterol: 15 mg | Sodium: 120 mg | Total carbohydrates: 15 g | Dietary fiber: 0 g | Sugars: 8 g | Protein: 1 g

Pumpkin Pie Mug Cake

Hands-On Time: 10 minutes
Total Time: 10 minutes
Yield: Serves 1

⅓ cup pumpkin purée
1 large egg
1 tablespoon whole milk
½ teaspoon vanilla extract
2 tablespoons light brown sugar
1 teaspoon pumpkin pie spice
⅛ teaspoon salt
2 small graham crackers, crushed
¼ cup whipped cream
1 tablespoon crushed walnuts

1. In a small bowl, whisk together pumpkin, egg, milk, vanilla, sugar, pumpkin pie spice, and salt. Whisk until smooth.

2. In a large microwavable mug, add crushed grahams and press down on bottom of mug. Pour in pumpkin mixture. Microwave on high for 2 minutes. Microwave ovens vary, so check every 30 seconds to ensure mixture is not bubbling over.

3. Carefully remove mug from microwave. Let stand 2 minutes to cool. Serve topped with whipped cream and walnuts.

Per Serving: Calories: 330 | Fat: 14 g | Saturated fat: 5 g | Cholesterol: 200 mg | Sodium: 490 mg | Total carbohydrates: 40 g | Dietary fiber: 4 g | Sugars: 25 g | Protein: 10 g

Banana Rolls

Hands-On Time: 30 minutes
Total Time: 30 minutes
Yield: Serves 12

5 medium ripe bananas, peeled
1 teaspoon tapioca flour
2 tablespoons water
2 cups warm water
25 rice paper wrappers
4 cups vegetable oil

1. In a small bowl, mash bananas into a paste.
2. Mix the tapioca flour with 2 tablespoons water and heat in the microwave on high for 30–40 seconds to make a paste.
3. Pour warm water into a shallow bowl. Dip one rice paper wrapper into the water until soft. Remove and lay flat on a work surface. Place 2 tablespoons of the mashed bananas in the bottom third of the wrapper. Roll the filling up to halfway. Fold the two sides over the middle and roll up to meet with the top. Glue with tapioca paste.
4. Heat the oil in a deep-frying pan to 350°F. Deep-fry each roll individually for 4 minutes. Drain on paper towels.

Per Serving: Calories: 195 | Fat: 11 g | Saturated fat: 2 g | Cholesterol: 4 mg | Sodium: 178 mg | Total carbohydrates: 24 g | Dietary fiber: 1 g | Sugars: 6 g | Protein: 0.5 g

Ambrosia

Hands-On Time: 5 minutes
Total Time: 20 minutes
Yield: Serves 8

1 (8-ounce) cup heavy whipping cream
1 tablespoon confectioners' sugar
1 teaspoon vanilla extract
⅓ cup pineapple juice from canned pineapple
2 (14-ounce) cans mandarin oranges, drained
1 (15-ounce) can crushed pineapple, drained, reserving juice
1 cup shredded coconut
½ cup chopped pecans
⅛ teaspoon ground cinnamon

1. In the bowl of a stand mixer fitted with whisk attachment, add whipping cream, confectioners' sugar, and vanilla. Beat until soft peaks form. Beat in pineapple juice. Fold in oranges, pineapple, coconut, and pecans.
2. Transfer to a serving bowl and sprinkle with cinnamon.
3. Cover and chill for 15 minutes before serving.

Per Serving: Calories: 280 | Fat: 20 g | Saturated fat: 11 g | Cholesterol: 35 mg | Sodium: 45 mg | Total carbohydrates: 26 g | Dietary fiber: 3 g | Sugars: 23 g | Protein: 3 g

Butterscotch Drop Cookies

Hands-On Time: 10 minutes
Total Time: 25 minutes
Yield: Makes 48 cookies

2½ cups all-purpose flour
1 teaspoon baking soda
½ teaspoon baking powder
½ teaspoon salt
½ cup unsalted butter
1½ cups packed dark brown sugar
2 large eggs
2 teaspoons vanilla extract
1 cup whole buttermilk (not skim or low fat)
1 cup chopped pecans

1. Preheat oven to 350°F. Lightly grease two baking sheets.
2. Stir dry ingredients together in a medium bowl; set aside.
3. In another medium bowl, cream together butter and brown sugar until light and fluffy. Beat in eggs and vanilla.
4. Add dry ingredients to wet ingredients alternately with buttermilk. Mix well after each addition. Stir in the pecans.
5. Drop by rounded teaspoons onto prepared baking sheets. Bake 10–12 minutes; do not overbake. Cool for 3–5 minutes before removing from baking sheets.

Per Cookie: Calories: 83 | Fat: 4 g | Saturated fat: 1.5 g | Cholesterol: 13 mg | Sodium: 64 mg | Total carbohydrates: 11 g | Dietary fiber: 0 g | Sugars: 7 g | Protein: 1 g

Raspberry Sorbet (pictured)

Hands-On Time: 5 minutes
Total Time: 15 minutes
Yield: Serves 6

4 cups frozen raspberries
2 teaspoons agave nectar
2 teaspoons vanilla extract
1 teaspoon chopped mint leaves

1. In a high-speed blender, combine the raspberries, agave nectar, vanilla, and mint and purée.
2. Once fully puréed, pour the raspberry mixture into 6 small cups and freeze for 10 minutes.
3. Serve with a spoon.

Per Serving: Calories: 60 | Fat: 0 g | Saturated fat: 0 g | Cholesterol: 0 mg | Sodium: 0 mg | Total carbohydrates: 13 g | Dietary fiber: 6 g | Sugars: 5 g | Protein: 1 g

Easy Peanut Butter Cookies

Hands-On Time: 20 minutes
Total Time: 30 minutes
Yield: Makes 24 cookies

1 cup peanut butter
1 cup sugar
1 large egg

1. Preheat oven to 350°F. Line a cookie sheet with parchment paper and set aside.

2. In a large bowl cream together the peanut butter and sugar. Once thoroughly mixed, stir in the egg.

3. The batter will be very thick and sticky. For small cookies, use a spoon to scoop out about 1 tablespoon of batter, roll it into a ball, and place on the cookie sheet about 1" apart. For large cookies, scoop out about 2 tablespoons of dough, roll into a larger ball, and place on the cookie sheet about 2" apart.

4. Using a fork, flatten cookies and make a crisscross pattern on them. Place in oven and bake for 8–10 minutes until golden brown. Allow cookies to cool on baking sheet for about 10 minutes before placing them on a cooling rack.

5. Store cookies in an airtight container on the counter for 2–3 days. Cookies and cookie dough can also be frozen for up to 1 month.

Per Cookie: Calories: 110 | Fat: 6 g | Saturated fat: 1 g | Cholesterol: 10 mg | Sodium: 40 mg | Total carbohydrates: 10 g | Dietary fiber: 1 g | Sugars: 9 g | Protein: 3 g

Pineapple Banana Freeze

Hands-On Time: 5 minutes
Total Time: 15 minutes
Yield: Serves 6

2 bananas, peeled
2 cups pineapple
2 teaspoons vanilla extract
1 cup ice

1. In a high-speed blender, combine the bananas, pineapple, and vanilla and purée. Add ice and blend until smooth.

2. Once smooth, pour the mixture into 6 cups and freeze for 10 minutes.

3. Serve with a spoon.

Per Serving: Calories: 70 | Fat: 0 g | Saturated fat: 0 g | Cholesterol: 0 mg | Sodium: 0 mg | Total carbohydrates: 17 g | Dietary fiber: 2 g | Sugars: 11 g | Protein: 1 g

Strawberry Whip

Hands-On Time: 15 minutes
Total Time: 15 minutes
Yield: Serves 4

1 large egg white
1¼ cups mashed strawberries
¼ cup sugar
¼ teaspoon lemon juice

1. In a medium bowl, whip together the egg white and strawberries. When the mixture begins to thicken, gradually add the sugar. Continue to beat until the mixture holds soft peaks. Stir in the lemon juice.

2. Chill well before serving.

Per Serving: Calories: 70 | Fat: 0 g | Saturated fat: 0 g | Cholesterol: 0 mg | Sodium: 15 mg | Total carbohydrates: 17 g | Dietary fiber: 1 g | Sugars: 15 g | Protein: 1 g

Crisp Lemon Cookies

Hands-On Time: 15 minutes
Total Time: 25 minutes
Yield: Makes 36 cookies

1½ cups unbleached all-purpose flour
1 cup white whole-wheat flour
1½ cups sugar
1 tablespoon baking powder
¾ cup olive oil
Juice and grated zest of 2 large lemons
1 tablespoon vanilla extract

1. Preheat oven to 350°F.

2. Measure flours, sugar, and baking powder into a medium mixing bowl and whisk well to combine. Add remaining ingredients and stir to form a stiff dough.

3. Drop by rounded tablespoons onto two ungreased baking sheets. Place sheets on middle rack in oven and bake 10 minutes until cookies are pale and have spread out.

4. Remove from oven, cool on baking sheets 5 minutes, then transfer to a wire rack to cool fully.

5. Serve cooled cookies or store in an airtight container for up to 3 days.

Per Cookie: Calories: 100 | Fat: 4.5 g | Saturated fat: 0.5 g | Cholesterol: 0 mg | Sodium: 40 mg | Total carbohydrates: 12 g | Dietary fiber: 1 g | Sugars: 6 g | Protein: 1 g

Apple Strawberry Crumble

Hands-On Time: 10 minutes
Total Time: 25 minutes
Yield: Serves 4

2 cups chopped green apples
2 cups chopped strawberries
¼ cup Egg Beaters
1 medium ripe banana, peeled
    and mashed
1 cup oatmeal
¼ cup Splenda brown sugar
½ teaspoon ground cinnamon

1. Preheat oven to 350°F.

2. Combine apples and strawberries and pour into a 6" x 6" baking dish. Combine other ingredients in a small bowl and pile on top of the fruit.

3. Bake for 10–15 minutes or until golden brown and bubbling.

Per Serving: Calories: 220 | Fat: 2 g | Saturated fat: 0.5 g | Cholesterol: 0 mg | Sodium: 30 mg | Total carbohydrates: 46 g | Dietary fiber: 6 g | Sugars: 25 g | Protein: 5 g

Chocolate Cupcakes (pictured)

Hands-On Time: 10 minutes
Total Time: 30 minutes
Yield: Makes 16 cupcakes

1⅔ cups white whole-wheat flour
¾ cup light brown sugar
¼ cup unsweetened cocoa
    powder
2 teaspoons sodium-free baking
    soda
1 cup water
½ cup unsweetened applesauce
1 teaspoon pure vanilla extract
½ cup semisweet chocolate chips

1. Preheat oven to 350°F. Line 2 muffin tins with paper liners and set aside.

2. Place the dry ingredients, except chocolate chips, into a medium mixing bowl and whisk together. Add the wet ingredients to the pan and mix until combined.

3. Pour batter into the muffin cups, filling each roughly ⅔ full. Sprinkle chocolate chips evenly over the batter.

4. Place pan on middle rack in oven and bake for 20 minutes. Remove from oven and place on wire rack to cool. Cool briefly before serving.

Per Cupcake: Calories: 100 | Fat: 1.5 g | Saturated fat: 1 g | Cholesterol: 0 mg | Sodium: 0 mg | Total carbohydrates: 20 g | Dietary fiber: 2 g | Sugars: 12 g | Protein: 2 g

Chocolate Mug Cake

Hands-On Time: 5 minutes
Total Time: 7 minutes
Yield: Serves 1

2 large egg whites
¼ cup pumpkin purée
2 tablespoons almond flour
1 tablespoon granulated stevia
1 tablespoon unsweetened cocoa powder
¼ teaspoon baking powder
¼ teaspoon vanilla extract
⅛ teaspoon salt
1 teaspoon unsweetened rice milk

1. Combine all ingredients in a large microwave-safe mug, making sure to mix thoroughly so there are no chunks or powder left over.

2. Microwave on high 2 minutes or until cake is set. Carefully remove mug from microwave. Let stand 2 minutes to cool.

Per Serving: Calories: 160 | Fat: 8 g | Saturated fat: 1 g | Cholesterol: 0 mg | Sodium: 700 mg | Total carbohydrates: 12 g | Dietary fiber: 5 g | Sugars: 4 g | Protein: 12 g

Old-Fashioned Strawberry Shortcake

Hands-On Time: 15 minutes
Total Time: 15 minutes
Yield: Serves 4

4 homemade or store-bought biscuits
1 pound ripe sliced strawberries
2 tablespoons sugar
1 cup light whipped cream

1. Slice biscuits in half. Place the bottom of each into a serving bowl and set the tops aside.

2. Place sliced strawberries in a medium mixing bowl, sprinkle sugar over top, and stir to coat. Let sit 5 minutes to allow strawberries to release their juice.

3. Spoon berries over the biscuit bottoms, then cover with the tops. Spoon excess syrup over top of the biscuits, then garnish with whipped cream. Serve immediately.

Per Serving: Calories: 390 | Fat: 24 g | Saturated fat: 13 g | Cholesterol: 35 mg | Sodium: 460 mg | Total carbohydrates: 40 g | Dietary fiber: 3 g | Sugars: 14 g | Protein: 5 g

Peanut Butter Fudge

Hands-On Time: 15 minutes
Total Time: 15 minutes
Yield: Serves 36

1 cup brown sugar
1 cup granulated sugar
½ cup powdered sugar
1 cup skim milk
⅓ cup corn syrup
1 (10-ounce) bag large
   marshmallows
1½ cups peanut butter
2 teaspoons vanilla extract

1. Grease a 13″ x 9″ pan with unsalted butter and set aside. In large microwave-safe bowl, combine brown sugar, granulated sugar, powdered sugar, skim milk, and corn syrup; mix well. Microwave on high for 2 minutes, remove and stir. Rinse spoon. Microwave on high for 2 minutes longer, remove, and stir. Microwave on high for 2 minutes, then remove.

2. Stir in marshmallows until melted. Add peanut butter and vanilla and mix well. Spoon into prepared pan and refrigerate until set. Cut into squares.

Per Serving: Calories: 140 | Fat: 6 g | Saturated fat: 1 g | Cholesterol: 0 mg | Sodium: 60 mg | Total carbohydrates: 21 g | Dietary fiber: 1 g | Sugars: 18 g | Protein: 3 g

Frozen Cookie Dough

Hands-On Time: 20 minutes
Total Time: 20 minutes
Yield: Makes 36 cookies

1 cup butter
½ cup sugar
½ cup brown sugar
2 large eggs
3 tablespoons heavy cream
2 teaspoons vanilla extract
2½ cups all-purpose flour
1 teaspoon baking powder
½ teaspoon baking soda
¼ teaspoon salt

1. Preheat oven to 350°F.

2. In large bowl, beat butter until soft. Add sugar and brown sugar and beat until smooth. Add eggs, cream, and vanilla and beat again.

3. Add flour, baking powder, baking soda, and salt and mix well. Form into 2 rolls on waxed paper, each 2″ wide and about 9″ long. Roll up with wax paper, place in freezer bags, and freeze until firm.

4. Each roll can be used for a roll of refrigerated cookie dough. Slice each roll into 18 (½″-thick) rounds and bake for 8–11 minutes until done.

Per Serving: Calories: 106 | Fat: 6 g | Saturated fat: 3.5 g | Cholesterol: 25 mg | Sodium: 40 mg | Total carbohydrates: 12 g | Dietary fiber: 0 g | Sugars: 5 g | Protein: 1 g

Mango Lemon Sorbet

Hands-On Time: 10 minutes
Total Time: 10 minutes
Yield: Serves 12

½ cup sugar
¼ cup water
3 cups mango purée
¼ cup lemon juice

1. Combine sugar and water in a medium saucepan and heat over medium-high heat until sugar dissolves. Remove from heat and chill until cooled.

2. Combine chilled sugar syrup, mango purée, and lemon juice.

3. Freeze in an ice-cream freezer according to manufacturer's instructions.

Per Serving: Calories: 70 | Fat: 0 g | Saturated fat: 0 g | Cholesterol: 0 mg | Sodium: 5 mg | Total carbohydrates: 17 g | Dietary fiber: 0 g | Sugars: 16 g | Protein: 0 g

Cornflake and Coconut Macaroons (pictured)

Hands-On Time: 15 minutes
Total Time: 30 minutes
Yield: Makes 36 cookies

2 large egg whites
1 cup sugar
1 teaspoon vanilla extract
½ teaspoon coconut extract
1 cup shredded coconut
2 cups crushed cornflakes

1. Preheat oven to 350°F. Line 2 large baking sheets with parchment and spray with nonstick spray.

2. In a medium bowl, beat egg whites until foamy. Gradually add sugar until stiff, glossy peaks form. Beat in vanilla and coconut extracts. Gently fold in coconut, then cornflakes.

3. Drop by tablespoonfuls onto baking sheets.

4. Bake 12–15 minutes. Remove from baking sheets immediately and set aside to cool.

Per Cookie: Calories: 46 | Fat: 1 g | Saturated fat: 1 g | Cholesterol: 0 mg | Sodium: 45 mg | Total carbohydrates: 10 g | Dietary fiber: 0 g | Sugars: 6 g | Protein: 1 g

Chocolate Pudding

Hands-On Time: 15 minutes
Total Time: 15 minutes
Yield: Serves 6

½ cup sugar
⅓ cup unsweetened cocoa powder
3 tablespoons cornstarch
¼ teaspoon salt
½ cup whole milk
½ teaspoon vanilla extract

1. In a medium saucepan, stir together the sugar, cocoa, cornstarch, and salt. Gradually blend in the milk. Cook over medium heat, stirring constantly, for about 10 minutes, until the mixture thickens. Cook for 2–3 minutes longer until set. Add the vanilla.

2. Pour into 6 custard cups. Chill before serving.

Per Serving: Calories: 100 | Fat: 1.5 g | Saturated fat: 1 g | Cholesterol: 0 mg | Sodium: 105 mg | Total carbohydrates: 24 g | Dietary fiber: 2 g | Sugars: 18 g | Protein: 2 g

No-Bake Peanut Butter, Oatmeal, and Chocolate Cookies

Hands-On Time: 15 minutes
Total Time: 15 minutes
Yield: Makes 24 cookies

2 cups sugar
½ cup butter
¼ cup cocoa
½ cup whole milk
¼ cup peanut butter
1 teaspoon vanilla extract
3 cups oatmeal

1. In a large saucepan, boil the sugar, butter, cocoa, and milk for 1 minute. Remove from the heat and add the peanut butter, vanilla, and oatmeal. Mix well.

2. Drop by full teaspoons on wax paper and let cool.

Per Cookie: Calories: 153 | Fat: 6 g | Saturated fat: 3 g | Cholesterol: 10 mg | Sodium: 16 mg | Total carbohydrates: 24 g | Dietary fiber: 1 g | Sugars: 17 g | Protein: 2 g

Bananas Foster

Hands-On Time: 15 minutes
Total Time: 15 minutes
Yield: Serves 4

4 medium bananas, peeled and
  sliced
¼ cup apple juice concentrate
1 tablespoon grated orange zest
¼ cup orange juice
1 tablespoon ground cinnamon
12 ounces frozen vanilla low-fat
  yogurt

1. Combine bananas, apple juice concentrate, zest, juice, and cinnamon in a medium nonstick skillet over medium-high heat. Bring to a boil.

2. Reduce heat to medium-low and cook until bananas are tender, about 10 minutes.

3. Put 3 ounces frozen yogurt each in four dessert bowls or stemmed glasses; spoon heated banana sauce over top.

Per Serving: Calories: 294 | Fat: 2 g | Saturated fat: 1 g | Cholesterol: 36 mg | Sodium: 39 mg | Total carbohydrates: 64 g | Dietary fiber: 4 g | Sugars: 42 g | Protein: 9 g

Yogurt Fruit Pops

Hands-On Time: 10 minutes
Total Time: 10 minutes
Yield: Makes 6 pops

8 ounces plain low-fat yogurt
2 cups chopped fresh fruit, such
  as strawberries and peaches

1. In food processor or blender, purée the yogurt and fruit until smooth.

2. Pour evenly into molds or cups. Freeze until set.

Per Pop: Calories: 40 | Fat: 0.5 g | Saturated fat: 0 g | Cholesterol: 5 mg | Sodium: 30 mg | Total carbohydrates: 6 g | Dietary fiber: 1 g | Sugars: 5 g | Protein: 2 g

Thin Mint Cocoa (pictured)

Hands-On Time: 10 minutes
Total Time: 10 minutes
Yield: Serves 4

3½ cups vanilla almond milk
¼ cup unsweetened cocoa
   powder
¼ cup light brown sugar
¼ teaspoon pure peppermint
   extract

1. Measure almond milk into a medium saucepan and place over medium-high heat.

2. Once milk begins to steam, roughly 3–5 minutes, add cocoa and brown sugar and whisk well to combine.

3. Remove from heat. Stir in the peppermint extract and serve immediately.

Per Serving: Calories: 80 | Fat: 3 g | Saturated fat: 0 g | Cholesterol: 0 mg | Sodium: 160 mg | Total carbohydrates: 15 g | Dietary fiber: 3 g | Sugars: 11 g | Protein: 2 g

Sweet Chai Tea

Hands-On Time: 5 minutes
Total Time: 10 minutes
Yield: Serves 6

5 cups water
1 cup almond milk
½ cup agave nectar
1 teaspoon vanilla extract
¼ teaspoon ground cloves
¼ teaspoon ground ginger
⅛ teaspoon ground allspice
⅛ teaspoon ground cardamom
⅛ teaspoon ground cinnamon
6 black tea bags, strings removed

1. Place water, milk, agave, vanilla, cloves, ginger, allspice, cardamom, and cinnamon in a large saucepan and whisk until combined. Add tea bags and stir well.

2. Heat over high until contents begin to steam but have not yet boiled, about 5 minutes. Turn off heat and let rest 1 minute.

3. Remove tea bags and ladle into a teapot or mugs. Serve immediately.

Per Serving: Calories: 90 | Fat: 0.5 g | Saturated fat: 0 g | Cholesterol: 0 mg | Sodium: 30 mg | Total carbohydrates: 20 g | Dietary fiber: 0 g | Sugars: 19 g | Protein: 0 g

Whole-Wheat Sugar Cookies

Hands-On Time: 10 minutes
Total Time: 20 minutes
Yield: Makes 20 cookies

1 cup all-purpose flour
½ cup whole-wheat flour
¾ cup plus 1 tablespoon sugar, divided
¼ teaspoon salt
1 teaspoon baking powder
3 tablespoons canola oil
1 large egg
2 tablespoons skim milk
2 teaspoons vanilla extract

1. Preheat oven to 350°F. Spray 2 large baking sheets with nonstick cooking spray.

2. Mix flour, ¾ cup sugar, salt, and baking powder in a large bowl.

3. Mix oil, egg, milk, and vanilla in a medium bowl; add to dry ingredients and mix thoroughly.

4. Drop cookie dough balls about 2" apart on baking sheets. Sprinkle with remaining sugar.

5. Bake 8–10 minutes or until slightly browned on edges.

Per Cookie: Calories: 80 | Fat: 2 g | Saturated fat: 0 g | Cholesterol: 10 mg | Sodium: 35 mg | Total carbohydrates: 14 g | Dietary fiber: 1 g | Sugars: 7 g | Protein: 1 g

Flaky Peach Tart

Hands-On Time: 20 minutes
Total Time: 30 minutes
Yield: Serves 18

½ cup peach jam, divided
6 sheets phyllo dough, thawed
8 tablespoons butter, melted
6 medium peaches, pitted and sliced

1. Preheat oven to 375°F. Line a baking sheet with parchment paper.

2. Place a fine-mesh strainer over a medium bowl. Press jam through strainer.

3. Working one phyllo pastry sheet at a time, place on the prepared baking sheet. Brush with melted butter and repeat for all 6 sheets. Brush the top of each sheet with ½ of the strained peach jam. Arrange peach slices into rows over the top of each phyllo sheet. Brush the peaches with the remaining strained jam.

4. Bake for 10–15 minutes or until pastry is dark golden brown and fruit is tender. Let sit for 15 minutes before cutting and serving.

Per Serving: Calories: 110 | Fat: 6 g | Saturated fat: 3.5 g | Cholesterol: 15 mg | Sodium: 35 mg | Total carbohydrates: 14 g | Dietary fiber: 1 g | Sugars: 9 g | Protein: 1 g

Snow Drops

Hands-On Time: 15 minutes
Total Time: 30 minutes
Yield: Makes 24 cookies

⅞ cup butter, softened

1 cup confectioners' sugar, divided

2 cups cake flour

1 cup chopped walnuts

2 teaspoons vanilla extract

1 teaspoon water

1. Preheat oven to 400°F.

2. In a large bowl, cream together the butter and ½ cup confectioners' sugar. Stir in the flour, walnuts, vanilla, and water. Mix well. Cover and chill until firm enough to shape with your fingers.

3. Form the dough into small balls and place on a greased baking sheet.

4. Bake for 10–12 minutes or until lightly browned. Remove from the oven and immediately roll in remaining confectioners' sugar to coat evenly. Let cool completely on a rack.

Per Cookie: Calories: 150 | Fat: 10 g | Saturated fat: 4.5 g | Cholesterol: 20 mg | Sodium: 0 mg | Total carbohydrates: 15 g | Dietary fiber: 1 g | Sugars: 5 g | Protein: 2 g

Apple Pie Cookies

Hands-On Time: 20 minutes
Total Time: 30 minutes
Yield: Makes 24 cookies

1 medium apple, peeled, cored, and finely chopped

1 large egg

¾ cup powdered honey

½ teaspoon vanilla extract

1 tablespoon molasses

1 cup plus 1 tablespoon spelt flour, divided

½ teaspoon baking soda

½ teaspoon sea salt

1 teaspoon ground cinnamon

¼ teaspoon ground nutmeg

1. Preheat oven to 350°F. Line 2 large baking sheets with parchment paper.

2. In a large bowl, add apple, egg, and powdered honey and mix well. Add vanilla and molasses. Add the flour, baking soda, salt, cinnamon, and nutmeg and mix until combined.

3. Spoon 1-tablespoon amounts of dough balls onto baking sheets 2" apart. Bake for 10 minutes, until cookies are browned. Remove from baking sheet and cool on a wire rack. Store in an airtight container.

Per Cookie: Calories: 40 | Fat: 0 g | Saturated fat: 0 g | Cholesterol: 10 mg | Sodium: 80 mg | Total carbohydrates: 9 g | Dietary fiber: 0 g | Sugars: 6 g | Protein: 1 g

Watermelon Mint Agua Fresca (pictured)

Hands-On Time: 20 minutes
Total Time: 20 minutes
Yield: Serves 6

¾ cup sugar
2 cups water, divided
½ cup fresh whole mint leaves
1 (6-pound) seedless watermelon,
    cubed and rind removed

1. In a small saucepan, bring sugar, 1 cup water, and mint to a boil over high heat. Stir to dissolve sugar.
2. Strain out mint and discard. Allow mixture to cool.
3. Place watermelon and sugar mixture in a food processor. Pulse until smooth. Strain through a wide wire mesh sieve into a pitcher. Stir in remaining water.

Per Serving: Calories: 143 | Fat: 0 g | Saturated fat: 0 g | Cholesterol: 0 mg | Sodium: 5 mg | Total carbohydrates: 39 g | Dietary fiber: 1 g | Sugars: 35 g | Protein: 2 g

Homemade Lemonade

Hands-On Time: 10 minutes
Total Time: 30 minutes
Yield: Serves 10

6 large lemons
1¼ cups brown sugar
8 cups boiling water, divided

1. Scrub the lemons and halve them. Squeeze the juice and pulp into a large bowl or pitcher. Add the sugar and pour 4 cups of water over it. Stir until the sugar dissolves.
2. Add the lemon halves and the rest of the water. Stir well, then cover and allow to cool. Serve over ice.

Per Serving: Calories: 160 | Fat: 0 g | Saturated fat: 0 g | Cholesterol: 0 mg | Sodium: 20 mg | Total carbohydrates: 41 g | Dietary fiber: 1 g | Sugars: 38 g | Protein: 0 g

Peach Creamsicle Smoothie

Hands-On Time: 10 minutes
Total Time: 10 minutes
Yield: Serves 2

2 cups fresh chopped peaches
1 medium banana, peeled
1½ cups vanilla almond milk
½ cup orange juice
2 cups ice

1. Combine peaches, banana, almond milk, and orange juice in a blender with ½ cup ice and blend until thoroughly combined.
2. Add remaining ice gradually while blending until desired consistency is reached.

Per Serving: Calories: 164 | Fat: 3 g | Saturated fat: 0 g | Cholesterol: 0 mg | Sodium: 135 mg | Total carbohydrates: 36 g | Dietary fiber: 5 g | Sugars: 25 g | Protein: 3 g

Oatmeal and Chocolate Chip Cookies

Hands-On Time: 10 minutes
Total Time: 30 minutes
Yield: Makes 24 cookies

1 (18-ounce) box yellow cake mix
⅔ cup rolled oats
½ cup margarine
1 large egg
½ cup chocolate chips

1. Preheat oven to 375°F.
2. Combine cake mix, oats, margarine, and egg in a medium bowl and mix well. Fold in chocolate chips. Drop by spoonfuls onto an ungreased cookie sheet.
3. Bake for 10 minutes or until lightly golden. Remove warm cookies from sheet and allow to cool on a wire rack.

Per Cookie: Calories: 140 | Fat: 6 g | Saturated fat: 1.5 g | Cholesterol: 10 mg | Sodium: 190 mg | Total carbohydrates: 21 g | Dietary fiber: 1 g | Sugars: 11 g | Protein: 2 g

Nilla Wafers

Hands-On Time: 10 minutes
Total Time: 25 minutes
Yield: Makes 24 cookies

½ cup unsalted butter
1 cup sugar
1 large egg
1 tablespoon vanilla extract
1⅓ cups all-purpose flour
¾ teaspoon baking soda
¼ teaspoon salt
⅛ teaspoon ground nutmeg

1. Preheat oven to 350°F.
2. In a large mixing bowl, cream butter and sugar. Beat in egg and vanilla. In a small bowl, combine flour, baking soda, salt, and nutmeg; blend into butter mixture.
3. Use a teaspoon-sized cookie scoop to drop onto two ungreased baking sheets.
4. Bake 12–15 minutes or until cookie edges are brown.

Per Cookie: Calories: 40 | Fat: 2 g | Saturated fat: 1 g | Cholesterol: 9 mg | Sodium: 34 mg | Total carbohydrates: 5 g | Dietary fiber: 0 g | Sugars: 3 g | Protein: 0 g

Maple Snickerdoodles

Hands-On Time: 15 minutes
Total Time: 30 minutes
Yield: Makes 36 cookies

2 cups all-purpose flour
1½ teaspoons baking powder
¼ teaspoon baking soda
1½ teaspoons ground cinnamon
¼ cup unsalted butter
¼ cup vegetable shortening
1½ cups granulated sugar, divided
3 tablespoons maple syrup
1 large egg
¼ cup maple sugar

1. Preheat oven to 350°F. In a large bowl, stir together flour, baking powder, baking soda, and cinnamon; set aside.

2. In a small bowl, cream butter, shortening, 1 cup granulated sugar, and maple syrup until light and fluffy. Add egg; beat well. Stir in flour mixture until well blended.

3. Mix remaining granulated sugar and maple sugar in a small saucer. Roll dough into 36 balls and then into sugar mixture.

4. Place on ungreased baking sheets 2″ apart. Bake each sheet for 8–10 minutes. Cookies should still look slightly underdone.

5. Cool on cookie sheets 5 minutes. Remove cookies from sheets and cool completely.

Per Cookie: Calories: 76 | Fat: 3 g | Saturated fat: 1 g | Cholesterol: 9 mg | Sodium: 11 mg | Total carbohydrates: 13 g | Dietary fiber: 0 g | Sugars: 8 g | Protein: 1 g

Limeade

Hands-On Time: 15 minutes
Total Time: 15 minutes
Yield: Serves 6

¾ cup fresh-squeezed lime juice
4 cups water
½ cup sugar
1 cup lemon-lime soda
Ice cubes to serve over

In a pitcher, combine lime juice, water, and sugar; add lemon-lime soda. Serve over ice.

Per Serving: Calories: 63 | Fat: 0 g | Saturated fat: 0 g | Cholesterol: 0 mg | Sodium: 10 mg | Total carbohydrates: 18 g | Dietary fiber: 0 g | Sugars: 17 g | Protein: 0 g

Lemon-Lime Soda (pictured)

Hands-On Time: 10 minutes
Total Time: 10 minutes
Yield: Serves 6

2 cups water

1 cup sugar

¼ cup fresh squeezed lemon juice

¼ cup fresh squeezed lime juice

4 cups crushed ice

6 cups sparkling water

1. In a medium saucepan combine water and sugar over medium heat and cook until sugar is melted, about 5 minutes. Set aside and cool.

2. Combine sugar syrup and citrus juice in a pitcher. Add crushed ice to 6 glasses and divide mixture into glasses; top with sparkling water. Stir gently and serve immediately.

Per Serving: Calories: 133 | Fat: 0 g | Saturated fat: 0 g | Cholesterol: 0 mg | Sodium: 0 mg | Total carbohydrates: 34 g | Dietary fiber: 0 g | Sugars: 34 g | Protein: 0 g

Strawberry Yogurt Frappé

Hands-On Time: 10 minutes
Total Time: 10 minutes
Yield: Serves 4

1½ cups cubed cantaloupe

1 cup strawberries, stems removed

½ cup strawberry low-fat yogurt

4 mint sprigs

Combine the cantaloupe and strawberries in a blender and process until smooth. With the blender running, add the yogurt gradually and process until smooth. Equally divide into 4 chilled glasses. Add a mint sprig to each glass and serve immediately.

Per Serving: Calories: 60 | Fat: 0 g | Saturated fat: 0 g | Cholesterol: 0 mg | Sodium: 25 mg | Total carbohydrates: 13 g | Dietary fiber: 1 g | Sugars: 10 g | Protein: 2 g

Strawberry Lemonade

Hands-On Time: 15 minutes
Total Time: 15 minutes
Yield: Serves 4

½ cup fresh hulled strawberries
¾ cup lemon juice
½ cup sugar
4 cups water
1 medium lemon, thinly sliced
Crushed ice to serve over

1. Purée strawberries in a blender or food processor.
2. In a large pitcher, stir together lemon juice, sugar, and water until sugar has dissolved. Stir in strawberry purée, lemon slices, and ice.

Per Serving: Calories: 77 | Fat: 0 g | Saturated fat: 0 g | Cholesterol: 0 mg | Sodium: 0 mg | Total carbohydrates: 23 g | Dietary fiber: 1 g | Sugars: 20 g | Protein: 0 g

Holiday Spiced Cider

Hands-On Time: 10 minutes
Total Time: 25 minutes
Yield: Serves 4

1 teaspoon whole cloves
¼ teaspoon ground nutmeg
⅛ teaspoon ground ginger
1 quart apple cider
5 cinnamon sticks
4 thin orange slices

1. Place the cloves, nutmeg, and ginger in a tea ball. Pour the cider into a large saucepan with one of the cinnamon sticks. Hang the tea ball on the side of the pan into the cider. Float the orange slices on top. Heat on medium-low to a temperature just below a simmer and allow to cook for at least 15 minutes.
2. To serve, place one cinnamon stick in each of four mugs and pour cider in, leaving the oranges and cinnamon stick in the pot.

Per Serving: Calories: 130 | Fat: 0 g | Saturated fat: 0 g | Cholesterol: 0 mg | Sodium: 10 mg | Total carbohydrates: 33 g | Dietary fiber: 3 g | Sugars: 26 g | Protein: 1 g

Mango Milkshakes

Hands-On Time: 10 minutes
Total Time: 10 minutes
Yield: Serves 2

1 medium ripe mango
1 cup vanilla nonfat frozen yogurt
1 cup mango juice

1. Peel mango and cut into cubes. Place into a blender or food processor and purée.

2. Add remaining ingredients and pulse until smooth. Serve immediately.

Per Serving: Calories: 250 | Fat: 0.5 g | Saturated fat: 0 g | Cholesterol: 5 mg | Sodium: 70 mg | Total carbohydrates: 59 g | Dietary fiber: 4 g | Sugars: 52 g | Protein: 6 g

Lemon Iced Tea

Hands-On Time: 5 minutes
Total Time: 15 minutes
Yield: Serves 6

6 tea bags
6 cups water
4 tablespoons lemon juice
4 tablespoons agave nectar

1. Place tea bags into a large heatproof pitcher.

2. Measure water into a kettle or medium saucepan and place over high heat. Once water begins to steam but not boil, remove from heat and pour into pitcher.

3. Let tea steep 3–5 minutes, depending upon taste. Remove tea bags from pitcher and discard. Add lemon juice and agave nectar and stir well to combine.

4. Let tea cool at room temperature or place pitcher in refrigerator and chill before serving.

Per Serving: Calories: 40 | Fat: 0 g | Saturated fat: 0 g | Cholesterol: 0 mg | Sodium: 10 mg | Total carbohydrates: 12 g | Dietary fiber: 0 g | Sugars: 11 g | Protein: 0 g

Chapter 14

Snacks and Dips

Banana Sorbet

Hands-On Time: 5 minutes
Total Time: 15 minutes
Yield: Serves 6

4 frozen whole bananas, peeled
   and chopped
2 teaspoons vanilla extract
1 teaspoon nutmeg
1 teaspoon agave nectar

1. In a high-speed blender, combine the bananas and vanilla and purée. While blending, add the nutmeg and agave nectar.

2. Once fully puréed, pour the banana mixture into 6 cups and freeze for 10 minutes.

Per Serving: Calories: 80 | Fat: 0.5 g | Saturated fat: 0 g | Cholesterol: 0 mg | Sodium: 0 mg | Total carbohydrates: 19 g | Dietary fiber: 2 g | Sugars: 11 g | Protein: 1 g

Animal Crackers

Hands-On Time: 15 minutes
Total Time: 30 minutes
Yield: Makes 36 cookies

½ cup old-fashioned oats
¼ teaspoon salt
¾ cup flour
¼ teaspoon baking soda
¼ cup unsalted butter, softened
¼ cup buttermilk
2 teaspoons honey
¼ teaspoon maple extract

1. Preheat oven to 400°F.

2. Grind oats in blender until it is like flour. Mix in rest of dry ingredients.

3. Cut in butter until mixture is like coarse crumbs. Add buttermilk, honey, and maple extract. Remove dough from blender and gather into a ball; knead lightly on work surface.

4. Roll dough to about ⅛″ thick and cut with animal-shaped cookie cutters. Place on ungreased baking sheets.

5. Bake each sheet 10–12 minutes or until crackers are golden. Cool completely.

Per Cookie: Calories: 26 | Fat: 1 g | Saturated fat: 1 g | Cholesterol: 4 mg | Sodium: 27 mg | Total carbohydrates: 3 g | Dietary fiber: 0 g | Sugars: 1 g | Protein: 0 g

Avocado Rancho Dip

Hands-On Time: 5 minutes
Total Time: 25 minutes
Yield: Serves 12

4 medium ripe avocados, peeled, pitted, and chopped
½ cup buttermilk
1 teaspoon chopped chives
½ teaspoon garlic powder
½ teaspoon onion powder
1 teaspoon kosher salt
½ teaspoon ground black pepper
2 teaspoons fresh lemon juice

Combine all ingredients in a blender and process until smooth. Refrigerate at least 20 minutes to allow ingredients to meld.

Per Serving: Calories: 115 | Fat: 10 g | Saturated fat: 2 g | Cholesterol: 1 mg | Sodium: 140 mg | Total carbohydrates: 7 g | Dietary fiber: 5 g | Sugars: 1 g | Protein: 2 g

Cheesy Potato Chips

Hands-On Time: 30 minutes
Total Time: 30 minutes
Yield: Serves 8

2 large russet potatoes, skins on
4 cups peanut oil
⅓ cup grated Parmesan cheese
1 teaspoon salt

1. Thinly slice potatoes and place slices in a large bowl of ice water.

2. In a large high-sided, heavy pot, heat peanut oil over high heat until it reaches 375°F. Remove a handful of potato slices from the ice water and dry thoroughly on kitchen towels. Carefully drop potato slices into the hot oil. Cook and stir to separate. Fry until golden brown.

3. Remove with a large strainer and place in a single layer on fresh paper towels to cool. Immediately sprinkle with some cheese and salt and toss. Repeat with remaining chips, cheese, and salt. Cool completely and store in airtight container for up to 1 week.

Per Serving: Calories: 150 | Fat: 9 g | Saturated fat: 2 g | Cholesterol: 5 mg | Sodium: 360 mg | Total carbohydrates: 16 g | Dietary fiber: 2 g | Sugars: 1 g | Protein: 3 g

Yummiest Play Dough Ever (pictured)

Hands-On Time: 15 minutes
Total Time: 15 minutes
Yield: Serves 10

1 (18.25-ounce) box white cake
    mix
½ cup margarine, softened
3 tablespoons water
Food coloring

Mix cake mix and margarine in a large bowl. Add water bit by bit until dough reaches the desired consistency. Divide dough into batches and color each batch.

Per Serving: Calories: 270 | Fat: 11 g | Saturated fat: 2.5 g | Cholesterol: 0 mg | Sodium: 440 mg | Total carbohydrates: 42 g | Dietary fiber: 1 g | Sugars: 22 g | Protein: 2 g

Fruit Kebabs

Hands-On Time: 30 minutes
Total Time: 30 minutes
Yield: Serves 4

1 cup green seedless grapes
1 cup pineapple chunks
1 cup halved strawberries
1 cup red seedless grapes
1 cup blueberries
4 (8") wooden skewers

Thread fruit onto skewers, alternating types of fruit.

Per Serving: Calories: 120 | Fat: 0.5 g | Saturated fat: 0 g | Cholesterol: 0 mg | Sodium: 0 mg | Total carbohydrates: 32 g | Dietary fiber: 3 g | Sugars: 26 g | Protein: 1 g

Mango Salsa

Hands-On Time: 15 minutes
Total Time: 15 minutes
Yield: Serves 8

1 medium ripe mango, peeled and
 diced
1 small tomato, chopped
2 cloves garlic, minced
1 medium jalapeño pepper,
 seeded and minced
Juice of 1 fresh lime
2 tablespoons chopped fresh
 cilantro
1 tablespoon apple cider vinegar
1 teaspoon agave nectar
1 teaspoon ground cumin

1. Place all the ingredients in a medium bowl and stir well
 to combine.
2. Serve immediately or cover and refrigerate until ready to
 serve.

Per Serving: Calories: 40 | Fat: 0 g | Saturated fat: 0 g | Cholesterol: 0 mg
| Sodium: 0 mg | Total carbohydrates: 9 g | Dietary fiber: 1 g | Sugars: 7 g |
Protein: 1 g

Super Healthy Chocolate Chip Cookies

Hands-On Time: 20 minutes
Total Time: 30 minutes
Yield: Makes 24 cookies

2 tablespoons coconut butter
2 tablespoons grapeseed oil
⅔ cup coconut sugar
2 tablespoons xylitol
¼ cup unsweetened applesauce
1 teaspoon vanilla extract
½ teaspoon natural butter extract
¼ teaspoon sea salt
½ teaspoon baking soda
¼ teaspoon baking powder
1 cup plus 3 tablespoons white
 spelt flour, divided
⅔ cup chocolate chips

1. Preheat oven to 350°F. Line two large baking sheets with
 parchment paper.
2. In a medium bowl, combine coconut butter and oil and
 mix well. Add the coconut sugar, xylitol, and applesauce
 and stir to combine.
3. Add the vanilla, butter extract, salt, baking soda, and
 baking powder. Stir the batter to combine well.
4. Add ½ cup of flour and stir to combine. Then add the
 chocolate chips with the remaining flour. The dough
 should be a bit sticky.
5. Spoon out rounded teaspoons of dough 2″ apart onto two
 baking sheets. Bake for 8 minutes or until golden brown.
 Remove from baking sheet and cool on a wire rack.

Per Cookie: Calories: 70 | Fat: 2 g | Saturated fat: 1 g | Cholesterol: 0 mg |
Sodium: 40 mg | Total carbohydrates: 13 g | Dietary fiber: 0 g | Sugars: 7 g |
Protein: 1 g

Hot Artichoke Dip

Hands-On Time: 5 minutes
Total Time: 30 minutes
Yield: Serves 10

1 (10.5-ounce) can artichoke
     hearts, drained and chopped
2 cloves garlic, minced
¼ cup mayonnaise
½ teaspoon Worcestershire sauce
½ cup grated Parmesan cheese
½ teaspoon salt
½ teaspoon ground white pepper
½ teaspoon minced chives
½ cup panko bread crumbs

1. Preheat oven to 350°F.

2. Combine all the ingredients except the panko in a 2-quart ovenproof glass dish. Mix well. Top with panko. Bake uncovered for 25 minutes.

Per Serving: Calories: 77 | Fat: 6 g | Saturated fat: 1 g | Cholesterol: 7 mg | Sodium: 318 mg | Total carbohydrates: 5 g | Dietary fiber: 1 g | Sugars: 0 g | Protein: 2 g

Homemade Whole-Wheat Pretzels

Hands-On Time: 10 minutes
Total Time: 25 minutes
Yield: Serves 4

½ tablespoon yeast
¾ cup warm water
½ tablespoon sugar
½ teaspoon salt
1 cup all-purpose flour
1 cup whole-wheat flour
1 teaspoon coarse salt

1. Preheat oven to 425°F. In a large bowl, mix together yeast, water, and sugar. Add ½ teaspoon salt and flours.

2. Place dough on a floured board. Knead 3–5 times and pinch off a small lump of dough. Roll into desired pretzel shape.

3. Place pretzel on an ungreased cookie sheet and sprinkle with coarse salt. Repeat with remaining dough. Bake 12–15 minutes until golden brown.

Per Serving: Calories: 230 | Fat: 1 g | Saturated fat: 0 g | Cholesterol: 0 mg | Sodium: 800 mg | Total carbohydrates: 48 g | Dietary fiber: 5 g | Sugars: 2 g | Protein: 8 g

Orange Honey Fruit Dip (pictured)

Hands-On Time: 10 minutes
Total Time: 10 minutes
Yield: Serves 8

1 cup plain low-fat yogurt

3 tablespoons orange juice

1 tablespoon honey

1 medium apple, cored and sliced

5 strawberries, sliced

1 medium banana, peeled and sliced

¼ cup grapes

In a small bowl, stir together yogurt, juice, and honey. Cover tightly. Refrigerate for up to 5 days until ready to serve with the assorted fresh fruit.

Per Serving: Calories: 60 | Fat: 0.5 g | Saturated fat: 0.5 g | Cholesterol: 0 mg | Sodium: 20 mg | Total carbohydrates: 13 g | Dietary fiber: 1 g | Sugars: 10 g | Protein: 2 g

Chocolate Krispy Rice Balls

Hands-On Time: 20 minutes
Total Time: 20 minutes
Yield: Makes 24 cookies

2 cups 100 percent puffed rice cereal

½ cup rolled oats

¼ teaspoon salt

½ cup coconut sugar

3 tablespoons honey

2 teaspoons water

1 ounce unsweetened chocolate, chopped

1½ teaspoons vanilla extract

1½ tablespoons cocoa powder

1. Line a baking sheet with parchment paper; set aside. Combine puffed rice cereal, oats, and salt in a large bowl.

2. In a small microwave-safe bowl, combine the coconut sugar, honey, and water. Microwave on high for 1 minute, stirring every 10 seconds. The mixture will bubble up, but this is okay. After 1 minute, add the chopped chocolate and stir. Microwave on high for another 5 seconds or so until the chocolate is completely melted.

3. Add the vanilla extract and cocoa powder to the chocolate mixture. The mixture should look like a chocolate ganache. Quickly pour over the rice and oats mixture while it is still warm. Work quickly to stir and coat everything evenly.

4. Use an ice cream scoop to form the mixture into balls. Place the balls on the prepared baking sheet. Serve immediately or store in a covered container.

Per Cookie: Calories: 45 | Fat: 1 g | Saturated fat: 0.5 g | Cholesterol: 0 mg | Sodium: 25 mg | Total carbohydrates: 9 g | Dietary fiber: 1 g | Sugars: 6 g | Protein: 1 g

Green Tea Kiwi Ice Pops

Hands-On Time: 15 minutes
Total Time: 15 minutes
Yield: Makes 4 pops

1½ teaspoons green tea matcha powder
1 tablespoon boiling water
2 kiwis, peeled and diced
12 ounces vanilla low-fat Greek yogurt
1 teaspoon fresh lemon juice
3 tablespoons honey

1. In a small bowl, combine matcha powder and boiling water. Stir to combine to create a smooth paste. Set aside.

2. In a large bowl, mix the diced kiwis, Greek yogurt, lemon juice, and honey. Stir in matcha paste and make sure it is thoroughly combined.

3. Spoon mixture into Popsicle molds or small cups, making sure to only fill ¾ of the way. Place in the freezer until frozen.

Per Pop: Calories: 150 | Fat: 0 g | Saturated fat: 0 g | Cholesterol: 0 mg | Sodium: 30 mg | Total carbohydrates: 29 g | Dietary fiber: 1 g | Sugars: 26 g | Protein: 8 g

Cinnamon Sweet Popcorn

Hands-On Time: 5 minutes
Total Time: 15 minutes
Yield: Serves 4

Spectrum Naturals Canola Spray Oil with Butter Flavor
4 cups air-popped popcorn
1 tablespoon granulated sugar
⅛ teaspoon ground cinnamon
⅛ teaspoon ground nutmeg
⅛ teaspoon ground cloves
⅛ teaspoon ground allspice

1. Preheat oven to 300°F. Treat a large baking sheet with the spray oil.

2. Spread the popcorn on the pan and lightly coat with the spray oil. Mix together the remaining ingredients in a small bowl; sprinkle over the popcorn. Lightly coat again with the spray oil, if desired.

3. Bake for 5 minutes. Toss the popcorn and rotate the pan, then bake for an additional 5 minutes. Serve warm or at room temperature.

Per Serving: Calories: 50 | Fat: 0 g | Saturated fat: 0 g | Cholesterol: 0 mg | Sodium: 0 mg | Total carbohydrates: 10 g | Dietary fiber: 1 g | Sugars: 3 g | Protein: 1 g

Blueberry Streusel Muffins

Hands-On Time: 10 minutes
Total Time: 28 minutes
Yield: Makes 12 muffins

⅓ cup plain low-fat yogurt

½ cup plus 2 tablespoons maple sugar, divided

1 large egg

½ teaspoon vanilla extract

⅓ cup unsweetened almond milk

¼ teaspoon lemon zest

1 teaspoon baking powder

½ teaspoon sea salt

1 cup plus 1 tablespoon white spelt flour, divided

½ cup fresh blueberries

¼ teaspoon cinnamon

2 tablespoons unsalted butter, diced

1. Preheat oven to 375°F and place muffin liners in a 12-cup muffin pan.
2. In a medium bowl, mix together yogurt, ½ cup maple sugar, egg, vanilla, almond milk, and lemon zest. When combined, mix in the baking powder, salt, and 1 cup flour.
3. Gently fold in the blueberries.
4. In a separate bowl, create the crumb topping by mixing 2 tablespoons maple sugar, 1 tablespoon flour, cinnamon, and diced butter.
5. Pour batter into prepared muffin tin cups and spoon the crumb topping over the tops. Bake for 18 minutes or until tops become golden brown.

Per Muffin: Calories: 110 | Fat: 2.5 g | Saturated fat: 1.5 g | Cholesterol: 20 mg | Sodium: 115 mg | Total carbohydrates: 20 g | Dietary fiber: 1 g | Sugars: 11 g | Protein: 2 g

Raw Applesauce

Hands-On Time: 10 minutes
Total Time: 10 minutes
Yield: Serves 6

4 medium apples, peeled and cored

4 teaspoons lemon juice

4 teaspoons maple syrup

1 teaspoon ground cinnamon

Chop apples finely in a food processor. Stir in remaining ingredients. Serve immediately or store in refrigerator for up to 2 days.

Per Serving: Calories: 76 | Fat: 0 g | Saturated fat: 0 g | Cholesterol: 0 mg | Sodium: 0 mg | Total carbohydrates: 20 g | Dietary fiber: 3 g | Sugars: 15 g | Protein: 0 g

No-Bake Honey Balls (pictured)

Hands-On Time: 15 minutes
Total Time: 15 minutes
Yield: Serves 15

½ cup honey
½ cup golden raisins
½ cup dry milk powder
2 cups gluten-free crushed crisp
   rice cereal, divided
¼ cup confectioners' sugar
1 cup finely chopped dates

1. In a food processor, combine honey and raisins; process until smooth.

2. Scrape mixture into a small bowl and add milk powder, 1 cup crushed cereal, confectioners' sugar, and dates and mix well. You may need to add more powdered sugar or honey for desired consistency.

3. Form mixture into ¾" balls and roll in remaining crushed cereal. Store in airtight container at room temperature.

Per Serving: Calories: 110 | Fat: 1 g | Saturated fat: 0.5 g | Cholesterol: 5 mg | Sodium: 20 mg | Total carbohydrates: 25 g | Dietary fiber: 1 g | Sugars: 24 g | Protein: 2 g

Plantain Chips (Chips de Banana da Terra)

Hands-On Time: 15 minutes
Total Time: 15 minutes
Yield: Serves 6

4 medium green plantains, peeled
2 cups vegetable oil
1 teaspoon sea salt

1. Working quickly, use a mandoline or very sharp knife to cut the peeled plantain lengthwise into the thinnest slices possible. (You can also cut the plantain crosswise at a slight angle, which is easier if you don't have a mandoline.)

2. Heat the oil in a deep skillet or large heavy saucepan to 350°F. Working in batches, cook the plantain slices until golden brown and crispy, about 3–4 minutes.

3. Remove plantain slices from the oil with a slotted spoon and drain on paper towels. Sprinkle with sea salt and serve warm or at room temperature.

Per Serving: Calories: 250 | Fat: 12 g | Saturated fat: 1 g | Cholesterol: 0 mg | Sodium: 390 mg | Total carbohydrates: 38 g | Dietary fiber: 3 g | Sugars: 18 g | Protein: 2 g

Creamy Edamame Jalapeño Dip

Hands-On Time: 10 minutes
Total Time: 10 minutes
Yield: Serves 12

2 cups shelled edamame
1 cup chopped cilantro leaves
2 small jalapeño peppers, seeded and chopped, divided
1 small red onion, peeled and chopped
1 cup sour cream
2 tablespoons lime juice
2 tablespoons olive oil
¼ teaspoon salt
¼ teaspoon ground black pepper

1. In the bowl of a food processor, pulse edamame, cilantro leaves, 1 jalapeño, and red onion until evenly chopped. Add sour cream, lime juice, olive oil, salt, and pepper. Process until smooth.

2. Top with the remaining chopped jalapeño.

Per Serving: Calories: 80 | Fat: 6 g | Saturated fat: 2 g | Cholesterol: 9 mg | Sodium: 58 mg | Total carbohydrates: 4 g | Dietary fiber: 1 g | Sugars: 2 g | Protein: 3 g

Cheesy-Flavored Seasoned Popcorn

Hands-On Time: 15 minutes
Total Time: 15 minutes
Yield: Serves 4

2 tablespoons nutritional yeast flakes
¾ teaspoon garlic powder
¾ teaspoon onion powder
½ teaspoon ground sweet paprika
¼ teaspoon dried thyme
¼ teaspoon ground black pepper
½ cup popcorn kernels
2 teaspoons olive oil

1. Measure the nutritional yeast, garlic powder, onion powder, paprika, thyme, and black pepper into a small bowl and stir well to combine. Set aside.

2. Place popcorn kernels into an air popper. Place a medium stockpot beneath the popcorn dispenser, turn appliance on, and wait until kernels have popped. Turn off popper and set aside.

3. Drizzle the oil over the popcorn and toss well to coat. Once popcorn is thoroughly coated with oil, sprinkle with the seasoning mixture and stir vigorously for 3 minutes until completely coated.

4. Serve immediately or store in an airtight container until serving.

Per Serving: Calories: 140 | Fat: 3.5 g | Saturated fat: 0 g | Cholesterol: 0 mg | Sodium: 0 mg | Total carbohydrates: 23 g | Dietary fiber: 5 g | Sugars: 0 g | Protein: 5 g

Cucumber and Cream Cheese Tea Sandwiches

Hands-On Time: 10 minutes
Total Time: 10 minutes
Yield: Serves 8

1 small cucumber (approximately 4"), peeled and thinly sliced
1 teaspoon salt
8 slices white bread, crusts removed
4 ounces cream cheese, softened

1. Arrange cucumbers in a single layer on a large plate or cutting board and sprinkle with salt.

2. On a work surface, lay out 4 slices of bread. Spread each with a thin layer of cream cheese. Add a couple layers of cucumber slices. Spread the remaining 4 slices of bread with a thin layer of the remaining cream cheese. Place bread on top of cucumbers.

3. Using a sharp knife, cut each sandwich into 4 equal pieces.

Per Serving: Calories: 135 | Fat: 6 g | Saturated fat: 3 g | Cholesterol: 14 mg | Sodium: 483 mg | Total carbohydrates: 17 g | Dietary fiber: 1 g | Sugars: 3 g | Protein: 4 g

Dip Mix

Hands-On Time: 10 minutes
Total Time: 10 minutes
Yield: Makes 1½ cups

⅓ cup dried dill weed
¼ cup dried minced onion
3 tablespoons granulated garlic
⅓ cup dried parsley
¼ cup dried chopped chives
1 tablespoon salt
1 tablespoon paprika

1. Combine all ingredients in a medium bowl and blend well. Spoon into sealed containers; label and use within 4 months.

2. To use, combine 3 tablespoons of this mix with 1 cup sour cream and 1 cup plain yogurt or 1 cup mayonnaise and 1 cup plain yogurt. Serve with vegetables as a dip.

Per Serving: Calories: 20 | Fat: 1 g | Saturated fat: 0 g | Cholesterol: 0 mg | Sodium: 590 mg | Total carbohydrates: 3 g | Dietary fiber: 1 g | Sugars: 1 g | Protein: 1 g

Easy Hummus (pictured)

Hands-On Time: 10 minutes
Total Time: 10 minutes
Yield: Makes 2 cups

6 cloves garlic, peeled
½ teaspoon salt
1 (15-ounce) can chickpeas, drained
⅓ cup tahini
2 tablespoons lemon juice
2 tablespoons olive oil
½ teaspoon ground cumin

1. Purée the garlic and salt in a food processor. Add the chickpeas and purée to a paste. Add the remaining ingredients and process until smooth, scraping down the sides of the bowl.

2. Transfer the finished purée into a serving bowl and serve.

Per Tablespoon: Calories: 70 | Fat: 5 g | Saturated fat: 0.5 g | Cholesterol: 0 mg | Sodium: 160 mg | Total carbohydrates: 5 g | Dietary fiber: 2 g | Sugars: 0 g | Protein: 3 g

Simple Pita Chips

Hands-On Time: 5 minutes
Total Time: 20 minutes
Yield: Serves 4

2 whole-wheat pitas
¼ teaspoon garlic powder

1. Preheat oven to 350°F.

1. Cut each pita into 8 wedges. Place wedges on cookie sheet and sprinkle with garlic powder. Bake for 10–15 minutes or until lightly brown and crisp.

Per Serving: Calories: 80 | Fat: 1 g | Saturated fat: 0 g | Cholesterol: 0 mg | Sodium: 110 mg | Total carbohydrates: 15 g | Dietary fiber: 2 g | Sugars: 1 g | Protein: 3 g

Figs with Coconut Cream

Hands-On Time: 10 minutes
Total Time: 10 minutes
Yield: Serves 2

8 large fresh ripe figs
¾ cup light coconut milk

1. Cut the figs into quarters and place in a medium bowl.

2. Add the coconut milk. Let the figs rest for 3 minutes before serving. This process will allow the juices to mix in with the milk.

Per Serving: Calories: 160 | Fat: 5 g | Saturated fat: 3 g | Cholesterol: 0 mg | Sodium: 30 mg | Total carbohydrates: 32 g | Dietary fiber: 5 g | Sugars: 25 g | Protein: 1 g

Bagel Chips

Hands-On Time: 5 minutes
Total Time: 15 minutes
Yield: Serves 6

3 small whole-wheat bagels
1 tablespoon olive oil
⅛ teaspoon garlic salt
⅛ teaspoon ground black pepper

1. Preheat oven to 350°F.

2. Thinly slice the bagels crosswise, discarding the tiny ends.

3. Spread the pieces on a baking sheet. Drizzle with olive oil and sprinkle with garlic salt and pepper.

4. Bake for 10 minutes. Cool on a wire rack.

Per Serving: Calories: 100 | Fat: 3 g | Saturated fat: 0.5 g | Cholesterol: 0 mg | Sodium: 160 mg | Total carbohydrates: 16 g | Dietary fiber: 1 g | Sugars: 2 g | Protein: 3 g

Spinach and Ricotta Dip

Hands-On Time: 10 minutes
Total Time: 10 minutes
Yield: Serves 12

1 (10-ounce) package frozen chopped spinach, thawed and drained
½ cup ricotta cheese
⅓ cup mayonnaise
¼ cup chopped green onions
¼ cup sour cream
3 tablespoons lemon juice
2 tablespoons grated onion (including juice)
⅛ teaspoon Worcestershire sauce
¼ teaspoon salt
½ teaspoon ground black pepper
1 tablespoon chopped fresh parsley
1 baguette, sliced and toasted

Combine all the ingredients in a food processor and pulse until smooth. Transfer to a medium bowl and chill thoroughly. Serve with toasted baguette.

Per Serving: Calories: 130 | Fat: 7 g | Saturated fat: 2 g | Cholesterol: 10 mg | Sodium: 240 mg | Total carbohydrates: 13 g | Dietary fiber: 1 g | Sugars: 2 g | Protein: 4 g

Herb Butter Cashews

Hands-On Time: 10 minutes
Total Time: 20 minutes
Yield: Serves 48

3 cups cashews
1 tablespoon unsalted butter, melted
1 tablespoon chopped fresh thyme
1 tablespoon chopped fresh rosemary
2 teaspoons brown sugar
1 teaspoon sea salt
½ teaspoon chili powder
¼ teaspoon Hungarian paprika

1. Preheat oven to 350°F.
2. In small bowl, combine melted butter, thyme, rosemary, brown sugar, salt, chili powder, and paprika. Set aside.
3. Spread nuts in a single layer on a large, rimmed baking sheet.
4. Roast for 10 minutes or until slightly browned and fragrant.
5. Toss warmed nuts with butter mixture.

Per Serving: Calories: 80 | Fat: 7 g | Saturated fat: 1 g | Cholesterol: 0 mg | Sodium: 40 mg | Total carbohydrates: 5 g | Dietary fiber: 1 g | Sugars: 1 g | Protein: 3 g

Baked Potato Chips (pictured)

Hands-On Time: 15 minutes
Total Time: 25 minutes
Yield: Serves 8

2 medium Idaho potatoes, cut into ⅛" slices

1 tablespoon extra-virgin olive oil

2 teaspoons all-natural sea salt, divided

2 teaspoons garlic powder, divided

1 teaspoon ground black pepper, divided

1. Preheat the oven to broil at 400°F and prepare an oven rack with olive oil spray.

2. In a medium bowl, toss the potato slices in the olive oil until evenly coated.

3. Spread the potato slices flat on the prepared oven rack, sprinkle top sides of slices with 1 teaspoon of salt, 1 teaspoon of garlic powder, and ½ teaspoon of pepper.

4. Broil for 5 minutes, checking frequently, or until golden brown. Remove rack, flip chips, sprinkle with remaining salt, garlic powder, and pepper and return to oven to continue broiling for another 5 minutes or until golden brown.

5. Remove from heat and allow to cool for 5 minutes before serving.

Per Serving: Calories: 60 | Fat: 2 g | Saturated fat: 0 g | Cholesterol: 0 mg | Sodium: 590 mg | Total carbohydrates: 9 g | Dietary fiber: 1 g | Sugars: 1 g | Protein: 1 g

Quick and Easy Salsa

Hands-On Time: 10 minutes
Total Time: 10 minutes
Yield: Serves 12

Combine all ingredients in medium bowl and mix gently. Serve immediately or cover and refrigerate.

Per Serving: Calories: 20 | Fat: 1 g | Saturated fat: 0 g | Cholesterol: 0 mg | Sodium: 100 mg | Total carbohydrates: 2 g | Dietary fiber: 0 g | Sugars: 1 g | Protein: 0 g

3 large Roma tomatoes, very finely diced and seeds removed

1 medium jalapeño pepper, seeded and minced

½ cup minced red onion

¼ cup chopped cilantro

1 clove garlic, peeled and minced

2 tablespoons lime juice

½ teaspoon salt

1 tablespoon olive oil

Celery Sticks with Peanut Butter and Raisins

Hands-On Time: 10 minutes
Total Time: 10 minutes
Yield: Serves 2

3 large celery stalks
3 tablespoons peanut butter
3 tablespoons raisins

1. Wash the celery stalks and cut each in half.
2. Spread peanut butter in the hollow of the celery.
3. Top with raisins.

Per Serving: Calories: 200 | Fat: 12 g | Saturated fat: 2.5 g | Cholesterol: 0 mg | Sodium: 150 mg | Total carbohydrates: 19 g | Dietary fiber: 3 g | Sugars: 14 g | Protein: 6 g

Spicy Cheese Dip

Hands-On Time: 5 minutes
Total Time: 30 minutes
Yield: Serves 32

2 pounds pasteurized processed cheese food, cut into cubes
8 ounces cream cheese, cut into cubes
1 (4-ounce) can chopped mild green chili peppers
1 (1.25-ounce) envelope taco seasoning mix
1 (16-ounce) jar chunky salsa or canned Mexican-style diced tomatoes

1. Combine all ingredients in a 3- to 5-quart slow cooker.
2. Cover and cook on low setting, stirring occasionally, until cheese is melted and mixture is hot, about 25 minutes.
3. Serve warm from the slow cooker or a chafing dish. Stir occasionally to keep smooth.

Per Serving: Calories: 97 | Fat: 5 g | Saturated fat: 3.5 g | Cholesterol: 20 mg | Sodium: 620 mg | Total carbohydrates: 6 g | Dietary fiber: 0 g | Sugars: 3 g | Protein: 6 g

Holy Guacamole

Hands-On Time: 10 minutes
Total Time: 10 minutes
Yield: Serves 6

1 medium ripe avocado
1 small ripe tomato, chopped
½ small red onion, peeled and chopped
Juice of 1 fresh lime
1 clove garlic, minced
1 tablespoon chopped fresh cilantro
½ teaspoon ground cumin
⅛ teaspoon ground cayenne pepper

1. Peel, pit, and dice the avocado. Place diced avocado in a deep bowl and mash with a fork as smoothly or coarsely as desired. Add remaining ingredients and mix well.

2. Serve immediately or cover and chill before serving.

Per Serving: Calories: 60 | Fat: 4.5 g | Saturated fat: 1 g | Cholesterol: 0 mg | Sodium: 0 mg | Total carbohydrates: 5 g | Dietary fiber: 3 g | Sugars: 1 g | Protein: 1 g

Baked Tortilla Chips

Hands-On Time: 5 minutes
Total Time: 20 minutes
Yield: Serves 10

10 (6") fat-free corn tortillas
2 teaspoons salt

1. Preheat oven to 400°F.

2. Spray 2 large baking sheets with nonstick cooking spray. Cut each tortilla into 6 wedges. Scatter wedges onto baking sheets.

3. Spray wedges with nonstick cooking spray and sprinkle with salt. Bake for 12 minutes.

Per Serving: Calories: 50 | Fat: 0 g | Saturated fat: 0 g | Cholesterol: 0 mg | Sodium: 490 mg | Total carbohydrates: 8 g | Dietary fiber: 1 g | Sugars: 1 g | Protein: 2 g

Zesty Black Bean Salsa

Hands-On Time: 15 minutes
Total Time: 15 minutes
Yield: Serves 6

1½ cups cooked black beans
1 cup finely chopped red onion
1 medium tomato, chopped
1 medium green bell pepper,
    seeded and chopped
1 medium jalapeño pepper,
    seeded and finely chopped
3 tablespoons lime juice
2 tablespoons olive oil
¼ teaspoon ground black pepper

1. In medium bowl, combine black beans, onion, tomato, bell pepper, and jalapeño.

2. In separate small bowl, whisk together lime juice, olive oil, and ground pepper. Pour over beans; mix well. Chill before serving.

Per Serving: Calories: 120 | Fat: 5 g | Saturated fat: 0.5 g | Cholesterol: 0 mg | Sodium: 5 mg | Total carbohydrates: 16 g | Dietary fiber: 5 g | Sugars: 3 g | Protein: 5 g

Easy Rosemary Snack Crackers (pictured)

Hands-On Time: 10 minutes
Total Time: 24 hours, 10 minutes
Yield: Serves 12

¼ cup light olive oil
2 tablespoons finely chopped
    fresh rosemary
½ teaspoon smoked paprika
½ teaspoon garlic powder
¼ teaspoon onion powder
1 (7-ounce) box Cheddar cheese–
    flavored snack crackers

In a gallon-sized resealable bag or a large plastic storage container with an airtight lid, combine the oil, rosemary, paprika, garlic powder, and onion powder and mix well. Add the crackers, seal the bag or cover the bowl, and gently rotate so all the crackers are evenly coated in the mixture. Let stand on the counter for 24 hours, occasionally rotating, before serving.

Per Serving: Calories: 130 | Fat: 9 g | Saturated fat: 2 g | Cholesterol: 0 mg | Sodium: 130 mg | Total carbohydrates: 10 g | Dietary fiber: 1 g | Sugars: 0 g | Protein: 2 g

English Muffin Pizza Snacks

Hands-On Time: 10 minutes
Total Time: 25 minutes
Yield: Serves 6

3 English muffins
1 cup marinara sauce
2 cups shredded mozzarella cheese
1 cup shredded Parmesan cheese

1. Split English muffins and toast the halves, either in a toaster or in the oven. Place muffin halves soft-side up on a baking sheet. Spread sauce over each muffin half. Combine the cheeses in a small bowl and sprinkle over the sauce on each muffin pizza.

2. Place muffins in a 350°F oven and bake for 12 minutes or until cheese is bubbly and browned. Let stand briefly before serving.

Per Serving: Calories: 250 | Fat: 13 g | Saturated fat: 7 g | Cholesterol: 35 mg | Sodium: 720 mg | Total carbohydrates: 18 g | Dietary fiber: 1 g | Sugars: 3 g | Protein: 19 g

Cinnamon Yogurt Dip with Apples

Hands-On Time: 5 minutes
Total Time: 25 minutes
Yield: Serves 1

½ cup plain nonfat Greek yogurt
2 teaspoons Splenda
½ teaspoon ground cinnamon
1 medium apple, cored and sliced

1. Mix the yogurt, Splenda, and cinnamon in a small bowl. Chill for 20 minutes.

2. Serve dip with apple slices.

Per Serving: Calories: 170 | Fat: 0 g | Saturated fat: 0 g | Cholesterol: 0 mg | Sodium: 45 mg | Total carbohydrates: 32 g | Dietary fiber: 4 g | Sugars: 23 g | Protein: 12 g

Energy Bites

Hands-On Time: 10 minutes
Total Time: 10 minutes
Yield: Makes 12 bites

½ cup honey
½ cup peanut butter
1 cup nonfat dry milk
1 cup quick-cook rolled oats
½ cup raisins
2 cups crushed corn flakes cereal

1. Mix the honey and peanut butter together in a medium bowl. Add the dry milk, oats, and raisins. Mix together well.

2. Roll the mixture into 2 dozen balls. Roll the balls in the crushed cereal.

3. Cover and refrigerate.

Per 2 Bites: Calories: 210 | Fat: 6 g | Saturated fat: 1 g | Cholesterol: 0 mg | Sodium: 120 mg | Total carbohydrates: 36 g | Dietary fiber: 2 g | Sugars: 25 g | Protein: 6 g

Standard US/Metric Measurement Conversions

VOLUME CONVERSIONS

US Volume Measure	Metric Equivalent
⅛ teaspoon	0.5 milliliter
¼ teaspoon	1 milliliter
½ teaspoon	2 milliliters
1 teaspoon	5 milliliters
½ tablespoon	7 milliliters
1 tablespoon (3 teaspoons)	15 milliliters
2 tablespoons (1 fluid ounce)	30 milliliters
¼ cup (4 tablespoons)	60 milliliters
⅓ cup	80 milliliters
½ cup (4 fluid ounces)	125 milliliters
⅔ cup	160 milliliters
¾ cup (6 fluid ounces)	180 milliliters
1 cup (16 tablespoons)	250 milliliters
1 pint (2 cups)	500 milliliters
1 quart (4 cups)	1 liter (about)

WEIGHT CONVERSIONS

US Weight Measure	Metric Equivalent
½ ounce	15 grams
1 ounce	30 grams
2 ounces	60 grams
3 ounces	85 grams
¼ pound (4 ounces)	115 grams
½ pound (8 ounces)	225 grams
¾ pound (12 ounces)	340 grams
1 pound (16 ounces)	454 grams

OVEN TEMPERATURE CONVERSIONS

Degrees Fahrenheit	Degrees Celsius
200 degrees F	95 degrees C
250 degrees F	120 degrees C
275 degrees F	135 degrees C
300 degrees F	150 degrees C
325 degrees F	160 degrees C
350 degrees F	180 degrees C
375 degrees F	190 degrees C
400 degrees F	205 degrees C
425 degrees F	220 degrees C
450 degrees F	230 degrees C

BAKING PAN SIZES

American	Metric
8 × 1½ inch round baking pan	20 × 4 cm cake tin
9 × 1½ inch round baking pan	23 × 3.5 cm cake tin
11 × 7 × 1½ inch baking pan	28 × 18 × 4 cm baking tin
13 × 9 × 2 inch baking pan	30 × 20 × 5 cm baking tin
2 quart rectangular baking dish	30 × 20 × 3 cm baking tin
15 × 10 × 2 inch baking pan	38 × 25 × 5 cm baking tin (Swiss roll tin)
9 inch pie plate	22 × 4 or 23 × 4 cm pie plate
7 or 8 inch springform pan	18 or 20 cm springform or loose bottom cake tin
9 × 5 × 3 inch loaf pan	23 × 13 × 7 cm or 2 lb narrow loaf or pâté tin
1½ quart casserole	1.5 liter casserole
2 quart casserole	2 liter casserole

Index